Ripley's Believe It or Not!

2011

Executive VP Norm Deska
VP, Exhibits & Archives Edward Meyer
Archives Assistant Anthony Scipio
Researcher Lucas Stram

Publisher Anne Marshall

Editorial Director Rebecca Miles
Researcher & Picture Manager James Proud
Editorial Assistant Charlotte Howell
Additional Research Rosie Alexander
Text Geoff Tibballs
Editors Judy Barratt, Sally McFall
Factchecker Alex Bazlinton
Indexer Hilary Bird

Art Director Sam South
Design Dynamo Design
Reprographics Juice Creative

Copyright ©2010 by Ripley Entertainment Inc.

First published in Great Britain in 2010 by
Random House Books
Random House, 20 Vauxhall Bridge Road,
London SW1V 2SA

www.rbooks.co.uk

Addresses for companies within The Random House
Group Limited can be found at:
www.randomhouse.co.uk/offices.htm

The Random House Group Limited Reg. No. 954009

All rights reserved. Ripley's, Believe It or Not!, and
Ripley's Believe It or Not! are registered trademarks of
Ripley Entertainment Inc.

ISBN 9781847945860
10 9 8 7 6 5 4 3 2 1

The Random House Group Limited supports The
Forest Stewardship Council (FSC), the leading
international forest certification organisation.
All our titles that are printed on Greenpeace
approved FSC certified paper carry the FSC logo.
Our paper procurement policy can be found at
www.rbooks.co.uk/environment

No part of this publication may be reproduced in
whole or in part, or stored in a retrieval system,
or transmitted in any form or by any means,
electronic, mechanical, photocopying, recording,
or otherwise, without written permission from the
publisher. For information regarding permission,
write to VP Intellectual Property, Ripley
Entertainment Inc., Suite 188, 7576 Kingspointe
Parkway, Orlando, Florida 32819
e-mail: publishing@ripleys.com

A CIP catalogue record for this book
is available from the British Library

Printed in China

PUBLISHER'S NOTE
While every effort has been made to verify
the accuracy of the entries in this book, the
Publishers cannot be held responsible for any
errors contained in the work. They would be
glad to receive any information from readers.

WARNING
Some of the stunts and activities in this book
are undertaken by experts and should not
be attempted by anyone without adequate
training and supervision.

Ripley's Believe It or Not!

2011

ENTER IF YOU DARE!

RIPLEY

PUBLISHING

a Jim Pattison Company

THE RIPLEY WORLD

The world of Ripley's is a vast, elaborate machine. There are researchers, curators, archivists and model-makers, as well as editors and correspondents who compile articles and write for the *Ripley's Believe It or Not!* books. Dedicated and passionate about what they do, these people never tire in their mission to uncover and preserve the unbelievable side of life.

Across the world, 31 museums showcase the Ripley's collection. On display are unforgettable exhibits supplied by the huge central archive that is kept in the vast storage warehouse at Ripley's headquarters in Orlando, Florida. This is also where all of the wax-work sculptures of extraordinary people, past and present, are conceived and lovingly brought to life (see page 8).

Forever on the look out for new bizarre exhibits to wow visitors, Ripley's regularly updates its museum collections. Here, a room in the newly remodeled museum in Brisbane, Australia, showcases just some of the unbelievable Ripley's pieces.

A display in the Ripley's museum in Brisbane, Australia, features tall man Robert Wadlow, 17-in-tall (43-cm) Alypius—imprisoned in a bird cage by an Egyptian pharaoh for treason—a Paduang woman with brass neck rings, three-legged performer Francisco Lentini, and Avelino Perez Matos who could dislocate his eyeballs from their sockets. Also shown is the tiny Peel P-50 car—big enough for one, and very easy to park!

ROBERT RIPLEY

Ripley's operates with the energy of its founder, Robert Ripley, who, in 1918, began his quest to expose the world's most unbelievable true stories.

At the time, he was working as a cartoonist at the New York Globe. At first, his column pinpointed unusual achievements in athletics, but he soon broadened his search into every aspect of life. Traveling endlessly to collect material, he covered more than 464,000 mi (747,000 km) in his lifetime, and his enthusiasm for the bizarre was matched only by that of his readership—the mailbags dumped on his desk contained as many as 170,000 letters a week from fans with a curious tale to tell.

Exhibits in the Ripley's museums encompass an incredibly diverse array of unusual items. This lifesize sculpture of a dog has been made from discarded toys by English artist Robert Bradford.

The 31 Ripley's museums around the world are often housed in buildings that are quite unbelievable themselves! This is the eye-catching façade of the Ripley's museum in Atlantic City, New Jersey. For a full list of Ripley's museums, see page 254.

Ripley's regularly presents spectacular public events—which are usually held at its museum locations—such as "Sword Swallowing Day." This features jaw-dropping stunts by dozens of experts at this incredible art.

IT'S YOUR CALL...

LET US KNOW IF YOU HAVE A STRANGE FACT THAT WE SHOULD KNOW ABOUT

WRITE TO US

BION Research,
Ripley Entertainment Inc.,
7576 Kingspointe Parkway, 188,
Orlando, Florida 32819,
U.S.A.
Please include photos where possible

Follow us on Facebook and Twitter

Or send an email to
bionresearch@ripleys.com

Contribute via our website
www.ripleybooks.com

Check out today's Believe It or Not! cartoon: www.comics.com/ripleys_believe_it_or_not

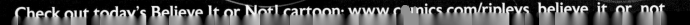

BEHIND THE SCENES

Integral to the success of every Ripley's museum are the exhibits. These are collected at our HQ in Orlando. This is also where hundreds of the museums' minutely detailed sculptures are created, in the Ripley's art department.

The walls here are stacked with shelves that heave with boxes of buttons, rolls of fabric and jars of glass eyes and teeth. On the floor stand silent, headless bodies, and elsewhere heads wait patiently for the processes that turn an inanimate object into a sculpture seemingly full of life.

Wax model Walter Hudson poses with members of the art team—from left: Olga Irrizary, Andy Howard, Barry Anderson and Bruce Miller (bottom left). Olga reports that the wrap around Walter's 152-in (3.8-m) waist required 6½ yd (6 m) of fabric.

Molding ①

Bodywork ②

Hairstyling ③

Painting ⑤

Dressing ④

The Ripley's art department in Orlando, Florida, where the sculptures for Ripley's museums are constructed. Grace McDaniels's wax head can be seen as a work in progress and in its final form.

"We receive photographs and cartoons from the archive department and often have specific dimensions to work from," explains Barry Anderson, the department's director and a working artist who began his career in film and television make-up special effects. "In the case of figures with extreme body sizes, we'll sculpt the shape in foam first, before laying clay over the top."

Molding 1

From the clay shape, a rubber mold is made, which is filled with wax. "We use resin for the bodies, wax for the heads usually, because wax has a translucent quality," says Andy Howard. "We use five different waxes to get the right amount of softness and durability. It's a secret recipe. We might add some fiberglass and plastic if the model's got fragile areas such as in the case of Grace McDaniel's lips!"

2 Bodywork

Bruce Miller worked for years at Universal Studios and for Disney at Epcot, constructing, among others, the E.T. and King Kong exhibits: "At Ripley's, the body is made from fiberglass and plastic. The limbs are made separately and are then slotted together, with wooden fittings for the shoulders and waist."

Hairstyling 3

Glass eyeballs and teeth are then inserted. Hair comes next. "We cut the eye of a needle so it becomes hook-shaped and use this to handle one hair at a time. We work with real hair—which is very expensive—punching each hair into the slightly softened wax. A single head of hair can take 80 hours to complete," says Debra Brozovich. "We normally keep the hair six to ten inches long, so it can be cut and styled later."

4 Dressing

After that, the sculpture can be dressed. Olga Irrizary has made the Ripley sculptures' costumes for 15 years. "I've made many suits in my time for tallest man Robert Wadlow. His three-piece suit uses seven to eight yards of material, and his shirt alone takes another three yards. His shoe size is 37EE and his shoes are custom made. A single pair costs $3,000. We go to a manufacturer who makes shoes for basketball players!" For tiny sculpture Pauline Muster's shoes—she stood just 1 ft 11.2 in (59 cm) tall—Olga shops in baby stores.

5 Painting

A detailed painting process then begins. "We take great pride in getting everything perfect," concludes Barry. "And keeping the sculptures that way. We're constantly making repairs. A museum may send a damaged model to us and when we open the crate, there are just pieces inside. But we send it back as good as new."

SEEKING THE WEIRD

When Edward Meyer took possession of a ball 7 ft (2.1 m) high, weighing 9,400 lb (4,265 kg) and made from 780,000 rubber bands, it had to be lifted by crane onto a flat bed truck and transported 250 mi (400 km) from Lauderhill, Florida, to Orlando. See page 162 for the full story.

Edward Meyer is the Ripley archivist in Florida. Here, he talks about some of his favorite memories of how some exhibits came to light.

● I've received over 100 shrunken heads over the years, but only one by surprise—in the mail. I bought two from a "walk-in" to our office. He was carrying them in a brown paper lunch bag!

● After searching high and low for ten years, I found a copy of the Lord's Prayer engraved on a pinhead. It was a totally flukish find, made while I was doing an inventory of a collection of miniature coin paintings on a freezing cold snowy day in Seattle, Washington.

● After paying $100.00 each for 20 intricately carved toothpicks, I received a phone call from our customs broker informing me they had just cleared a box from customs, but all it had in it was toothpicks. I had visions of him using one of my precious toothpicks to clean his teeth!

● We once discovered a stuffed albino moose head in a funky rundown bar in Cochrane, Canada. We offered to buy the whole bar, because we wanted the moose so bad, but were unsuccessful in making a deal. Many years later, the owner phoned me out of the blue and we bought it. It's now in our museum in Branson, Missouri.

Doctors were surprised at a hospital in Wuhan, China, when they saw a four-year-old girl with six fingers on her right hand. What was particularly unusual was that the fingers were each almost identical, with no obvious thumb. As the hand prevented the girl from gripping objects tightly, doctors performed surgery to remove one of the extra fingers and reconstruct the muscles.

LAVA JUNKY

PATRICK KOSTER WILL DO ANYTHING TO GET A GOOD PICTURE—EVEN SLEEP ON THE EDGE OF AN ACTIVE VOLCANO! THE DUTCH ENGINEER BEGAN PHOTOGRAPHING NATURAL PHENOMENA OVER TEN YEARS AGO. HE BECAME OBSESSED WITH CAPTURING THE VIOLENT POWER OF VOLCANOES, CALLING HIMSELF A "LAVA JUNKY," AND EVEN PROPOSING TO HIS WIFE NEXT TO A SIMMERING CRATER.

TO GET THE BEST SHOTS, KOSTER RISKS INHALING TOXIC GAS, SUFFOCATION FROM HOT ASH AND LETHAL VOLCANIC BOMBS— LUMPS OF MOLTEN ROCK VIOLENTLY EJECTED FROM ERUPTING VOLCANOES, NOT TO MENTION THE UNSTOPPABLE FLOW OF SUPER- HOT LAVA SURGING PAST HIS CAMERA. DESPITE THE DANGERS, KOSTER WEARS REGULAR CLOTHING, WITH ONLY A GAS MASK FOR PROTECTION FROM NOXIOUS GAS. HE HAS PHOTOGRAPHED VOLCANOES ON THE CANARY ISLANDS, AND IN ETHIOPIA, ITALY, GREECE AND HAWAII AMONG OTHERS, AND HAS A LONG LIST OF OTHER LAVA-SPEWING CRATERS HE INTENDS TO VISIT.

At this burning lava lake in the crater of active volcano Erta Ale, the surface is constantly moving and bubbling, spewing potentially lethal sulphur dioxide gas. The surrounding terrain is rough and crumbling, meaning Patrick has to watch his footing very carefully to avoid falling in to the lava lake.

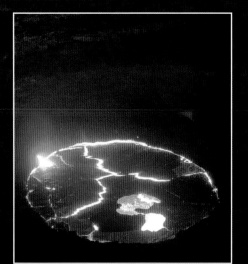

Lava from Kilauea pouring into Pacific Ocean, Big Island, Hawaii. The lava can explode on contact with the sea, throwing lava unpredictably into the air. Another danger here is the appearance of plumes of toxic gas, which contain hydrochloric acid, volcanic ash and needle-sharp lava pieces.

Colorful salt flats, Dallol, Ethiopia. The earth's crust is very thin here, resulting in striking volcanic features when very hot salt water rises to the surface. The area is extremely hot, temperatures can reach over 140°F (60°C) so dehydration is a real risk.

Patrick standing on the edge of a lava fountain on the most active volcano on earth, Kilauea, Big Island, Hawaii. The molten lava here is over 2,012°F (1,100°C).

RIPLEY'S _ask_

There are many different places to photograph, why volcanoes in particular?
After putting in a lot of effort each time, I hope to witness one of nature's most destructive forces, capture its beauty, and walk away from it safely with a lot of pictures. There are only a handful of people doing this kind of photography worldwide. In my country, The Netherlands, I am the only one. Experiencing a real volcanic eruption for the first time is unbelievable. It is all about the smell of sulfur, the sound like a jet engine, the explosions like bombs going off, ash and stones falling down, poor visibility. The feeling of adrenaline combined with fear while taking photographs is addictive. You just want more.

How hot does it get?
Lava can get extremely hot. A sudden lava fountain in the Erta Ale pit crater generated so much extra heat that I fled the crater's edge afraid that my clothes would catch fire.

What is the worst aspect of photographing volcanoes?
The extreme conditions. Cameras, tripods and lenses have all failed because of volcanic ash and gases. There is also the risk of being hurt while hiking up a volcano's summit or through lava fields, and the worst form of altitude sickness is also a problem. There is danger from inhaling toxic gas or volcanic ash, or being hit by lava bombs during an explosion.

What is the best aspect?
After the extreme effort of getting to the volcano's crater, actually experiencing— seeing, hearing, feeling, smelling—

Do you ever get scared?
Yes and it's a good thing. You stay alert and sharp to react immediately if something extraordinary happens. It also makes you more careful. The best picture is not necessarily the one taken closest to the action.

Have you ever been caught out?
I have had some narrow escapes. In Tanzania a small lava "bridge" collapsed in the boiling lava pit moments after I left. In Hawaii I stood on edges that were gone the next day (so called bench collapse). They had fallen into the ocean. The seawater is extremely hot at these places so survival is almost impossible. Another time on Stromboli the conditions at the summit were so poor, with wind blowing ash and toxic gases right over the summit, that a gas mask and helmet needed to be used. Taking pictures was

Silk Cocoon

A motorist returned to his car in Rotterdam, the Netherlands, in 2009 to find it buried beneath a giant silk cocoon created by an army of caterpillars. His Honda car had somehow been mistaken for food by spindle ermine larvae, which weave silk webs to protect themselves from birds and wasps, allowing them to gorge on leaves for six weeks before transforming into butterflies.

℞ BIRD LOVER

A male traveler arriving at Los Angeles International Airport, California, in 2009 was found to have 14 live birds strapped to his legs under his pants. Customs officials became suspicious after spotting bird feathers and droppings on his socks, and tail feathers protruding beneath his pants.

℞ HIDING PLACE

Two-year-old Natalie Jasmer from Greenville, Pennsylvania, did such a good job of hiding during a 2009 game of hide-and-seek that her family had to call police and firefighters to help find her. After an hour's search, she was finally found by the family dog, having fallen asleep in a drawer beneath the washing machine.

℞ INSEPARABLE TWINS

Identical twins Peter and Paul Kingston from West Sussex, England, have been almost inseparable for over 75 years. They worked for the same electronics firm and then as entertainers at the same holiday camp, and for the past 40 years they have shared the same house with their respective wives.

℞ BOXED CLEVER

A prisoner escaped jail in Willich, Germany, in November 2008 by hiding in a box, which was part of a courier's shipment.

℞ ID PROBLEM

A judge presiding over a drug trafficking case in Kuala Lumpur, Malaysia, released the defendants—identical twins—because police officers couldn't prove which one had originally been arrested.

℞ GRAVE DISCOVERY

In March 2009, while planting bushes, Sheila Woods of Devon, England, uncovered a grave, complete with headstone, coffin and corpse from 1833, in the middle of her garden.

Scissor Spider

Security guards at American airports confiscate hundreds of scissors and other potential weapons every day. Artist Christopher Locke collects these spiky tools and bends them into sculptures, including spiders made from twisted scissors and creepy crawlies made from knives and multi-tools.

℞ STRAY BULLET

In July 2009, Janifer Bliss was accidentally shot while sitting on the toilet, when the person in the next-door cubicle dropped their gun and it went off. Bliss was sitting in the cubicle in a hotel bathroom in Tampa, Florida, when she was hit in the leg by the stray bullet, which was fired as the handgun fell to the ground.

℞ BABY SWITCH

Kay Rene Reed Qualls and DeeAnn Angell Shafer learned at the age of 56 that they had been accidentally switched at birth and had grown up with each other's parents. The girls were born at Pioneer Memorial Hospital in Heppner, Oregon, in 1953, but the mistake was only uncovered when they took DNA tests in 2009.

℞ BEETLE TERROR

In December 2008, police in Osaka, Japan, arrested a man for releasing thousands of beetle larvae onto an express train to scare female passengers.

℞ SWALLOWED PHONE

When Andrew Cheatle lost his cell phone on a beach at Worthing, West Sussex, England, he thought it had been swept out to sea and that he would never see it again, but a week later it turned up—in the belly of a huge cod. The 25-lb (11-kg) cod had been caught by fisherman Glen Kerley, who was gutting it for his fish stall when he found the phone—which still worked—inside the fish's stomach.

℞ LEAP DAY

The Keogh family have three generations born on 29 February, beating odds of 3,118,535,181 to one. Peter Keogh was born in Ireland on leap day—February 29—1940, his son Eric was born in the U.K. on leap day 1964 and granddaughter Bethany was born in the U.K. on leap day 1996.

℞ WILD CHILD

A Russian girl spent the first five years of her life being brought up by cats and dogs. The girl, from the Siberian city of Chita, adopted the behavior of the animals she lived with, even barking like a little dog and jumping at the door when people left the room.

℞ CLOSE RELATIVES

After not seeing each other for 60 years, long-lost siblings George Culwick and Lucy Heenan discovered in 2008 that they had been living just 4 mi (6.5 km) apart in Birmingham, West Midlands, England.

℞ CLOUD NINE

To mark the ninth day of the ninth month of 2009, a budget supermarket chain in Los Angeles, California, offered nine couples cut-rate wedding ceremonies for 99 cents. After getting hitched, the couples were handed $99.99 in cash and taken to a romantic location for their honeymoon.

℞ CASH CATCH

Two Australian teenagers who went on a fishing trip to Tuntable Creek, near Nimbin, New South Wales, in September 2009 landed a surprise catch—a plastic package containing $87,000 in cash.

TRAVELING TWINS

CHANG AND ENG BUNKER (1811–74) WERE THE ORIGINAL SIAMESE TWINS, THE RARE CONDITION BEING NAMED AFTER THEIR BIRTHPLACE OF SIAM (MODERN-DAY THAILAND). THEY WERE JOINED AT THE STOMACH BY A SMALL PIECE OF CARTILAGE AND WERE LATER EXHIBITED AS A CURIOSITY. THEY WENT ON TO MARRY TWO SISTERS AND HAD A TOTAL OF 21 CHILDREN. IN 1874, CHANG SUFFERED A STROKE IN HIS SLEEP AND WHEN ENG AWOKE TO FIND HIS BROTHER DEAD, HE REFUSED TO BE SEPARATED FROM HIM AND BLED TO DEATH THREE HOURS LATER, BECAUSE THE BLOOD WAS NOT BEING PUMPED BACK FROM HIS TWIN'S BODY.

JULY

Past pheasant given up the ghost on the Warwick Highway.

		1	SAT	17	
		2	SUN	18	
THU		3	MON	19	
FRI		4	TUE	20	
SAT		5	WED	21	
SUN		6	THU	22	
MON		7	FRI	23	
TUE		8	SAT	24	
WED		9	SUN	25	
THU		10	MON	26	
FRI		11	TUE	27	
SAT		12	WED	28	
SUN		13	THU	29	
MON		14	FRI	30	
TUE		15	SAT	31	
WED		16			
THU					
FRI					

ROADKILL CALENDAR

KEVIN BERESFORD TRAVELED ALL OVER BRITAIN TAKING PHOTOGRAPHS OF ROADKILL FOR A 2010 CALENDAR THAT BECAME A BEST-SELLER. HE SOLD HUNDREDS OF COPIES OF HIS QUIRKY ROADKILL CALENDAR, WHICH FEATURED PICTURES OF SQUASHED SQUIRRELS, FLATTENED FOXES AND MASHED MAGPIES.

ROAD KILL

CALENDAR 2010

No animal was deliberately killed or maimed in the production of this calendar

® MOON CHECK

A $10.50 check signed by Neil Armstrong hours before he took off for the Moon was sold for $27,350 at an auction in Amherst, New Hampshire, in July 2009—40 years to the day after it was written. Armstrong had written the check—for money borrowed from a NASA manager—in case anything happened to him on the lunar mission.

® DENTAL DISCOVERY

A customer shopping at a Walmart store in Falmouth, Massachusetts, said he found ten human teeth hidden in a zipped compartment of a wallet he was about to buy. Police said the teeth belonged to an adult, but since there was no blood or gum tissue present, it would not be possible to perform DNA tests to identify whose teeth they were.

® DELAYED DELIVERY

Dave Conn of Hudson, Ohio, received a postcard in his mailbox 47 years after it was sent. The card had been sent by a woman from Helena, Montana, in 1962, but the delay meant it never reached its intended recipient, who had died in 1988.

® BOTTLE VOYAGE

A bottle with a note inside thrown into the ocean in 1969 off the coast of New Jersey was discovered 39 years later—just 400 mi (645 km) away in Corolla, North Carolina.

® FREE SALAMI

Motorists in the Bulgarian capital Sofia were awarded free salami in 2009 for driving courteously. As part of a police road-safety initiative, a salami factory offered lunch to any driver who yielded to pedestrians at marked street crossings.

® DOUBLE MONEY

In August 2009, customers flocked to a faulty cash machine that was paying out double money at a supermarket in London, England. The store closed the machine as soon as it learned of the fault, but by then lucky customers had taken over $7,500 from it.

Ⓡ ROWERS' RESCUE

The pilot of a light aircraft forced to bale out in the middle of the Irish Sea had a lucky escape when he was spotted by a team trying to row its way around Britain. The four-man crew was ten days into its time challenge when one of them saw the plane half-submerged in the freezing water. Pilot John O'Shaughnessy, who had been flying from Wales to Ireland, was standing on the wing.

Ⓡ INCRIMINATING EVIDENCE

Vlado Taneski, a Macedonian crime reporter, covered a series of murders in such detail that police eventually discovered in June 2008 that he was responsible for them!

Ⓡ GREENBRIER GHOST

A ghost once helped convict a murderer. Zona Shue's death in Greenbrier County, West Virginia, in 1897 was presumed natural until her spirit appeared to her mother and described how she was killed by her husband Edward. Her mother persuaded the local prosecutor to reopen the case and an autopsy on the exhumed body verified that Zona had been murdered. Edward was subsequently convicted of the crime.

Ⓡ UNWANTED CUSTOMERS

Shoppers at a food store in Puyallup, Washington State, were forced to flee in 2009 after cattle broke away from a fair parade and ran amok in the aisles. A year earlier, in 2008, a bull from the same fair charged into a bank.

Ⓡ BAR BLAZE

In 2008, a fire crew from the town of Bournemouth in Dorset, England, was sent to extinguish a blaze at a bar called The Inferno—which was situated next to another bar called The Old Fire Station.

Ⓡ CORK ATTACK

After a truck carrying bottles of wine crashed and caught fire on a highway in Wamsutter, Wyoming, emergency crews came under attack from a hail of corks as the bottles exploded in the heat.

Ⓡ BANK ERROR

After Josh Muszynski of Manchester, New Hampshire, swiped his debit card at a gas station to pay for a pack of cigarettes in July 2009, he checked his account online and saw that he had been charged over $23 quadrillion. The Bank of America corrected the error the following day.

Car Crazy

After spending 17 years building his own Lamborghini sports car in the cellar of his Wisconsin home, Ken Imhoff realized that he had no way of getting it out. Undeterred, he built a ramp and hired a mechanical digger to gouge out a slope in his garden, even removing a section of the house's foundations. At the end of a delicate 2½-hour operation, the new car finally emerged above ground.

Ⓡ FAMILY LINE

After six generations spanning 217 years, the last Dr. Maurice of the town of Marlborough in Wiltshire, England, finally hung up his stethoscope in 2009. Dr. David Maurice's retirement brought to an end an unbroken line of family members caring for the town's sick people dating back to 1792.

Ⓡ BODY HOAX

After receiving a tip-off about what appeared to be a body wrapped in a sleeping bag in a forest near Izu City, Japan, police officers took it back to the station for a post-mortem examination—but when the medical examiner opened the bag, he found it contained a life-size doll wearing a brown wig, a blouse and a skirt.

Ⓡ BUCKET CEREMONY

In keeping with a tradition in Xi'an, China, that the bride's feet should not touch the ground during the journey from home to the ceremony, a couple got married in 2008 in midair in two large tractor digger buckets. The bride and two bridesmaids stood in one bucket, while the groom and two best men stood opposite them in a second bucket.

Something Fishy

An unidentified 4½-ft-long (1.4-m) fish caught near Taizhou City in eastern China, had a large sucker pad on its head. No villager would eat the weird-looking creature in case its appearance was the result of toxic poisoning.

BODY SNATCHERS

WELCOME TO THE WORLD OF THE PARASITE, AND WHAT A WORLD IT IS! THESE GUYS ARE FRIGHTENINGLY SMART—THEY LIVE ON, OR IN, ANOTHER ORGANISM AND MANIPULATE THE BEHAVIOR OF THEIR UNSUSPECTING HOSTS TO THEIR ADVANTAGE, OFTEN KILLING THEM IN THE PROCESS.

Deadly Mushroom

Spores invade, insect dies, fungi grows out of corpse

These fungi infect caterpillars and other insects, killing them and mummifying the body as they spread. Some fungi make insects into zombies, whereby the insects crawl along and die in the best place for the fungi spores to spread into the air and infect other insects.

Brain Eaters

Fly drops larva that will eat ant's brain until its head falls off

The fly lands on the head of an ant, laying an egg that releases a brain-eating larva. The larva eventually decapitates the ant and lives in the head for two weeks until it emerges as an adult Phorid fly.

This parasite invades snails, making their eyestalks swollen and colorful to encourage birds, which then attack the snails and rip off their eyestalks. The flatworms breed in the birds' guts. Other snails then eat bird droppings infected with the parasite, and the endless cycle continues.

Stuck for Life

Male fish fuse with females for life!

Male anglerfish are much smaller than female anglerfish. They bite onto the body of females until their skin and eventually their blood vessels fuse together. The withered male then becomes part of the female body forever, useless except for his role in fertilizing the female's eggs.

Eye Catching

Infected snail eyestalks look like pulsating green caterpillars

Mind Control

Hairworms begin life as tiny creatures living in the guts of insects, which they start eating from the inside until they grow to be longer than their hosts—up to 3 ft (1 m) in length! The presence of the worm drives the insect to seek out water, where it then drowns. The adult worm then squeezes itself out of its host and lives in the water.

Makes insects drown themselves so water-dwelling worm can escape into water

Womb Invader

Parasite takes over crab egg pouch

A parasitic barnacle attaches itself to crabs, invades the egg pouch and forces the crab to look after parasite eggs. If the crab is male, the parasite sterilizes it and makes its abdomen bigger, essentially turning the male crab female.

Hunter Hunted

Paralyzes tarantula so young wasp can eat it

Tarantula Hawk wasps hunt tarantulas and paralyze them with a powerful sting—one of the most painful ever recorded. The spider is dragged back to its own nest, where the wasp lays an egg on its body. When the wasp larva hatches, the paralyzed spider is eaten alive.

Taste Buddy

Replaces fish tongue to feed on blood and mucus

This creature clamps onto the tongue of a fish, sucking blood from the tongue until it withers and dies. The parasite then remains firmly attached in the fish's mouth, working just like the original tongue, dining on blood, mucus and scraps of food.

R LATE DEMAND

A German mathematician, who had been dead for 450 years, received a letter in 2009 demanding that he pay long-overdue TV licence fees. The bill was sent to the last home address of algebra expert Adam Ries, even though he had died in 1559—centuries before the invention of television.

R GRATEFUL THIEF

An Italian thief thanked police for rescuing him from a group of irate Korean tourists whom he had just robbed. The thief had stolen a handbag from the family during their visit to Rome, but they gave chase and floored him with taekwondo moves, before subjecting him to a beating. They stopped only when an officer arrived to arrest the 48-year-old man.

R DOLPHIN GAMES

A woman who had been playing with a friendly bottlenose dolphin called Moko in the sea off Mahia Beach on New Zealand's North Island got into difficulty when the dolphin stopped her from returning to shore. Her cries for help eventually alerted rescuers who rowed out to find her exhausted and cold, clinging to a buoy. Locals say the dolphin gets lonely in the winter when there are fewer people around and just wanted to keep playing.

R CUCUMBER THEFTS

In 2009, police in Adelaide, Australia, investigated a series of thefts involving cucumbers. More than $8,500 worth of cucumbers were stolen in 11 separate burglaries on market gardens over a period of three months.

R LOTTERY LUCK

In 2002, Mike McDermott from Hampshire, England, won the lottery twice with the same numbers, beating odds of 5.4 trillion to one.

R HOARD UNCOVERED

An elderly Japanese businessman lost $4 million in cash when a thief found it buried in his garden.

R GUILTY CONSCIENCE

A man who robbed a Walnut Creek, California, bank in July 2009 apparently felt so guilty that three days later he walked into a church, confessed to the crime and handed over $1,200 to a priest before leaving.

R WAYWARD SHOT

History buff William Maser, whose hobby is re-creating 19th-century military firearms, accidentally fired a 2-lb (1-kg) cannonball through the wall of his neighbor's home in Georges Township, Pennsylvania, in September 2009. He fired the cannonball, about 2 in (5 cm) in diameter, outside his own home, but it ricocheted and hit a house 400 yd (365 m) away, smashing through a window and a wall before landing in a closet.

HAIR SCULPTURE

CHINESE HAIRDRESSER HUANG XIN SPENT SEVEN DAYS AND NIGHTS CREATING THIS SCULPTURE OF BARACK OBAMA FROM 9 LB (4 KG) OF HUMAN HAIR COLLECTED IN HIS SHOPS. AFTER WASHING AND DYING THE HAIR—HE USED ONLY WOMEN'S HAIR BECAUSE IT WAS SOFTER—HE GLUED IT ON TO PAPER BEFORE ROLLING IT INTO DIFFERENT SHAPES. HUANG XIN HAS ALSO CREATED A DETAILED MODEL OF BEIJING'S TIANANMEN GATE TOWER FROM HAIR.

Ram Raid

A ram in Helgoysund, Norway, was stranded 15 ft (4.5 m) up a telegraph pole for an hour after it tried to abseil down an electricity cable to reach a field of ewes. The lovelorn sheep slid down the cable from a higher field with his horn stuck on the wire, before stopping against the pole. Eventually a group of German tourists managed to loop a rope around the sheep and lower it to the ground.

℞ ELDERLY GRADUATE

Eleanor Benz, who dropped out of high school to help her family during the Great Depression, finally received her diploma in 2009—73 years later. She left Chicago's Lake View High School at age 17 to take a job, but at her 90th birthday party she was presented with the diploma, gown and cap, complete with a 1936 tassel.

℞ CARDBOARD CUTOUTS

Flat daddies and flat mommies, life-sized cardboard cutout photos of U.S. soldiers stationed abroad, are used to connect families with absent spouses and parents.

℞ EXPLODING FRIDGE

Kathy Cullingworth of West Yorkshire, England, was woken with a start one night when her fridge suddenly exploded. She found the fridge doors had been blown off, scattering food all over the kitchen.

℞ BOTTLE VOYAGE

A message in a bottle dropped off a cruise ship by a U.S. teenager in the Bahamas in 2004 was found five years later on a beach in Cornwall, England—4,000 mi (6,440 km) away. The message had been written by Daniel Knopp of Baltimore, Maryland.

Family Likeness

Dhanna Ram of Rajasthan, India, has been growing his mustache since 1988—and by 2009 it measured 4½ ft (1.4 m) long. He was inspired by the death of his father, Karna Ram Bheel, who himself had a mustache that measured a whopping 6½ ft (2 m) long!

MAORI MUMMIES

MAORI TRIBES OF NEW ZEALAND USED TO MUMMIFY HEAVILY TATTOOED HEADS OF WARRIOR ADVERSARIES, SKIN, HAIR, TEETH AND ALL. MAORI WARRIORS WOULD COLLECT AS TROPHIES THE DECAPITATED, TATTOOED HEADS OF NOTABLE ENEMIES THEY HAD KILLED IN BATTLE, AND THE HEADS OF THEIR OWN DEAD LEADERS AND FAMILY MEMBERS WERE ALSO REMOVED AND TREATED WITH RESPECT—SOMETIMES TO PREVENT OTHER TRIBES ESCAPING WITH THEM. IT HAS BEEN REPORTED THAT ENTIRE BODIES WERE PRESERVED, ALTHOUGH NONE REMAIN. MAORI FACIAL TATTOOS, KNOWN AS *TA MOKO*, WERE A LONG AND PAINFUL PROCESS, WHICH MADE USE OF CARVED BONE CHISELS TO MAKE CUTS IN THE FACE. IN THE 18TH CENTURY, EUROPEAN VISITORS BEGAN TO BUY THE SKULLS AS INTERESTING ARTIFACTS, AND SOON THE TRADE IN MUMMIFIED *TA MOKO* BECAME SO POPULAR THAT APPROPRIATELY TATTOOED ENEMIES WERE KILLED SOLELY IN ORDER TO SUPPLY THE MARKET WITH FRESH HEADS. THIS MURDEROUS PRACTICE WAS EVENTUALLY OUTLAWED IN THE 19TH CENTURY.

RIPLEY'S RESEARCH

IN ORDER TO MUMMIFY A HEAD, THE MAORIS WOULD FIRST REMOVE THE BRAIN AND THE EYES FROM THE DECAPITATED HEAD. THEN THE EMPTY SKULL AND EYE SOCKETS WERE STUFFED WITH PLANT FIBERS. THE HEAD WAS THEN DRIED OVER A PERIOD OF 24 HOURS USING BOILING, STEAMING AND SMOKING METHODS.

℞ MODERN CANNIBALS

The journalist Paul Raffaele reported in 2006 that he had discovered a modern headhunter tribe on the island of New Guinea that still removed the heads of their enemies and cannibalized their remains, and they have the skulls to prove it.

℞ DEATH EATERS

The ancient Greek historian Herodotus wrote of a nomadic tribe in Iran that killed and ate members of their community when they became old and weak, cooking them with their cattle. According to his writings, this was the way that they preferred to go.

℞ FROZEN MUMMY

In 1995, two climbers in the Andes discovered the mummified body of a young girl, frozen solid on the side of Mount Ampato. Although it is thought she died in the 15th century, her body was remarkably well preserved.

It is not just heads that could be shrunk. The Jivaros once captured a gold-seeking Spanish army officer and reduced his entire body from a height of 5 ft 9 in (1.75 m) to a shrunken mummy just 31 in (0.78 m) tall.

Robert Ripley holds up a shrunken head from the Jivaro tribes of South America.

℞ UNBURIED HEADS

Headhunting rituals took place in Europe well into the 20th century. Tribes in Montenegro would remove the heads of people they had killed to prevent them receiving a proper burial.

℞ BLUE DOTS

Headhunters of Borneo would mark one finger joint with a blue dot for each victim they had killed. Chief Temonggong Koh had completely blue hands by the time of his death in the late 20th century.

℞ TROPHY BODIES

The Sausa tribe from Peru would skin their enemies, before filling the skin with ash, sewing it back up and displaying the stuffed skin as a trophy and status symbol.

Head Shrinkers

Some of the most unbelievable discoveries that Robert Ripley made on his travels were the shrunken heads of South America. The Jivaro tribes of Ecuador and Peru would take the heads of fallen enemies, remove the skin whole, and shrink it to the size of a fist. *Tsantas*, as the shrunken heads were known locally, were used to banish the vengeful spirits of their previous owners, with their lips sewn shut to stop the spirits from escaping. When Western tourists began to visit the area in the 19th and 20th centuries, a demand for gruesome souvenirs fueled the practice, and it is said that people were killed just to keep up the supply. Robert Ripley reported in his journal that a German scientist who attempted to find Jivaro headhunters came out of the forest as nothing more than a shrunken head with a red beard. A TV documentary team recently unearthed a Polish videotape from the early 1960s that not only seemed to prove that *tsantas* were still being made by the Jivaro tribe at that time, but also provides remarkable video footage of the head-shrinking process.

℞ GOOD LUCK HEADS

The feared Wa tribe from the jungles of Burma (Myanmar) would regularly cut off people's heads, and did so up until the 1970s, as they thought the severed heads prevented disease and brought good luck.

℞IPLEY'S RESEARCH

THE JIVARO USED TO TAKE A DECAPITATED HEAD AND MAKE AN INCISION IN THE BACK OF THE SCALP SO THAT THEY COULD SLICE THE SKIN, FLESH AND HAIR OFF THE BONE, MAKING SURE IT REMAINED INTACT. THEN THEY WOULD TAKE THE BONELESS HEAD, SEW THE EYELIDS SHUT, AND SEAL THE MOUTH WITH WOODEN PEGS. THE NEXT PART OF THE PROCESS INVOLVED BOILING THE HEAD FOR NO LESS THAN TWO HOURS IN HERBS THAT CONTAINED TANNIN TO DRY OUT THE HEAD. ONCE REMOVED FROM THE BOIL, THE FLESH WAS SCRAPED FROM THE SKIN AND THE HEAD WAS SHRUNK FURTHER WITH HOT ROCKS AND SAND, BEFORE BEING GRADUALLY MOLDED BACK INTO ITS ORIGINAL SHAPE. FINALLY, THE MOUTH WAS SEWN SHUT WITH STRING AND THE HEAD DRIED OVER A FIRE FOR SEVERAL DAYS.

Snap!

Conjoined crocodile twins were born at the Samut Prakarn Crocodile Farm and Zoo near Bangkok, Thailand. The animals, named Chang and Eng after the world's most famous Siamese twins (see page 15), each had a head and four legs, but shared a common lower body with one tail.

℞ CASH FIND

While walking to his car in Syracuse, New York, in 2009, David Jenks noticed a number of bags apparently containing trash lying by the side of the street—but when he went to move them he discovered that they were filled with $250,000 in banknotes.

℞ CHILD'S PLAY

Three-year-old Pipi Quinlan from Auckland, New Zealand, visited an online auction site in 2009 and bought a mechanical shovel for $12,000 while her parents were asleep.

℞ SNAP DECISION

An anti-Mafia police unit in Naples, Italy, seized a crocodile that was used by an alleged mobster to intimidate local businessmen. Officers said the gangster would invite extortion victims to his home and threaten them with the crocodile, which weighed 88 lb (40 kg) and was 5 ft 7 in (1.7 m) long, unless they paid him protection money.

℞ MISSILE CATCH

Commercial fisherman Rodney Salomon from St. Petersburg, Florida, landed the catch of his life in 2009—an 8-ft-long (2.4-m), American-made, air-to-air guided missile that could have exploded at any moment. Despite the danger, he reeled in the missile, strapped it to the roof of his boat and kept fishing in the Gulf of Mexico for another ten days—even during electrical storms—before returning to port.

℞ DOUBLE LIFE

Two women who worked at the same factory in Zhengzhou, China, were shocked to learn they were both married to the same man. Cui Bin divided his time between the two households, making excuses for his frequent absences. Meanwhile, the two wives had become friends through a shared love of karaoke, never dreaming that they were also sharing a husband.

℞ WINNING TICKET

Two months after her husband Donald's death, Charlotte Peters of Danbury, Connecticut, checked through his belongings and found a $10 million winning lottery ticket. He had bought the ticket just hours before suffering a fatal heart attack in November 2008.

℞ SNAIL MAIL

In July 2009, Wendy Bosworth from Wolverhampton, West Midlands, England, received a postcard from a Greek island—22 years after it was sent. The card had been posted by her niece, Joanne Bosworth, who was holidaying on the island of Nisyros in 1987.

Head Drill

Chinese kung fu master Hu Qiong can insert a fast-spinning electric drill into his temple and belly for a full minute and walk away unharmed. Known as "The Unbreakable Body," Hu can also catch a running electric saw with his bare hands.

ⓡ ANGRY JEDI

The founder of the Jedi religion inspired by *Star Wars* threatened legal action after he was asked to leave a supermarket for wearing the sect's traditional hood. Daniel Jones from Holyhead, North Wales, leader of the International Church of Jediism, claimed the supermarket victimized him for his beliefs.

ⓡ JELLYFISH ASSAULT

In September 2009, a 41-year-old man was arrested on Madeira Beach, Florida, accused of throwing jellyfish at teenagers.

ⓡ MISTAKEN IDENTITY

Assistants at a convenience store in Waterloo, Ohio, that had been robbed twice in two months mistook a drunken customer for a robber and threw a bag of cash at him. The man ignored the money and staggered out of the store.

ⓡ DECAPITATED DUKE

In 1851, builders working in a church near the Tower of London in London, England, discovered a severed head in the vaults. It was discovered to be the Duke of Suffolk, an aristocrat decapitated at the Tower in 1554, his head well preserved by sawdust from the scaffolding on which he lost his head.

ⓡ CHIMP CANDIDATE

A bad-tempered chimpanzee that had a habit of throwing excrement at visitors to Brazil's Rio de Janeiro Zoo was nominated by a satirical magazine to run for the city's 1988 mayoral election. Tiao polled more than 400,000 votes, finishing third out of the 12 candidates.

ⓡ SCORPION HOME

Suang Puangsri has given up the bottom floor of his two-story home in Thailand to more than 4,600 pet scorpions. A practicing Buddhist, he spends an hour every day meditating inside their enclosure, often placing scorpions in his mouth. He says he has been stung so many times that he has become immune to their venom.

ⓡ LAWN RANGER

Stan Hardwick of North Yorkshire, England, owns a lawn mower for every day of the year. Known as the Lawn Ranger, he has spent thousands of dollars on over 365 mowers, some dating back to the mid-19th century. He keeps his favorites in the house for visitors to admire, and stores the rest in his garden shed.

TOP-HEAVY TURBAN

FOR A 2009 SIKH CELEBRATION IN AMRITSAR, INDIA, BABA BALWANT SINGH WORE A 130-LB (60-KG) TURBAN ON HIS HEAD THAT WEIGHED MORE THAN HE DOES! WHEN UNWOUND, THE TURBAN STRETCHED FOR AN INCREDIBLE 2,300 FT (700 M) — THAT'S EQUAL TO THE LENGTH OF SEVEN FOOTBALL FIELDS.

MAN OF STEEL

BUILDER HU ZHUYIN HAD A LUCKY ESCAPE AFTER IMPALING HIMSELF ON A CROWBAR 1 IN (2.5 CM) THICK WHEN HE SLIPPED WHILE CLIMBING SCAFFOLDING IN QINGDAO, CHINA. THE SOLID STEEL CROWBAR SLICED THROUGH HIS CHEST, MISSING HIS AORTA BY JUST 1/2 IN (1 CM). BEFORE MEDICS COULD OPERATE, FIREFIGHTERS HAD TO CUT THROUGH THE BAR SO THAT HU COULD LIE FLAT ON THE OPERATING TABLE.

℞ LODGED IN BRAIN

A large metal pin broke off and lodged itself in the brain of 19-year-old Chris Clear from Penrose, Colorado, while he was helping a friend move a rototiller. Luckily, the pin narrowly missed several major arteries and, after a nine-hour operation to remove it, Clear was able to return to work as a volunteer firefighter. There is not even a scar to remind him of the accident, but he kept the pin as a souvenir.

℞ BROKEN LEG

After suffering decades of pain, Steve Webb from Essex, England, discovered he had been walking around with a broken leg for 29 years. He broke his left leg in a motorbike crash when he was 20 and in 2009 found that it had never actually healed.

℞ ALL'S WELL

An 84-year-old man survived with only minor injuries after spending four days trapped in a well in June 2009. Bob Bennett had entered the 8-ft-deep (2.4-m) well shaft on his remote property at Benson Lake, British Columbia, Canada, while searching for a water source.

℞ HIDDEN PAIN

In April 2009, doctors treated Mrike Rrucaj of Albania for severe head pain and found a bullet that had been lodged in her cheek for 12 years without her knowing it.

℞ ELDERLY MOM

In November 2008, Rajo Devi from the state of Haryana, India, gave birth to a healthy baby at 70 years of age.

℞ CONCEALED WEAPON

Despite being searched several times, obese 540-lb (255-kg) George Vera was able to smuggle a gun into two different Texas jails by hiding it within his rolls of fat.

℞ NEW SKULL

A man whose skull was partially removed after an accident over 50 years ago has stunned doctors by growing a new one—something that is thought to have happened only once before. Gordon Moore of Northumberland, England, had worn a metal plate for half a century after being involved in a car crash, but when surgeons removed the plate in 2009 to treat an infection, they were amazed to find he had grown a completely new skull underneath.

℞ UTENSIL REMOVED

Doctors puzzled by the coughing fits that plagued a man for almost two years found the answer in 2009 by removing a 1-in (2.5-cm) fragment of a plastic eating utensil from his lung. John Manley of Wilmington, North Carolina, said he probably inhaled the piece of plastic while gulping a drink at a fast-food restaurant.

℞ MAGGOT INFESTATION

After suffering from constant nosebleeds for five days, a 70-year-old woman had 40 maggots removed from her nose by doctors at a hospital in Sion, India. A housefly had entered her nose and laid eggs inside it. When the eggs hatched, the larvae started feeding on her flesh, causing her nose to bleed.

℞ STRETCHED LEGS

In an attempt to be taken more seriously at work, Hajnal Ban, a politician from Logan, Queensland, Australia, paid a Russian surgeon $30,000 to break her legs and stretch them so that she would be 5 ft 4 in (1.62 m) tall, three inches taller than her original height.

℞ TEARS OF BLOOD

Teenager Calvino Inman of Rockwood, Tennessee, has a medical condition that leads to him crying tears of blood. The bleeding, which can last for up to an hour, occurs at least three times a day.

Swallowed Scissors

A man in Putian, China, accidentally swallowed a pair of scissors 3½ in (9 cm) long and 1½ in (4 cm) wide. Mr. Lin was using the scissors as a toothpick but when he suddenly laughed, they slipped down into his throat. He tried unsuccessfully to cough them back up and the scissors eventually had to be removed by surgery.

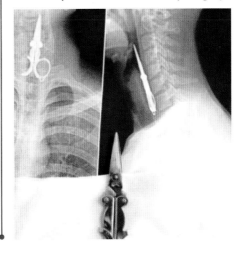

℞ AIRPLANE DEBRIS

Wissam Beydoun of Dearborn, Michigan, was standing outside his home talking in 2009 when he was hit on the shoulder by a piece of metal that had fallen from an airplane. The aluminum scrap, which measured 8 x 6 in (20 x 15 cm) and weighed about a quarter of an ounce, left him with nothing worse than a bump.

Giant Grave

After 990-lb (450-kg) José Luis Garza died in Juarez, Mexico, in 2008, carpenters built him a special extra-large coffin, which had to be lowered into a massive grave by 20 people.

℞ PARROT TALK

A U.S. firefighter who lost his power of speech in a road accident in 1995 has been taught to speak again by parrots. Brian Wilson from Damascus, Maryland, suffered such a serious head injury that doctors told him he would probably never be able to speak coherently again. However, two of the pet parrots that he had kept since childhood continually talked to him, and eventually he began to respond. To show his gratitude, he now provides a home for around 80 abandoned or unwanted parrots.

℞ SECOND BABY

Julia Grovenburg of Fort Smith, Arkansas, stunned doctors by conceiving for a second time while already pregnant. When Mrs. Grovenburg went for her first ultrasound scan, she thought she was about eight weeks pregnant—and she was, with a baby boy. However, she was also almost 11 weeks pregnant with a baby girl, who was developing next to her younger brother in their mother's womb. The non-twins are thought to represent an extremely rare case of superfetation.

Sumo Cyst

A Chinese woman thought she was pregnant with her first child, only to find that she was instead carrying an ovarian cyst weighing 7 lb 11 oz (3.5 kg). Surgeons at a hospital in Haikou successfully removed the cyst—the largest ovarian cyst found in over 20 years.

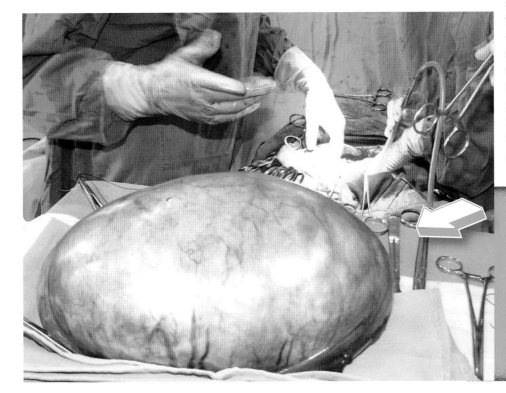

Wooly Wedding

Shepherdess Louise Fairburn from Lincolnshire, England, got married in a wedding dress made of wool from one of her own flock. Husband Ian wore a woolen waistcoat made from the same sheep. The dress took 120 hours to make and cost around £3,000. Louise, who even carried a Bo Peep-style crook on her big day, loves her sheep so much that they featured in her wedding photos.

R SAME NAME

Kelly Hildebrandt, a student from Miami, Florida, announced her engagement in 2009 to... Kelly Hildebrandt. Bored one evening, she had entered her name on the social networking website Facebook to see what would appear and found one match—a Kelly Hildebrandt from Lubbock, Texas. She sent him a message, they became friends and after visiting her in Florida, he proposed.

R TEXT DOCTOR

Caroline Tagg, a postgraduate academic at Birmingham University, England, has been awarded a doctorate in text messaging. She spent 3½ years writing an 80,000-word thesis on SMS texts and their language after studying more than 11,000 texts (that contained a total of around 190,000 words) sent by friends.

R MARATHON MARRIAGE

Rachel Pitt and Garry Keates of Hertfordshire, England, got married while running the 2009 London marathon. They took a detour 24 mi (38.6 km) into the race to jog down the aisle of St. Bride's church, on Fleet Street. Still wearing running shoes, they later completed the remaining 2¼ mi (3.5 km) hand-in-hand before the groom carried his new bride over the finish line as she threw her bouquet into the crowd.

R DOUBLE EGG

Farmer Jeff Taylor from Herefordshire, England, got the shock of his life when he found an egg inside another egg! Both eggs were intact and perfectly formed. Double eggs are thought to be the result of some malfunction in the hen's rhythmic muscular action, which moves a developing egg down the oviduct.

Musical Heights

In 2008, extreme cellists set themselves a 48-hour time limit to climb the four highest mountains in Britain and Ireland with cellos, perform a concert and cover the 1,000 mi (1,600 km) between the peaks. The challenge, completed successfully, followed performances in or on the roofs of 42 British cathedrals—a feat that they managed in just 12 days—and a concert at every street on the London Monopoly board in a day.

ⓡ ICING ON THE CAKE

When Neil Berrett of San Francisco, California, decided to quit his job at a naval shipyard in 2009, he had his letter of resignation written in icing on top of a cake.

ⓡ ZERO GRAVITY

A couple from Brooklyn, New York, proved they were head over heels in love during their wedding by getting married in zero gravity. Science fiction fans Noah Fulmor and Erin Finnegan paid over $15,000 to have their wedding at Kennedy Space Center in a converted Boeing 727 jet airplane which, in the course of a special 90-minute flight, undertakes spectacular roller-coaster-style dives, which simulates the weightlessness experienced by astronauts on space walks. As they floated on air, the couple exchanged rings made from precious metal fragments of a meteorite that crashed to Earth in Namibia 30,000 years ago.

ⓡ FALLING FISH

Leighann Niles was driving near Marblehead, Ohio, in August 2009 when her car windshield was smashed by a falling fish dropped from the talons of an eagle. She said the impact of the fish—a Lake Erie freshwater drum—felt like a brick hitting her car.

ⓡ MAKING HAY

A farmer's son, Markus Schmidt, spelt out his marriage proposal to girlfriend Corinna Pesl by rolling 150 bales of hay to form the words "Will you marry me?" Each bale of hay weighed 661 lb (300 kg) and each letter was 11½ ft (3.5 m) high. Corinna saw the 227-ft-long (70-m) message when she looked out of the bedroom window of her home in the Upper Bavaria region of Germany.

ⓡ PARKING TICKET

A traffic warden in Darwin, Northern Territory, Australia, gave a dog a parking ticket after it was left outside a shopping market. An elderly lady left the dog tied to a fence outside the Rapid Creek market while she went shopping, but when she returned she found that an inspector had attached a ticket to the dog's lead.

ⓡ WEDDING RUSH

Tens of thousands of Chinese people rushed to get married on September 9, 2009, believing that the 09/09/09 date was a good omen for a long marriage. The ninth day of the ninth month, "*jiu, jiu*" in Chinese, is a homonym for "*jiujiu*," which means "for a very long time."

LIGHT SNACK

A CUBAN TREE FROG THAT TRIED TO CATCH AN INSECT IN A PALM BEACH, FLORIDA, GARDEN ENDED UP GLOWING IN THE DARK AFTER SWALLOWING A FAIRY LIGHT. THE BUG HAD LANDED ON THE COLORED LIGHT IN WILDLIFE PHOTOGRAPHER JAMES SNYDER'S GARDEN, BUT WHEN THE FROG WENT IN FOR THE KILL, IT SWALLOWED THE ENTIRE BULB, TOO.

The Kjeragbolten is a granite boulder wedged between the narrow walls of a ravine on the Kjerag Mountain, near Stavanger in Norway. If your nerves—and your balance—allow, you can clamber onto the rock and enjoy the views of the Lysefjord waterway, a frightening 3,280-ft (1,000-m) drop below.

SHED THEATER

Eighty-one-year-old Don Parr from Birmingham, England, spent $15,000 on turning his garden shed into a 1940s movie theater. In a tribute to the picture house where he worked as a projectionist back in 1943, he fitted his shed, which measures 18 x 9 ft (4.8 x 2.4 m), with 14 seats from a real cinema. Now fans travel miles to watch old movies on his shed's 6 ft 6 in x 3 ft 3 in (2 x 1 m) screen, which is complemented with hi-tech surround sound.

AWESOME VIEWS

Chicago's Sears Tower, America's tallest building, installed four glass box viewing platforms in 2009 to make visitors feel like they are floating above the city—at a height of 1,353 ft (412 m). The Ledge, which can hold a weight of five tons, has glass that is 1½ in (3.8 cm) thick. It protrudes from the 103rd floor of the 1,725-ft-high (526-m) building as an extension to the tower's Skydeck and—for those brave enough to look down—offers unobstructed views of the city's streets and the Chicago River below.

CONTAINER CLASSROOMS

Shipping containers are being used as classrooms to provide education for children who live on the garbage dumps of Manila, the Philippines.

SEPARATE TOILETS

Russian cosmonauts on the International Space Station revealed in 2009 that they have been told by their officials to use only the Russian-built toilet and not the U.S. one.

Room with a View

Artists Tiago Primo and his brother Gabriel hung out in an alternative home built on the exterior wall of a building in Rio de Janeiro, Brazil, in the summer of 2009, attracting thousands of visitors. The pair had attached items of furniture, including a bed, a couch and a dresser, 30 ft (9 m) above the street, where they spent up to 14 hours a day.

FREE HOUSE

Gerry and Cindy Mann from Battle Creek, Michigan, came up with a novel way of selling their house—they offered a miniature replica of the home for $169,000 with the real house thrown in for free. The dollhouse, accurate in every detail, had been made by Cindy's father, Ron Caldwell, who built it on a 1:12 scale.

DEBT PAID

When the Skylab space station fell to Earth over Western Australia in 1979, the community of Esperance fined the U.S.A. $400 for littering. The fine was paid 30 years later—in April 2009—when radio-show host Scott Barley of Highway Radio, based in Barstow, California, raised the funds from his morning-show listeners. He sent Esperance a check for the outstanding amount on behalf of NASA.

FITNESS CHURCH

Developer and bodybuilder Al Horvath has converted an old church in Barberton, Ohio, into a gym. He created a Superman theme for the church's sanctuary, replaced the pews with rows of workout equipment and added murals depicting such fitness-related biblical characters as David and Goliath and Samson and Delilah.

HOUSE RAFFLE

Brian Wilshaw sold 46,000 raffle tickets at $35 each—with first prize in the draw being his $1.5 million estate at Morchard Bishop in Devon, England. Owing to the recession and falling U.K. house prices, he had been losing nearly $20,000 a month while trying to sell his 11.5-acre (4.6-ha) property, which came complete with a five-bedroom house, four holiday lodges, some woodland and a fishing lake.

Stone Home

This stunning and mysterious home is made of limestone rocks and is in Fafe, northern Portugal. Made by an unknown artist, there has been some speculation over the house's very existence, because of its extraordinary appearance and the few pictures that have been taken of it, but it is indeed real and has become a local icon over the years.

PINK HOSPITAL

To ease the stress of childbirth, the 30-bed Huasheng maternity hospital in Yuanlin, Taiwan, is decorated entirely in pink "Hello Kitty" décor. The nurses wear pink uniforms with cat-themed aprons and the cartoon cat's likeness even appears on birth-certificate covers.

ROOFTOP BATH

Silvia Mertens and Pieter Peerlings, architects from Antwerp, Belgium, built a four-story home/office building with a transparent front wall in a space less than 8 ft (2.4 m) wide—and with the bathtub on the roof.

JOKE KINGDOM

The kingdom of Wallachia, located in the Czech Republic, was founded in 1997 as a practical joke by photographer Tomás Harabis in a bid to attract tourists. King Boleslav the Gracious (aka Czech comedian Bolek Polivka) became ceremonial head of state and Harabis served as foreign minister. Wallachia adopted its own currency, passport, flag, university, state limousine and navy.

CAVE MOUTH

Predjama Castle in Slovenia was built in the 12th century in the middle of a 400-ft (123-m) overhanging limestone cliff, in the mouth of a cave.

SMALL SCREEN

A cinema in Coventry, England, measures just 10 x 8 ft (3 x 2.4 m) and seats only four people. Brian Sexton converted a derelict indoor stall in the city's market into the tiny Market Cinema, complete with small screen.

NARROW HOUSE

New York City's narrowest house went on sale for a fat $2.7 million in 2009. The 9^1/$_2$ x 42 ft (2.9 x 13 m), three-story home was built in Greenwich Village in 1873, sandwiched between two larger buildings.

GREEN SAND

Papakolea Beach, near South Point, Hawaii, has green sand as a result of olivine crystals found in the surrounding lava cone. Over the years, the sea has eroded the headland, depositing olivine on the beach. The waves have then washed away the lighter grains of sand leaving the darker olivine crystals to form the beach.

ROOF ATTACK

AN ORDINARY SMALL TERRACED HOUSE IN OXFORDSHIRE, ENGLAND, BECAME AN INTERNATIONAL TOURIST ATTRACTION AFTER A 25-FT (7.6-M) FIBERGLASS SHARK WAS STUCK HEADFIRST INTO THE ROOF. KNOWN AS THE "HEADINGTON SHARK," THE SCULPTURE WAS ERECTED IN 1986 BY THE HOME'S OWNER, BILL HEINE, AS A PROTEST AGAINST MAN'S INHUMANITY TO MAN. THE BUILDING STARTED A SIX-YEAR BATTLE WITH OXFORD CITY COUNCIL WHO WANTED IT REMOVED, BUT THEY RELENTED IN 1992 DECIDING TO ALLOW IT TO STAY ON CREATIVE GROUNDS.

ACID ADVENTURE

STORM CHASER GEORGE KOUROUNIS FROM CANADA WAS CRAZY ENOUGH TO TAKE A RIDE IN A RUBBER DINGY IN THE WORLD'S LARGEST ACID LAKE, NEXT TO THE 8,660-FT (2,640-M) KAWAH IJEN VOLCANO IN INDONESIA. WHEN THE VOLCANO ERUPTS, THE SURROUNDING AREAS CAN BE SHOWERED WITH ACID UP TO 2,000 FT (610 M) AWAY, AND THIS HAS CREATED A HOT LAKE THAT CONTAINS A DEADLY MIX OF OF SULFURIC ACID AND HYDROGEN CHLORIDE.

The powerful mixture of volcanic gases and rainwater in the lake creates the vast acid concoction that can reach temperatures of up to 93°F (34°C).

Volcano Bath

The thermal baths near Lake Rotomahana, New Zealand, were a rare natural phenomenon, known to some as the eighth wonder of the world. In the 1880s, these men were photographed there, in the shadow of an active volcano, taking a dip in one of the large natural mineral basins filled with warm spring water. These were formed from the mineral silica as water from boiling hot geysers cooled. The "Pink and White Terraces," as they were known, were popular tourist attractions until 1886, when nearby Mount Tarawera erupted, killing more than a hundred local people and destroying the terraces.

℞ REVERSE PLANET

A new planet—twice the size of Jupiter—has been discovered, and unlike any other planet, it travels counterclockwise around its star. The planet, spotted 1,000 light years away in the constellation of Scorpius, has been named WASP-17 because it is the 17th to be recorded outside the Solar System by the Wide Area Search for Planets run by U.K. universities.

℞ TADPOLE DELUGE

In separate incidents throughout Japan, hundreds of dead tadpoles fell to the ground in June 2009. In Nanao, 100 dead tadpoles were found on car windshields and in a parking lot over an area of 100 sq ft (10 sq m), and another 70 were found on a bridge walkway. Experts were mystified by the falls as there were no reports of tornadoes or strong winds at the time.

℞ METEORITE COLLECTOR

Rob Elliott from Fife, Scotland, has collected 1,000 meteorites from around the world, including one that is 110 million years old. He has spent more than 13 years building up his collection, using an old golf club with a magnet on the end as a homemade metal detector. Some of his rarest meteorites are valued at over $130,000 and his entire collection is worth millions.

℞ TALL CACTUS

At a dental college in Sattur, India, there is a 77-ft-tall (23-m) cactus. It was planted in 2002 and has flowers up to 8 in (20 cm) long.

℞ DUST STORM

A huge dust storm covered the Australian city of Sydney, in a blanket of red dust in September 2009. The storm originated in the Australian outback before sweeping 725 mi (1,167 km) east to shroud Sydney with dust, forcing people to stay indoors and international flights to be diverted.

℞ WHISTLING ISLAND

On the small island of La Gomera in the Canaries, people communicate with each other from miles apart by using a whistling language. Known as Silbo, the language has a vocabulary of more than 4,000 "words" and is used to send messages across the island's many mountains and valleys. Silbo was once on the verge of extinction, but now children in Gomeran schools are learning it as part of the curriculum.

℞ MELON SKIING

At the biennial Chinchilla Melon Festival in Queensland, Australia, competitors go skiing with scooped-out water melons on their feet. Wearing the melon footwear, they are dragged down a slippery course on a rope. The winner is the skier who stays upright for the longest distance.

℞ BUTTER BRIDGE

Government officials ordered the surfaces of a 1,000-ft-long (305-m) steel bridge in Guangzhou, China, to be smeared with butter to make it hard for people to climb up it to commit suicide by jumping from it. In just one month, eight people killed themselves on the bridge and several others climbed up it with the intention of jumping before changing their minds.

℞ DECIMAL TIME

Following the French Revolution, for two years from 1793 to 1795, France used "decimal time," which had a 10-hour day and 100-minute hours. Clocks and watches were produced with faces showing both standard time with numbers 1 to 24 and decimal time with numbers 1 to 10.

Hole in the Sky

A camera onboard the International Space Station witnessed the early stages of a volcanic eruption back on Earth that appeared to blow a gigantic hole in the clouds. The vast mushroom shape stretching above the Sarychev volcano on the Kuril Islands near Japan was thought to consist of brown volcanic ash and steam, which caused warm clouds to evaporate on either side of the eruption plume, leaving a clear hole in the cloud cover.

LAKE IN LAKE

The 40-sq-mi (104-sq-km) Lake Manitou in Ontario, Canada, is a lake inside a lake. It is located on 1,067-sq-mi (2,765-sq-km) Manitoulin Island, which in turn is located in Lake Huron.

SHIFTING BORDERS

The mountainous border dividing Italy and Switzerland includes glacier ridges. As the glaciers melt, the borders have shifted, prompting the two nations to redraw their borders by up to 330 ft (100 m) in places.

CANYON CHURCH

Las Lajas Cathedral, near Ipiales, Colombia, was built inside the canyon of the Guaitara River. It was constructed on a bridge spanning the river in such a way that the canyon cliff forms the back wall of the church.

SOUL-AR POWER

The above-ground mausoleums in the town of Santa Coloma de Gramenet, Spain, are outfitted with hundreds of solar panels—and they generate electricity for the town.

FIRE WHIRLS

Wind currents and temperature changes can turn a wildfire into a tornado-like column several hundred feet high.

LOW LYING

Although there are nearly 1,200 islands in the Maldives in the Indian Ocean, their combined landmass is only 115 sq mi (300 sq km)—twice the size of Washington, D.C. Most of the islands are less than 5 ft (1.5 m) above sea level, the highest point in the entire archipelago being just 8 ft (2.4 m) above sea level.

DOMINANT SUN

The Sun makes up 99.8 percent of all the mass in our Solar System. Everything else—including planets, asteroids, dust and moons—is just 0.2 percent.

HOT JUMP

An adventure company in Pucón, Chile, allows people to bungee jump from a helicopter over an active volcano. They are flown into the heart of the smoking volcano and plunge around 450 ft (140 m) toward the molten lava.

WATERS PARTED

When the black waters of the Rio Negro join the brown waters of the Rio Solimões at Manaus, Brazil, to form the Amazon River, they run side by side for miles without actually mixing.

℞ VANISHING RAIN

Evaporation rates in the desert are often faster than the speed at which rain falls, causing rain drops to disappear before they hit the ground.

℞ MOVING CLOSER

New Zealand's biggest earthquake in 78 years—recorded in the Tasman Sea in 2009—has brought the country's South Island a foot closer to Australia. The 7.8 magnitude quake expanded South Island westward by about 12 in (30 cm), making a tiny inroad into the 1,400-mi (2,255-km) gap separating it from Australia.

℞ TIME ZONES

Geographically, China falls into five time zones—but officially the entire country adheres to the same time.

℞ DEBRIS COLLECTION

Nearly 400,000 volunteers from around the world picked up 7 million lb (3.2 million kg) of debris from 17,000 mi (27,360 km) of coastline and waterways across the world on a single day—September 20, 2008.

℞ LIGHTNING STORM

A lightning storm in Saturn's atmosphere lasted for more than eight months in 2009, and emitted radio waves about 10,000 times more powerful than lightning discharges on Earth. They originate from huge thunderstorms with diameters of around 1,900 mi (3,000 km).

℞ ICE LAYER

Owing to its massive layer of ice, the continent of Antarctica has an average altitude 1.4 mi (2.2 km) above sea level.

℞ GHOST TERRITORY

The landmass of the Canadian territory of Nunavut is a million times larger than the European principality of Monaco, but has a smaller population.

℞ SECRET TREES

The location of Australia's Wollemi pine trees, once thought to be extinct, is secret. Anyone studying them arrives at the site blindfolded.

℞ TEMPERATURE SWING

Surface temperatures on the planet Mercury can change by more than 1,000°F (538°C) between day and night.

℞ DOUBLY LANDLOCKED

There are only two "doubly landlocked" countries. Liechtenstein and Uzbekistan are both surrounded by landlocked countries.

ROUGH WEATHER

KEN PRIOR, A MEMBER OF THE U.K.-BASED CLOUD APPRECIATION SOCIETY, PHOTOGRAPHED A BRAND NEW TYPE OF CLOUD IN 2009. THE FORMATION IS NOT OFFICIALLY RECOGNIZED AS YET, BUT THE CLOUD SOCIETY HAVE NAMED THE CLOUD "ASPERATUS," FROM THE LATIN FOR "ROUGH" BECAUSE OF THE BUMPY NATURE OF THE FORMATION. WEATHER DATA IS BEING GATHERED TO HELP DISTINGUISH THE STRANGE-LOOKING CLOUD. IF THE RELEVANT AUTHORITIES ACCEPT ASPERATUS, IT WILL BE THE FIRST TIME IN OVER 50 YEARS THAT A NEW TYPE OF CLOUD HAS BEEN FOUND.

AERIAL ALPHABET

GRAPHIC DESIGNER RHETT DASHWOOD FROM MELBOURNE, VICTORIA, AUSTRALIA, SCOURED SATELLITE IMAGES OF HIS HOME STATE ON THE INTERNET UNTIL HE HAD FOUND EVERY LETTER OF THE ALPHABET. THE LETTERS CAN BE SEEN IN BUILDINGS, BRIDGES, RIVERS, TREES AND FIELDS, AND MOST WOULD BE ALMOST IMPOSSIBLE TO RECOGNIZE FROM GROUND LEVEL. IT TOOK RHETT SIX MONTHS TO COMPLETE HIS SUPER-SIZED ALPHABET WITH LETTER LANDMARKS INCLUDING PATTERSON LAKES MARINA (G) AND MELBOURNE CRICKET GROUND (O).

R WHERE'S WALDO?

As part of her Media Arts degree, student Melanie Coles created a 54-ft-high (16.5-m) painting of children's book character Waldo on a rooftop in Vancouver, British Columbia, Canada, so that everyone looking on Google Earth could play *Where's Waldo*.

R OPRAH'S HEAD

A farmer in Queen Creek, Arizona, has created a crop circle in the image of Oprah Winfrey's head that can be seen properly only from the skies.

R JESUS IMAGE

On Google Earth, an image of the face of Jesus can be seen formed by the wind and the landscape in a Peruvian sand dune.

R BIG BALL

A basketball can be seen on Google Earth! Measuring 30 ft (9 m) in diameter and weighing 10 tons, the ball sculpture is located outside the Women's Basketball Hall of Fame building in Knoxville, Tennessee.

R CANYON MOUTH

From the air, the sides of a 130-ft-high (40-m), 3,000-ft-wide (1-km) rocky canyon in the West Darfur region of Sudan appear to form the shape of pouting female lips.

R MUSICAL CHIEF

A rock formation near Medicine Hat, Alberta, Canada, known as the "Badlands Guardian" resembles the face of a Native American Indian listening to an MP3 player. The contours of the face are formed by natural soil erosion while the "earphones" are actually a man-made road and an oil well.

R SMILEY FACE

Although the magnificent Palace of Versailles, near Paris, France, covering 2,000 acres (800 ha) of land, was built in the 17th century, it was not until it was viewed by aerial photography on the Internet that a smiley face was found hidden in the grounds, created by the landscape of the gardens.

R ROCK BIRD

From piles of more than 1,500 tons of rock, sculptor Andrew Rogers has created a birdlike geoglyph with a 330-ft (100-m) wingspan in You Yangs National Park, Victoria, Australia. Best viewed from the sky, the mythical avian creature, called a Bunjil, resembles an eagle and is the indigenous Aborigines' sky god.

Famous Face Ciudad Evita, a city of 70,000 inhabitants located in Greater Buenos Aires in Argentina, was founded in 1947 on the orders of Argentinian president Juan Peron. It was shaped to resemble a profile of his wife, Eva Peron, popularly known as Evita.

© Google Maps

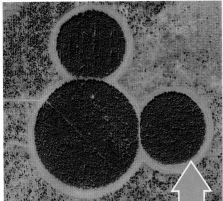

Bird's Eye Mouse

A pine forest shaped like Mickey Mouse's silhouette can be seen in Florida. The giant Mickey stretches for 2,000 ft (610 m), and despite its proximity to Disney World, its origins are unknown.

® FOREST FACE

From the air it is possible to see a face-shaped forest in Denmark. "The Sun as a Face" was planted in Odense in 2005 as part of the bicentennial celebrations of the birth of fairytale author Hans Christian Andersen.

® VISIBLE SHIPWRECK

The wreck of the SS *Jassim*, a Bolivian cargo ferry, which ran aground and sank on the Wingate Reef off the coast of Sudan in 2003, can be seen clearly on Internet aerial photography.

® FISH RAIDS

Thieves in Britain have been using aerial Internet photography to steal valuable fish. They use the online technology to pinpoint the location of garden ponds that cannot be seen from street level and that contain collections of highly prized koi carp.

® FOG NETS

When dense fog sweeps in from the Pacific Ocean, plastic mesh nets erected on a hillside near Lima, Peru, catch the moisture and provide valuable water to a region that gets little rainfall. The droplets of fog water fall from the nets into gutters and on to collection tanks. Since 2006, the nearby village of Bellavista has received hundreds of gallons of water during the foggy winter months.

® STARDUST SECRET

Traces of an amino acid called glycine have been discovered by NASA in wisps of stardust from the tail of the Wild 2 comet, suggesting that life could have begun in space before being delivered to Earth by meteorite and comet impacts. Glycine is a basic component of proteins without which life as we know it could not exist.

Really Big Reptile The Gagadju Crocodile Holiday Inn in Jabiru, Northern Territory, Australia, is built in the shape of an 820-ft (250-m) crocodile.

WALL OF SKULLS

A TOWER MADE FROM HUMAN SKULLS STILL STANDS IN THE SERBIAN CITY OF NIS, 200 YEARS AFTER IT WAS FIRST BUILT. TURKISH FORCES BUILT THE 10-FT (3-M) TOWER AFTER THEY HAD DEFEATED SERBIAN REBELS IN 1809. A TOTAL OF 952 SERBIAN SKULLS BECAME PART OF THE CONSTRUCTION, THE SCALPS STUFFED WITH COTTON AND SENT BACK TO CONSTANTINOPLE AS PROOF OF THE VICTORY. WHEN SERBIA WAS LIBERATED, THE CHAPEL WAS KEPT AS A MEMORIAL, AND 52 OF THE SKULLS REMAIN.

℞ A THOUSAND WINDOWS

A new, nine-story office block in Jinhua, China, has around 1,000 windows—with one room alone boasting 21 windows. All of the rooms in the building, designed by Japanese architect Sako Keiichiro, have irregular shapes and each floor features its own miniature garden.

℞ HIGH SCHOOL

A school in Gulu village, Sichuan Province, China, stands halfway up a mountain. Climbing up from the base takes five hours and children walking to school must negotiate a narrow, zigzagging path that is just 16 in (40 cm) wide in places and has a sheer drop on one side. The school has a basketball hoop, but children are allowed only to pat the balls, because if the balls are thrown and go over the edge of the cliff, it would take half a day to retrieve them.

℞ CHURCH STOLEN

A large church in rural Russia was stolen in October 2008. The Church of Christ's Resurrection had stood in the central Russian village of Komarovo for nearly 200 years before thieves dismantled it and took it away brick by brick.

℞ SUBURBAN TEMPLE

Travelers from around the world—as far away as Canada and Nepal—line up in their hundreds to visit Dhirajlal and Sushila Karia's suburban home in the seaside town of Clacton-on-Sea, England, to see a Hindu temple built inside their spare bedroom.

℞ CLIFF BASE

A church in Brittany, France, is built into the base of a cliff. The Chapel of St.-Gildas nestles under a huge granite outcrop on the bank of the Canal du Blavet.

℞ BRIDAL WAY

Unmarried men in the remote Indian village of Barwaan Kala are building a new road that they hope will bring them brides. More than 120 men in the village, located high in the Kaimur hills, remain bachelors because they say it is difficult for outsiders to reach their home through the rocky terrain.

℞ TRENCH ART

Ružica Church, located within the Kalemegdan Fortress in Belgrade, Serbia, has chandeliers made from bullets, swords and cannons. Soldiers made them during World War I.

℞ STATUE PARADE

At Las Fallas Festival, held each March in Valencia, Spain, hundreds of giant papier-mâché statues—some up to 30 ft (9 m) high—are paraded through the streets and then thrown on to bonfires.

ℛ AGE RESPECT

Each year on September 15, Respect for the Aged Day is celebrated in Japan and all citizens who reach age 100 are given a silver cup and a letter from the prime minister.

ℛ ELEPHANT BATTLE

In 1592, King Naresuan of Siam and the Crown Prince of Burma fought a duel while riding elephants. Centuries later, Naresuan's victory is still celebrated as a holiday in Thailand.

ℛ LEGEND COMES TRUE

In a case of life imitating art, on November 18, 2008, officials in Hamelin, Germany—home to the Pied Piper legend—announced that the town was overrun with rats.

ℛ RESTLESS GOATS

Some 400 goats on Taiwan's Penghu archipelago are believed to have been killed by lack of sleep caused by late-night noise from a wind farm adjoining their pasture. A local farmer says the constant noise from the eight turbines left his goats exhausted.

ℛ HARROWING EXPERIENCE

A 3,000-year-old barrel of butter has been found in an Irish bog. Two farm workers harrowing the land discovered a buried oak barrel, cut from the trunk of a tree, full of the ancient butter. Experts say it dates back to the Iron Age.

ℛ DONKEY DELIVERY

More than 3,000 donkeys were brought in to help deliver millions of ballot papers to remote mountain regions of Afghanistan for the country's 2009 presidential elections.

ℛ CHEESE ROLLERS

Competitors in Berne, Switzerland, roll lightweight wheels of cheese around an obstacle course as fast as possible. The race re-creates an old practice whereby wheels of cheese up to 3 ft (1 m) in diameter, 11 in (27 cm) thick and weighing 220 lb (100 kg) were rolled around dairies by hand.

ℛ HAIR HOUSE

Paula Sunshine built an extension to her house in Bury St Edmunds, Suffolk, England, from human hair mixed with plaster.

Rat Temple

ℛ COFFIN REST

The Wat Prammanee Monastery in Nakhon Nayok, Thailand, offers death and rebirth ceremonies for distressed worshipers, which include a brief rest in a coffin to mark the occasion.

ℛ ECHO CHAMBER

Harajuku, a futuristic Protestant church in Tokyo, Japan, was designed in 2005 with a ceiling specially made to reverberate natural sound for two seconds, thereby providing a unique listening experience for worshipers.

ℛ ROMANTIC NUTS

At the San Juan Fiesta, held in Ciudadela, Menorca, each June, large crowds of people gather to hurl hazelnuts at each other. Every time a nut hits another person, it is said to represent a kiss.

ℛ TUNNEL PEOPLE

Hundreds of people have built homes— some complete with double beds, furniture and kitchens—in the dark, damp storm drains that run under Las Vegas, Nevada. Despite the risks to their health from disease and venomous spiders, and a general risk of flooding, the "tunnel people" have set up elaborate camps with beds, bookshelves, wardrobes and even a makeshift shower created from an office water drinking dispenser.

Rats are not usually welcome house guests, but the hordes of rodents that swarm around the Karni Mata temple in Deshnoke, India, are always treated with great respect. The rats are kept well fed, and any food or drink that has been sampled by a rat is considered blessed. Spotting a white rat bodes particularly well, but if a visitor accidentally kills one of the rodents, they are expected to buy one made of gold or silver to replace it. Hindu legend has it that the 14th-century holy woman Karni Mata reincarnated dead storytellers into rats and they are given protection in her temple, which was built in the early 20th century.

Tentacle Terror

Resembling something from outer space, this mass cluster of tentacles shocked vacationers when it swept onto a beach on the Gower Peninsula in Wales, U.K. Measuring 6 ft (2 m) in length and slightly thicker than a telegraph pole, tourists who witnessed the alien-like sea monster thought it was a UFO invasion! Scientists later revealed the writhing creature to be thousands of goose barnacles clinging to a log, the result of bad weather sweeping them up from the bottom of the ocean.

LONG PROJECT

Romans in the ancient province of Syria (modern-day Jordan and Syria) spent 120 years building a 100-mi-long (160-km) aqueduct, most of which is chiseled from stone at depths of up to 260 ft (80 m).

GOLDEN SEWAGE

The burned waste at a sewage refinery in Nagano prefecture, Japan, is a more concentrated source of gold than the country's largest gold mine! Tens of thousands of dollars worth of gold were found at the Suwa treatment facility in 2008—because a number of precision equipment manufacturers in Nagano use gold in their work and lots of tiny particles of it end up in the sewer system.

TOAD KILL

The Australian state of Queensland has an annual one-day holiday for residents to cull cane toads.

ABANDONED CITY

In 2008, a long-abandoned 1,000-year-old city carved into the side of a mountain by the Cloud People tribe was discovered in Peru's Utcubamba province—untouched by looters.

GALAXY BLING

433 Eros, a banana-shaped asteroid 21 mi (33 km) long, contains precious metals worth at least $20,000 billion, including more gold than has ever been mined by humans on Earth. It orbits the sun, mainly between the orbits of Earth and Mars, and on January 31, 2012, is expected to pass within around 16 million miles (26 million km) of Earth, about 70 times the distance to the Moon.

DOUBLE DRAINAGE

The 1,035-sq-mi (2,681-sq-km) Wollaston Lake in Saskatchewan, Canada, drains naturally in two directions. It flows northwest into the Mackenzie River basin and northeast into Hudson Bay.

SALT PALACE

Constructed in 1993, the Salt Palace was built with pure rock salt from Grand Saline, Texas—an area of the U.S.A. that has enough salt to supply the world for 20,000 years.

RAT FREE

In 2003, New Zealand's Campbell Island became the world's largest island to be freed of a rat infestation after a massive poisoning campaign killed off the entire population of 200,000 rats.

Salted Shores

Situated on the shoreline of San Francisco Bay, these stunning red and green salt ponds are a vital habitat for more than 70 bird species. For over a century, approximately 80 percent of these shallow man-made ponds have been filled and developed for salt mining. The ponds create salt using only the sun and wind, while the input of varying amounts of algae, minerals, microorganisms and brine shrimp create the beautiful colors. These colors also indicate the salinity of the ponds, which produce around 5–8 in (13–20 cm) of salt at the end of their five-year process.

SENSELESS LAW

A local law in Skamania County, Washington, details penalties for harming a sasquatch—a mythical beast whose existence has never been confirmed!

WET LANDS

Canada has an estimated two million lakes, covering approximately 7.6 percent of the country's landmass.

FEW LOCALS

Only 10 percent of the 1.7 million people living in the Arab Emirate of Dubai are actually native to the country.

HAPPY HARRY

Harry Hallowes, an Irish tramp who squatted for more than 20 years in one of London's most expensive suburbs, was awarded a plot of land that could be worth up to $6 million. He was awarded squatters' rights to a 120 x 60 ft (36 x 18 m) patch of land on Hampstead Heath, where he has lived in a tiny shack since 1986.

FREE LAND

In 2009, the village of Rappottenstein, Austria, began offering free land to anyone willing to move there and start a family.

FIELD OF GOLD

Armed with a simple $4 metal detector, in 2009 Terry Herbert unearthed 1,500 pieces of medieval treasure from a field in Staffordshire, England, that together are worth millions of dollars. The 1,300-year-old treasure includes beautiful gold sword hilts, dazzling jewels from Sri Lanka and ornate early Christian gold crosses. The gold objects alone weigh more than 11 lb (5 kg) and Herbert's haul filled nearly 250 bags.

SALT HOTELS

Bolivia's Uyuni Salt Flats contain 10 billion tons of salt and are home to several hotels that are built from blocks of salt. Some even have beds made from salt.

TYPHOON GUST

Winds from a 2009 Chinese typhoon were so powerful that they blew a bathtub onto 40-ft-high (12-m) power cables. The 75-mph (120-km/h) winds from Typhoon Morakot swept the bathtub up from the balcony of a nearby hotel and deposited it on the overhead cables in Wenzhou, Zhejiang Province.

HIDDEN MOUNTAINS

Antarctica's Gamburtsev mountain range is located beneath 2.5 mi (4 km) of ice. Only discovered just over 50 years ago, the range has peaks as high as 10,000 ft (3,000 m) and, stretching for 750 mi (1,200 km), it covers as big an area as the European Alps.

HEIGHT RESTRICTION

Residents of Munich, Germany, have voted that new buildings must be no taller than 325 ft (99 m), the height of the city's cathedral towers, to avoid spoiling the skyline.

WALKING HOUSE

Danish artists have teamed up with engineers from Massachusetts to design a house that walks. The 10-ft-high (3-m) solar- and wind-powered home has a living room, kitchen, toilet and bed, plus a computer that controls the six hydraulic legs on which the house stands. These legs enable the house to stroll across all terrains and to walk away from flooded areas if necessary.

ONLY VOTER

The Banej polling station in Gujarat, India, has only one voter—Guru Bharatdas Darshandas, the sole caretaker of a temple in the middle of a forest.

ROOF GARDEN

The Courthouse Tower in Greensburg, Indiana, has had a tree growing from its roof for more than a century. A small sprig was first spotted there in the 1870s, and two of the trees that subsequently took root in the crevices of the roof are now growing happily 110 ft (33 m) above the ground.

ABANDONED APARTMENT

In January 2009, architect Mark Aretz discovered a small, one-bedroom apartment in Leipzig, Germany, that had been untouched since before the fall of the Berlin Wall, nearly 20 years earlier. It had been hastily abandoned by its occupants as the old Communist East German state disintegrated in 1989.

LOCKED IN

In an attempt to combat vandalism, the council of Klaipeda, Lithuania, announced in 2009 that all public toilets in the town would automatically lock in customers if they took longer than five minutes inside.

CROWDED BENCH

A wooden bench in Masuhogaura, Japan, is over 1,510 ft (460 m) long—that's more than a quarter of a mile—and can seat up to 1,350 people.

IRON PILLAR

The 22-ft-tall (6.7-m) Iron Pillar of Delhi, India, has stood outside in the rain and sun for 1,600 years and yet exhibits little sign of corrosion.

BEFORE

Patchwork Pumps

Jennifer Marsh, an artist from Syracuse, New York, wanted to make a statement about oil consumption, so she decided to give the abandoned gas station she walked past each day a much-needed splash of color. Jennifer entirely covered the building and the gas pumps with 5,000 sq ft (464 sq m) of patchwork material. The project received hundreds of colorful panels from all over the world, and Jennifer enlisted a team of volunteers to help her sew them into fabric panels to cover the derelict building, which stands 35 ft (10.6 m) tall and 40 ft (12 m) wide.

AFTER

Garage Illusion

THOMAS SASSENBACH, A DESIGNER FROM COLOGNE, GERMANY, WAS TIRED OF THE GRAY, UGLY GARAGE DOORS IN HIS HOMETOWN AND DECIDED TO GIVE THEM A MAKEOVER. HIS DESIGNS ARE DECEPTIVELY REALISTIC AND INTENDED TO MAKE PEOPLE STOP AND STARE. NOW YOU CAN PERSUADE YOUR NEIGHBORS THAT YOU HAVE A FORMULA-1 RACING CAR, A SPEEDBOAT, A REAL HORSE OR A JET FIGHTER IN YOUR GARAGE INSTEAD OF YOUR OLD CAR. (THEY ARE ACTUALLY JUST AMAZINGLY PAINTED TARPAULINS FIXED WITH VELCRO!)

℞ REFRIGERATED BEACH

The world's first refrigerated beach has been built in Dubai to prevent tourists burning their feet. A computer-controlled system of coolant-filled pipes under the sand keeps temperatures comfortable at the beach next to the Palazzo Versace hotel.

℞ BOTTLE TEMPLE

Around 20 buildings in the grounds of the Wat Pa Maha Chedi Kaew Temple in Sisaket, Thailand, are made almost entirely out of glass beer bottles. Buddhist monks started collecting the bottles in 1984 for their "Temple of a Million Bottles" project and found the medium so favorable that even the temple's mosaics of Buddha have been created with recycled beer-bottle caps.

℞ CROSSWORD BLOCK

An apartment block in Lvov, Ukraine, has a crossword puzzle 100 ft (30 m) high filling the whole of one external wall. Clues to the crossword—which is 19 squares across and 34 squares high—are scattered around the city's major landmarks and at night fluorescent letters placed inside every square are turned on to reveal the solution.

℞ ONE HOME

Alfonso de Marco of Eastbourne, East Sussex, England, celebrated his 107th birthday in April 2009—in the house where he had lived for the past 100 years. He had moved to Britain from Italy in 1909 as a seven-year-old to live above the ice-cream parlor that his father ran.

℞ FLYING LESSONS

Children at Kingsland Primary School in Stoke-on-Trent, Staffordshire, England, have some of their lessons in a disused airplane. The decommissioned S-360, which used to fly to Ireland and Spain, has been fitted out with desks and laptops.

℞ FAMILY STREET

No fewer than 69 members of one family live in the same street in Gateshead, Tyne and Wear, England. The Hall family have monopolized Cotswold Gardens since Catherine Hall settled there in 1958. Six of her eight children and their families currently live in the street, along with three uncles and a mother-in-law, and together they occupy 15 houses and have more than 50 pets.

AMAZON MARATHON

British ex-army officer Ed Stafford began the trip of his life in April 2008, when he set out to walk the entire length of the Amazon River in South America, from its source to the Atlantic Ocean. He hopes to become the first man ever to do this and to highlight rainforest deforestation in the process. The river is 4,000 mi (6,400 km) long, but Ed thinks he will have walked almost 6,000 mi (9,650 km) by the time he is finished because the river is so wide and deep in so many places that he can't always take the shortest route. By February 2010, Ed had passed the halfway point of his 4,000-mi (6,400-km) trek, accompanied by a local guide, Cho, and with much of his "walk" spent chest deep in murky water. Hiking through one of the wildest environments on earth, Ed has faced venomous snakes, flooding, electric eels, piranhas and jaguars. He has been pursued by armed Peruvian tribespeople and been wrongly arrested on suspicion of murder. Traveling light with only a backpack, he is also at risk of scurvy or even starvation, often forced to forage in the jungle and catch piranhas for breakfast.

Preparing for the day

"Every morning I wake with the sun. I click my stiff neck from side to side and reach for my malaria tablets. These get swigged down with iodinated water that is hanging in a bottle above my head.

As we are usually in the middle of nowhere, I roll out of my hammock without any kit on. I slip into my Crocs to stumble to my washing line. Cho, my guide, and I live with just two sets of clothes—one for the day that is usually gritty and wet, and one for the evening that is always clean and dry.

The wet clothes don't dry on the line overnight as the humidity is high and the airflow stifled by the thick trees. The line is there more to keep the clothes off the wet ground. I put them on without too much thinking and I hardly notice throughout the day that they are wet. On go my socks (with holes in them) and my jungle boots. It's now five past seven and I wander over to the fire area whilst brushing my teeth.

Usually the wood is wet, as neither Cho nor I have the ability to collect wood for the following morning and try and dry it. This is part laziness, part cockiness that we don't need to. One of us heads off with our machete and looks for dead wood that is hanging in the trees. Dead wood found on the floor is too wet. I snap a twig to make sure it is dead enough: If the wood bends beyond 90 degrees, and doesn't break cleanly in two, then it's too green and won't burn.

Once back at the fire area we make a small platform of logs, and light a piece of tree resin that will act as tinder and burn for ages. I then either add small twigs or shavings from the inside of large logs that are wet on the outside—but nice and dry inside. Usually we have water on the boil by half past seven.

Breakfast is always white rice and sometimes we get a reasonable catch of river fish and we don't need to open a can of tuna. The job of collecting the fishing net from the river is unpopular because the water is cold at this time in the morning and you have to swim to retrieve it. Removing a piranha from the net requires certain caution as, although their reputation as maneaters is largely unfounded, they do have very sharp teeth. The fish are usually catfish, trout and piranha and they get gutted and barbecued while the rice is cooking.

Concurrently, Cho and I nip back to our hammocks and pack everything away. Everything goes into a huge rubber sack that sits inside our backpacks – that way it's all 100% waterproof and we can swim with our packs on our backs and know that the Macbook and sat phone are fine.

We make enough rice to put half in our Tupperware boxes and save it for lunchtime. By the time we've finished eating breakfast, we are normally ready and packed. Between 8 and 8.30, we haul the 32–35-kg packs onto our mosquito-bitten backs and we are on the move once more."

49

Living the High Life

In Torajaland on the island of Sulawesi, Indonesia, when a person dies, an effigy, or doll, is made in their likeness. These dolls are called *Tau Tau*, and are put in graves, or in the homes of the living, as a blessing. In some places, life-size *Tau Tau* are placed in cliff faces where they peer down at travelers as they pass. Dug into the same cliffs are the graves of the dead, which are also hung on platforms high up on the cliffs, to prevent possessions being stolen.

ℝ LANDOWNERS

Sixty-nine percent of the land in Great Britain is owned by just 0.6 percent of the population—this is mostly landowning families who have held their land since the 19th century.

ℝ REDUCED ALPHABET

Rotokas, a language spoken by around 4,000 people on the island of Bounganville, Papua New Guinea, has only 12 letters in its alphabet—A, E, G, I, K, O, P, R, S, T, U, V.

ℝ HUSBAND CARRYING

As a part of a fall festival, women in the town of Winesburg, Ohio, compete in a husband-carrying contest.

ℝ MOZART'S STONE

The Austrian town of Raschala has a plaque on a stone where Wolfgang Amadeus Mozart once stopped to urinate by the side of the road. Each year, so many visitors flock to see the Mozart Pinkelstein ("Mozart pee-stone") that the town has now arranged a festival of music and drinking in memory of the composer's unscheduled visit.

ℝ ROYAL TIME

Until 1936, all 180 clocks in the royal collection at Sandringham House, Norfolk, England, were set on "Sandringham Time," half an hour ahead of Greenwich Mean Time. It was the idea of King Edward VII, who enjoyed shooting game birds on the Sandringham estate and wanted to lengthen daylight hours during the winter.

ℝ GLACIER PRAYERS

For more than 300 years, inhabitants of the Swiss Alpine villages of Fieschertal and Fiesch gave prayers to stop the growth of the Aletsch glacier, Europe's longest, which had caused their homes to flood. However, in 2009, they sought the blessing of Pope Benedict to change their prayers to stop the glacier shrinking. Climate change has seen Switzerland's glaciers, which are a key source of water for hydroelectric plants, melt by 12 percent over the past decade.

ℝ SOLE TENANT

In 2009, a luxury new 32-story apartment block in Fort Myers, Florida, had just one tenant. Victor Vangelakos, his wife and three children had the large swimming pool, games room and gym to themselves, as most of the other prospective residents backed out because of the global financial crisis.

ℝ LONG TUNNEL

The 10-mi-long (17-km) St. Gotthard road tunnel under the Swiss Alps is almost twice as long as Mount Everest is high.

ℝ GREATER WALL OF CHINA

A 2009 study revealed that the 2,000-year-old Great Wall of China is 2,400 mi (3,850 km) longer than previously thought. Using modern mapping technologies, the study uncovered extra sections of the wall that had been hidden by hills, trenches and rivers, making its total length around 5,500 mi (8,850 km).

ℝ BABY BOOM

A small village in Cambridgeshire, England, has a higher birth rate than India, China, Indonesia, Brazil or the U.S.A. Cambourne has just 7,600 residents, but produced 24.1 births per 1,000 women in 2009—almost double the U.K. average. The village has an unusually high concentration of young couples.

ℝ CORAL ROADS

Roads on the Pacific island of Guam are made with coral. Guam has little genuine sand on its beaches, just ground coral. Instead of importing real sand from other countries, the coral is mixed with asphalt to build the island's roads.

ℝ STRANGE BONE

Hikers walking in a forest near Landshut, Germany, in 2009 found a mysterious-looking bone. The police were summoned and discovered a hipbone with artificial joints. They could see no other remains, until they spotted a skeleton in a fir tree 36 ft (11 m) above them. Investigations concluded that a 69-year-old man had committed suicide when he climbed up the tree almost 30 years previously and roped himself to a branch. He managed this despite having hip replacements, as the tree was then shorter. As the tree grew, his bones fell to the ground.

ℝ LIMITED TRANSPORT

The principality of Andorra, located in the mountains between Spain and France, has no airports, trains or ports.

ISLAND OF THE DOLLS

Teshuilo Lake lies among the canals of Xochimilco near Mexico City, and on the lake there is a tiny island known as Isla de las Muñecas ("Island of the Dolls"). Many years ago, a young girl drowned there, and it became a haunted area that people were afraid to enter. A homeless man, Julián Santana, lived on the island for over 50 years, and began to collect and display children's dolls to remember the dead girl and keep her spirit happy. Santana would trade fresh vegetables, which he grew on the island, with local people for their discarded dolls. Although Santana died in 2001, there are still thousands of dolls scattered around the area, mostly hung in the trees.

A calf with three nostrils was born on a farm in Cheiry, Switzerland. Her extra nasal feature made her so popular with the locals that her owner, farmer Urs Herrmann, guaranteed her a permanent home at the farm instead of being sent to market with the other calves.

Fly-vertising

At the 2009 Frankfurt Book Fair, a German publishing company started a new advertising craze, attaching very small banners to flies and letting them loose around the halls of the fair. Eichborn, whose logo is a fly, decided to attach the lightweight banners saying "The Publisher of the Fly" to 200 flies to promote their advertising stand. The banners were attached using string and wax that would fall off naturally without harming the fly. However, the flies did have some difficulty staying in the air and kept landing on people all over the convention.

Fortunate Feline

When Chase, a kitten from Lexington, Kentucky, was hit by a car she lost her nose, eyelids and the skin on her face, as well as one of her legs. Surgeons were unable to rebuild her features, so she was left with pink tissue instead of fur on her face. She was adopted by Melissa Smith, the veterinary technician who had helped look after her, and has since become a "therapy cat" in the local area, helping people with disfigurements to improve their confidence. Chase has even become an online celebrity with her own blog that reassures her fans that she is happy and not in any pain.

℞ LUCKY FELIX

In April 2009, Felix, a 12-year-old cat belonging to Andrea Schröder of Cologne, Germany, was found alive despite having been trapped in the rubble of a collapsed apartment building for nearly five weeks.

℞ FOXY THIEF

Over several months, a fox in Germany stole more than 120 shoes from homes and gardens near Föhren. A forestry worker found the missing footwear in and around the fox's lair, the tiny tooth marks on the leather suggesting that the vixen may have used them as toys for her cubs to play with.

℞ DANCING COLLIE

Samson, a border collie dog from Manchester, England, loves disco dancing. He can perform twirls, spins and jumps in time to his favorite music, and can even stand on his back legs to do his own version of Michael Jackson's moonwalk.

℞ TOILET PYTHON

Erik Rantzau found a python almost twice his size coiled up in the toilet bowl of his house near Darwin, Northern Territory, Australia. The 10-ft-long (3-m) carpet python had been seen roaming in the garden for years before deciding to set up home in his toilet.

℞ CAMEL IMPORTS

Camels aren't native to Australia, but the continent has about one million of them roaming its rural interior.

℞ FREAK EGG

Thelma, a chicken owned by Margaret Hamstra of Lynden, Washington State, laid an oversized egg—8 in (20 cm) in circumference—with a normal egg inside. Both eggs had both a white and a yolk.

℞ PAINTING POOCH

Ziggy, a Pekingese dog owned by Elizabeth Monacelli of southern California, paints works of art that have sold for up to $250 at auction. He creates his masterpieces by putting his teeth around a paper towel roll, which is attached to a paintbrush. Monacelli plays him special Chinese music to get him in the artistic mood, but even then he manages an average of only three brushstrokes per painting session before curling into a ball and falling asleep.

℞ ELEPHANT SLIPPERS

In a bid to soothe painful abscesses on her front feet, Gay, a 40-year-old Asian elephant at Paignton Zoo, Devon, England, has been fitted with a pair of $750 slippers. To ensure a good fit, keepers had to draw an outline around her two front feet to make patterns that were then sent off to a specialist firm in Australia. Each slipper boot measures about 16 in (40 cm) in diameter and comes with laces that elephants can't undo.

Purrfectly content!

MEAT FEAST

MANE MEAL ENCOURAGING HUNGRY LIONS TO LEAP ONTO YOUR CAR MIGHT NOT SEEM VERY SMART, BUT THAT IS THE IDEA BEHIND A NEW EXHIBIT AT WERRIBEE OPEN RANGE ZOO IN VICTORIA, AUSTRALIA. ALTHOUGH IT LOOKS AS IF THERE IS NOTHING PROTECTING THE TOURISTS FROM BECOMING THIS LION'S NEXT MEAL, A CLOSER LOOK REVEALS A SHEET OF GLASS IN FRONT OF THE STEERING WHEEL, SO THAT PASSENGERS CAN GET CLOSE TO BIG CATS AS THEY FEED.

® FELINE PASSENGER

For over four years, a cat in Plymouth, England, has been catching the same bus every day. Casper boards the number 3 bus at 10.55 a.m. outside his home and travels the entire 11-mi (18-km) route before returning home an hour later. He is such a regular passenger that bus drivers look out for him to make sure he gets off at the right stop.

® FLUFFY FISH

A pet goldfish survived out of water for seven hours after apparently jumping out of his tank. Sparkle was found covered in dog hair and fluff behind the tank's stand in North Yorkshire, England, but after being washed under the tap, he started breathing again and made a full recovery.

® TEN-INCH TONGUE

The pangolin, a rare African animal, has a tongue that can extend up to 16 in (40 cm), which it uses to lap up termites and ants.

® DRUNKEN BADGER

German police were called to deal with a dead badger on the road near the town of Goslar—only to find that the animal was not dead at all, merely drunk! The badger had staggered into the middle of the road after eating overripe cherries that had fermented.

® SEA BUDGIE

A budgerigar that had escaped from its aviary in the coastal town of Brixham in Devon, England, was found floating half a mile out to sea. The bedraggled bird was plucked from the water by a dive-boat crew and reunited with its owner, budgie breeder Mike Peel.

® GOAT ARRESTED

A vigilante group in Kwara State, Nigeria, turned a goat over to police in January 2009, convinced that it was a car thief who had used black magic to change his form.

® GUCCI POOCHES

Dogs wearing designer outfits ranging from polka-dot bathing suits to glitzy evening wear took to the catwalk during a fashion show in Taipei, Taiwan, in July 2009.

® NON-SWIMMERS

Although adult hippos can see and breathe underwater and are adapted to aquatic life, they can't swim or even float. Their bodies are too dense for them to have any natural buoyancy, so they move around either by pushing off from the bottom of the river or simply by walking along the riverbed.

® CLEVER DOGS

Dogs may be as intelligent as two-year-old children. Animal psychologists at the University of British Columbia in Vancouver, Canada, have found that dogs are able to understand up to 250 "human" words and gestures, can count up to five and can even perform simple mathematical calculations.

BUNNY BOOM

In June 2009, Nancy Haseman of Rio Rancho, New Mexico, was found to be keeping 334 rabbits in her garden. She said her husband rescued a rabbit 12 years earlier after a neighbor abandoned it, then the couple began rescuing more rabbits. She had tried to keep the males separate from the females but the males kept hopping the fence.

IN A SPIN

A seven-week-old kitten survived in July 2009 after being trapped in a washing machine for a full cycle, including a spin. Toby is believed to have crawled into the machine at his home in Aberdeenshire, Scotland, before it was switched on, in an attempt to escape the summer heat wave.

REST PERIOD

Groundhogs breathe only once every five minutes during periods of hibernation.

PAW CHOICE

Domestic cats can be either left-handed or right-handed, according to their sex. Particularly when faced with difficult tasks, females prefer to use their right paw while tom cats tend to use their left paw.

MOTHER HEN

A hen in China adopted two orphaned puppies after their mother died. Owner Cao Fengying of Jiashan said the hen was best friends with the mother dog, and then looked after the puppies, fighting off other chickens who were trying to steal the puppies' food.

EXTRA HEAD

In July 2009, a baby cow was born at a farm in Rivera, Colombia, with two heads but only one brain. The weight of the extra head meant the calf—named Jennifer—could not stand without help, so farmer Marino Cabrera built a sling to support her.

FROG WEDDING

Two frogs were married in a solemn ceremony in the western Indian state of Maharashtra in June 2009 in an attempt to bring on delayed monsoon rains. Tradition says that if frogs are married off with full Vedic or Hindu rituals, the rain god is pleased and the heavens will open within days.

Young Angler

Eleven-year-old angler Jessica Wanstall from Kent, England, couldn't believe her eyes when she landed a monster fish twice her size while fishing with her family on a river in Spain in 2009. At nearly 9 ft (2.7 m) long and weighing 193 lb (87.5 kg), the catfish dwarfed Jessica, who weighs only 77 lb (35 kg), and her dad had to help her drag it up the bank in order to take some pictures.

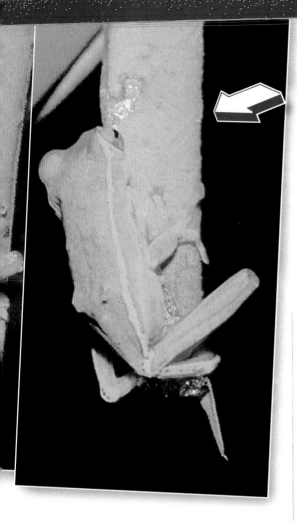

Frog's Eggs

Dr. S.D. Biju of the University of Delhi has discovered the ingenious method by which a type of Indian tree frog protects its young. The female frog carefully wraps its frogspawn in a leaf to make a foam-sealed container that prevents the embryos from drying out in the sunlight, then leaves them to develop on their own.

R DOLLAR NEST
A mouse made its home inside an ATM at a gas station in La Grande, Oregon, building its nest from 16 chewed-up $20 bills.

R FISH FAST
In some species of whalefish, the males stop eating entirely as they mature, their jaws waste away and they live exclusively on energy stored in their massive, fatty liver.

R WINGED CAT
Born perfectly normal, a long-haired white cat in Chongqing, China, began sprouting winglike growths on either side of his spine when he was a year old. Some experts believe the bony "wings" are a freak mutation in the form of a Siamese twin growing inside the cat. Others think the cause may be genetic, the result of chemicals absorbed during his mother's pregnancy.

R FLUSHED AWAY
A pet goldfish survived being flushed down a toilet in East Kilbride, Scotland, and was eventually rescued from a sewage plant. The fish was put down the toilet because its owners thought it was dying, but it revived as it made its way through the town's underground waste water network and was spotted flailing about on a mesh filtering screen at the Scottish Water sewage site.

R LOST DEER
While fishing in Chesapeake Bay, Chad Campbell from Washington state and Bo Warren from Virginia found a whitetail deer swimming in 80 ft (25 m) of deep water 1.5 mi (2.4 km) from the nearest coast.

R ROLE REVERSAL
Although toads are normally the prey of venomous snakes, some mountain toads in Qingcheng Mountain Park, Sichuan, China, have turned nature on its head by eating one of their chief predators, Jerdon's pit vipers.

R WHEEL TRAP
An inquisitive cat that poked its head into the wheel of a car had to be rescued by firefighters after becoming stuck in the small hole in the center. Using specialist cutting gear, it took fire crews from Bury St Edmunds in Suffolk, England, an hour to free Casper the Siamese.

R DRINKING HABIT
The thorny devil lizard from Australia drinks water through its feet. Using cracks in its scales, it can absorb water through its feet and into its body.

R WINNING STREAK
Bertie the Labrador dog won his owner Dave Hallett from Sussex, England, $300 in a pub lottery five weeks in a row, beating odds of 282-million-to-one. He predicted the winning bonus ball by putting his nose up to a number on a board.

RIPLEY'S RESEARCH
Compared to other creatures, it is relatively common (although still rare) for Bearded Dragons to be born with two heads in captivity. This may be owing to inbreeding and the fact that pet Bearded Dragons can produce large numbers of eggs each year. Two-headed dragons have two separate brains, but can often coordinate their bodies surprisingly well.

HEADS AND TAIL

Frank and Barbara Witte of Fresno California, have a highly unusual pet. Their Bearded Dragon, Zak-n-Wheezie, has two names because it was born with two heads. Experts predicted that the lizard would not live for long, but Zak-n-Wheezie is still going strong and is possibly the longest living two-headed Bearded Dragon in the world.

QUINCAILLIERS !!
EXIGEZ LA VERITABLE **TAPETTE E.**
POUR **RATS** ET **SOURIS**
DÉTENTE MÉTALLIQUE PERFECTIONNÉE
Robuste et Sensible
ec **PORTE-APPAT**

RESSORT TRÈS PUISSANT
En acier 1re qualité
A TRÈS HAUTE RÉSISTANCE

MARQUE DÉPOSÉE **E. A.** PARIS
GARANTIE DE **FABRICATION SUPÉRIEURE**

REGLAGE ET FONCTIONNEMENT GARANT

VE
GROS ICI

Rat-busters

The famous exterminator shop Julien Aurouze & Co, located on the rue des Halles in Paris, France, has always specialized in pest control or, more specifically, catching and killing rats. Founded in 1872, the shop window gives an obvious explanation of what they do, with stuffed rats hanging from traps by their mouths, and taxidermied rats scattered all over the displays inside.

℞ VENOMOUS MAMMAL

The *Hispaniolan solenodon*, a small mammal from Haiti and the Dominican Republic, is one of only a couple of mammals that has a venomous bite.

℞ MUSICAL ELEPHANT

An elephant at an English safari park entertains keepers and visitors by playing the harmonica. Five, a female African elephant at West Midlands Safari Park, discovered the harmonica after it was accidentally left on the side of her enclosure and soon learned to place the instrument in her trunk and blow out to produce some notes.

℞ GENTLE GIANT

Sancho, a longhorn steer from a New Holland, Ohio, farm, has horns measuring more than 10 ft (3 m) from tip to tip.

℞ EXPENSIVE SHEEP

A young male Texel sheep—a breed highly prized for its lean meat—was sold at a Scottish livestock market for over $350,000 in 2009. The young ram, who could father up to 1,000 lambs per year, cost more than $1,500 per pound, which means that a lamb chop from it would cost about $600!

℞ FALSE FOOT

A three-year-old Asian elephant whose front left foot was caught in a trap is able to walk again after he was fitted with a prosthetic foot. After cutting away 5 in (12 cm) of infected tissue, surgeons in Cambodia made a cast of Chhouk's stump so that a false foot could be created by a prosthetics' team. He needed no anesthetic while the limb was being attached—just a steady supply of turnips and bananas.

℞ RECYCLED PHONE

In 2009, a pelican at Tautphaus Park Zoo, Idaho, swallowed and later regurgitated a cell phone that a visitor had dropped into the pool.

℞ EARTHQUAKE PACKS

Pet owners in earthquake zones can buy special kits to ensure their cats and dogs survive. The Japanese-manufactured emergency packs contain a padded jacket and rain hat, special boots to protect paws, a bell in case the pet is lost in rubble, food, water and bowls, and aromatherapy oil to soothe stressed animals.

℞ TWO NOSES

A rabbit with two noses and four nostrils was discovered at a pet store in Milford, Connecticut, in 2009.

Inside Snout

In 2009, three piglets were born with their nostrils bizarrely inside the upper part of their lip. Half of a litter, born in the village of Jingdezhen, eastern China, had the rare deformity, but they still managed to eat, drink and breathe normally despite having no snouts.

ℛ SUPER RAT

A new species of rat has been discovered in Papua New Guinea that is as big as a domestic cat! Found in the crater of the extinct volcano Mount Bosavi, the Bosavi woolly rat measures more than 32 in (80 cm) from nose to tail and weighs 3 lb (1.4 kg).

ℛ ARROW SURGERY

A puppy from Kent, England, survived after swallowing a 10½-in (27-cm) plastic arrow that was almost as long as her. Betty, an eight-month-old Staffordshire bull terrier, underwent emergency surgery to remove the arrow, which had become lodged in her body from the esophagus to the small intestine.

22 POUNDS!

ℛ ODD TWINS

When farmer Vic Phillips from Somerset, England, mated his Aberdeen Angus bull with a Simmental heifer, the latter gave birth to twins—of different breeds. The male calf is a Simmental, yet the female is an Aberdeen Angus.

ℛ WANDERER RETURNS

A dog that vanished on the Gold Coast in Queensland, Australia, in 2000 was found nine years later and 1,250 mi (2,000 km) away in Melbourne, Victoria. While cleaning terrier-cross Muffy, animal carers spotted the microchip that identified her and enabled her to be reunited with her owners, the Lampard family.

ℛ LUCKY BREAK

After chasing a rabbit over a 40-ft (12-m) cliff on the Isle of Wight, England, Mac the golden retriever escaped plunging to his death when his collar caught on some rocks, breaking his fall.

ℛ CONTACT LENSES

A German company has invented a range of contact lenses for animals that suffer from cataracts, a condition that invariably leaves them blind. Among animals that may be able to be treated are lions, giraffes, bears, sea lions, kangaroos and tigers.

Porky Puss

IN 2009, THE PEOPLE'S DISPENSARY FOR SICK ANIMALS STARTED A FAT-FIGHTING CLUB FOR ANIMALS WITH WEIGHT PROBLEMS, AND SOCRATES THE CAT WAS ONE OF NINE CHOSEN ANIMALS. THE FAT CAT FROM NEWCASTLE, ENGLAND, LOVES TO EAT CHEESE-AND-ONION POTATO CHIPS AND WEIGHS A MASSIVE 22 LB (10 KG). THIS IS MORE THAN DOUBLE HIS IDEAL WEIGHT AND MAKES HIM "MORBIDLY OBESE." THE ANIMALS IN THE FITNESS CLUB ARE PUT ON A STRICT DIET AND EXERCISE REGIME FOR 100 DAYS TO INCREASE THEIR LIFE "PET-SPECTANCY" AND THE MOST IMPROVED CREATURE (AND OWNER) WINS A VACATION.

℞ MATERNAL INSTINCT

King penguins often adopt other penguins' chicks as their own and have been seen trying to raise a young skua—a species of bird that feeds on young penguins!

℞ NO JAWS

Horseshoe crabs have no jaws to chew with. Instead, they shove food straight into their open mouths with a pair of arms.

℞ FLOOD DIVERSION

During floods, Amazon River dolphins leave the river to swim through submerged forests lying in the flood plains.

℞ ETERNAL YOUTH

The fully grown, jellyfish-like creature *Turritopsis nutricula* can transform itself back into a juvenile an infinite number of times, keeping it from ever dying of old age.

℞ DUNG DWELLERS

Frogs in Sri Lanka's Bundala National Park have set up home in piles of Asian elephant dung. The frogs normally live among leaf litter on the ground, but because that can be in short supply during the dry season, they use elephant dung as an alternative habitat.

℞ UNINVITED GUEST

When Vickie Mendenhall from Spokane, Washington, bought a used couch for $27 in 2009, she found a cat living inside it. The cat had climbed in through a small hole on the underside when the couch's previous owner had donated it to the Value Village store.

℞ GREEN ENERGY

In 2008, the state of Michigan passed a new law that allows roadkill and other rotting animal carcasses to be converted into green energy. Bacteria and enzymes break down the carcasses and produce gas that can be used in engines and create electricity.

℞ SMOOTH SKIN

Elephants at Belfast Zoo in Northern Ireland have been given a brand of supermarket moisturizer to keep their bottoms smooth. Keeper Aisling McMahon recommended the moisturizing cream she used on her own skin and now the elephants receive regular applications to soften unwanted dry skin around their lower feet and butt.

℞ SLEEPY CEPHALOPOD

The Australian giant cuttlefish spends a remarkable 95 percent of its day resting and hiding in crevices from predators.

℞ SHARK SHOCK

A bamboo shark was born out of water in 2009 while being moved at an aquarium in Cheshire, England. The egg was being carefully transferred to a quarantine section at the Blue Planet Aquarium when it unexpectedly hatched in a diver's hands.

℞ TRAPPED UNDERGROUND

A Jack Russell terrier was trapped for 25 days underground in a rabbit warren in 2009—until he lost so much weight that he was able to crawl out. Six-year-old Jake was out walking with his owner Richard Thomas in Haverfordwest, Wales, when he chased a rabbit down a hole. When he failed to reappear, he was feared dead, but nearly a month later a new slimline Jake finally scrambled out, courtesy of his enforced diet.

℞ DOLPHIN TALK

In addition to using audible clicks and whistles, dolphins "talk" to each other by slapping their tails. Spanish scientists have observed that dolphins use various body movements, which also include diving and flopping sideways on the surface, as a means of communication.

Whale of a Tongue

When an unfortunate Finback whale washed up dead on a beach in Provincetown, Massachusetts, in 2009, the gases that were given off during the decomposition process caused its tongue to swell up like a giant balloon. Finbacks are the second biggest creatures on Earth after the Blue Whale and this young specimen was 40 ft (12 m) long and weighed about 22,000 lb (10,000 kg).

RIPLEY'S RESEARCH

ALBINISM IS A GENETIC TRAIT CHARACTERIZED BY A LACK OF MELANIN IN THE BODY, WHICH RESULTS IN A LACK OF PIGMENT. THIS GIVES ALBINO ANIMALS, AND PEOPLE, THEIR DISTINCTIVE WHITE COLORING. IT IS HIGHLY UNUSUAL, HOWEVER, FOR AN ALBINO ANIMAL, SUCH AS THIS DOLPHIN, TO BE SO UNIFORMLY AND BRIGHTLY PINK IN COLOR. MANY ALBINO ANIMALS SUFFER IN THE SUN AS MELANIN PROTECTS AGAINST ULTRAVIOLET LIGHT, BUT APART FROM SPENDING A LITTLE MORE TIME UNDER THE SURFACE, "PINKY" IN CALCASIEU LAKE SHOWS NO SIGNS OF THIS.

℞ SWEET TOOTH

A bear with a sweet tooth broke into a San Bernardino County, California, home and ate a 2-lb (900-g) box of chocolates from the refrigerator. He pushed aside vegetables in the fridge and went straight for the chocolates. He also tried unsuccessfully to open a bottle of champagne.

℞ POODLE STANDS

A poodle in Xi'an City, China, goes for a walk every day—on two feet. Gou Gou draws large crowds by walking hand-in-paw with owner Wang Guoqiang who taught the dog to walk on its two back legs as a puppy.

℞ DEEP DIVE

Sperm whales can dive to depths of nearly 2 mi (3 km) and can stay underwater for up to 90 minutes at a time without needing to surface for breath.

℞ JUMPING SQUID

Some species of squid leap from the water and glide through the air to evade predators.

Pink Dolphin

Never before seen, a bright pink albino Bottlenose dolphin has been catching the eye of sailors on coastal Calcasieu Lake, Louisiana. The dolphin, which has grown up in the area, is perfectly healthy apart from its flawless pink finish. The young creature swims with a small pod of fellow dolphins in the lake and is an unforgettable attraction for those lucky enough to catch a glimpse.

℞ SURFING DOG

An eight-month-old Border terrier can ride waves up to 3 ft (1 m) high near his home in Cornwall, England. Trained by owner Tim Kevan, Jack regularly surfs on a 9-ft (3-m) board and can even perform tricks such as a "hang five," where he walks up and down the board while surfing.

℞ FISH FANGS

Danionella dracula, a species of fish in Myanmar, has bone spurs that grow through the skin of its mouth and act as fangs.

℞ SWIMMING AID

A shark's skin is covered in tiny toothlike structures called denticles, which help it swim with a minimum of friction.

℞ FANTASTIC FINBACK

For many years Cambridge University in England has displayed the 70-ft (21-m) skeleton of a Finback Whale at its Zoology Museum. The specimen was found in 1865 on a beach in Sussex, England, and would have weighed 176,000 lb (80 tons).

Sea Pig

This curious creature was caught in deep water by the Cabrillo Marine Aquarium in California. It is about the size of an apple and can be found in most of the world's oceans at depths greater than 330 ft (100 m). It is actually a type of squid, and what looks like hair is actually a crop of tentacles attached to its head. Orange pigments on its body can look like facial features when its body swells with water. Add to this a protruding noselike "siphon," which it uses to propel itself, and you have what is commonly known as the Piglet Squid.

flea CIRCUS

The big top tent for Maria's Cardoso Flea Circus in Philadelphia.

QUEEN OF THE FLEAS

MARIA FERNANDA CARDOSO, AN ARTIST FROM COLOMBIA, HAS MADE HER CAREER EXPLORING THE PHYSICAL CAPABILITIES OF ANIMALS—AND HER FAMOUS CARDOSO FLEA CIRCUS PROJECT IS NO EXCEPTION. IN 1996, CARDOSO SET UP A BIG TOP TENT, MADE BY THE FABRIC WORKSHOP AND MUSEUM IN PHILADELPHIA, AND TWO OTHER ARENAS FOR HER FLEA PERFORMERS TO USE. HER TROOP CONSISTED OF FLEA TRAPEZE ARTISTS, WIRE-WALKERS AND FLEAS SHOT OUT OF CANNONS. CARDOSO LEADS HER FLEAS, WHILE WEARING HER CIRCUS ATTIRE, THROUGH STUNTS THAT ARE DESIGNED TO TEST THEIR RESPONSES TO HEAT, LIGHT AND CARBON DIOXIDE. ONCE THE FLEAS HAVE PERFORMED, THEY ARE REWARDED WITH HALF AN HOUR OF HER BLOOD.

One of her well-trained fleas balancing on a tightrope with a pole.

Flea-tastic Facts!

- A flea can pull up to 160,000 times its own weight, that's the same as a human pulling 2,679 double-decker buses.
- There are at least 2,000 different species of flea.
- Fleas are thought to have been sucking blood for more than 100 million years.
- A flea can jump 200 times its own length, that's the same as a human jumping to the top of the Empire State building.
- The largest infestation of fleas recorded was approximately 133,378,450 on a U.K. pig farm in 1986.
- A flea can produce up to 500 offspring in its lifetime.

Ripley's Revealed

A female cat flea tows a 19th-century cart in Germany at a circus.

The Alberti Flea Circus

The long-running, family-owned Alberti Flea Circus first opened in North Carolina in 1880. The current impresario is Jim Alberti, who learned how to train fleas from his grandfather at the age of 12.

RIPLEY'S ask

Tim Cockerill is a flea-circus expert, and tells us why fleas really are the best performers in the world…

When was the first flea circus created?
Jewelers first used fleas when, after making smaller and smaller gold chains, someone had the idea of harnessing a flea to a chain. There are reports of chained fleas throughout the 1500s and 1600s and of fleas pulling miniature carriages as early as 1745. The man who is credited with making flea circuses popular as a performance in its own right is Louis Bertolotto, who performed with his "Educated Fleas" in London's Regent Street from around 1830, before touring the world with his act.

What is it about fleas that make them good circus performers?
Fleas have very strong legs and good balance. They can be harnessed with a wire loop around their neck like an ox's yoke. Once harnessed, they can then pull weights much larger than their own body mass. Fleas are good at tightrope walking and their strong legs can also be put to use kicking balls in miniature football matches. This does not harm the fleas, but their lifespan is not long, so a performer needs to regularly replace his fleas.

How can you learn to train fleas for your very own circus?
The training is really a process of selection. Some fleas don't take well to being harnessed and refuse to feed once enslaved. Some fleas are oversensitive to noise and lights, others are docile and not well suited to performing. However, many fleas just love walking around pulling chariots or kicking balls, so these are the ones that are used in performances.

Famous Fleas

William Heckler started his flea circus in New York in 1900 with his son Roy at the forefront by 1925. When World War II restricted his intake of fleas, Roy started breeding his own. As circus director Roy would regularly feed his little performers with his own blood, allowing them to help themselves to his "quality human blood" and perform to their maximum potential. Choosing to breed females over males, as they are twice the size, Heckler would train them using a horizontal glass tube to walk or crawl instead of jump. Once they had hit their heads a few times, they knew to stay low!

A UNIQUE NOVELTY.
Direct from Earls Court Industrial Exhibition, London.

PROFESSOR KONTILI'S
WONDERFUL ROUMANIAN

Flea Circus

MUST BE SEEN TO BE BELIEVED,
PATRONISED BY ROYALTY, NOBILITY, & CLERGY.

Come and see the
LIVELY FLEAS
Dance a Ballet,
Fight a Duel, with
Swords,
Walk the Tight
Rope à la Blondin

Harnessed like
horses and drawing
and driving
Hansom Cabs, Mail
Vans, Funeral Cars,
Cabriolets, Milk
Cars, Artillery Fleas
firing a Cannon.

The
Smallest Performers
in the World.
Interesting alike.
to
Old and Young,
Rich and Poor.

TO BE SEEN WITHIN.

Cheapest Steam Printers, 38, Church Lane, (corner) Commercial Road, London, E

A Soaring Squeeze

Swallows travel at an amazing 35 mph (56 km/h), and when faced with an obstacle, such as a 2-in (5-cm) gap, they simply maneuver their 14-in (36-cm) wings and continue flying. The birds use their v-shaped tails to make sudden dramatic turns that enable them to squeeze through tiny gaps as well as snatch bugs out of the air.

R CORPSE CARPET

Thousands of generations of Bogong moths have been spending their summers in caves in the Australian Alps, their dead bodies forming a carpet 5 ft (1.5 m) deep.

R ADOPTED OWL

An orphaned baby eagle owl was adopted by a springer spaniel at a bird of prey rescue center in Cornwall, England, in 2009. The pair became inseparable and Sophie the spaniel even gave Bramble the owl a daily wash by licking her.

R GIANT WORM

The giant Gippsland earthworm, which lives in Victoria, Australia, can reach lengths of 10 ft (3 m). The young are already 8 in (20 cm) long when they hatch and take about five years to reach maturity. When the giant worm was first discovered in the 1870s, its size led scientists to think it was a snake.

R FATAL REPAIRS

Some aphids use goo from their bodies to patch holes in their colony's home—but often die in the process.

R PEPPERMINT SPRAY

Australia's peppermint stick insects spray an irritating, peppermint-scented fluid to defend themselves against predators.

R PIGEON SMUGGLERS

In March 2009, Brazilian police discovered inmates raising homing pigeons within Danilo Pinheiro Prison, Sorocaba, for the purpose of smuggling in contraband. Guards intercepted two pigeons carrying cell phones and chargers to detainees.

R STAR WITNESS

In April 2009, Judge James Martz of Palm Beach County, Florida, ordered a parrot to appear in court for a custody dispute involving the bird.

R DOG'S GUIDE DOG

A blind Border collie has his own guide dog! Five-year-old Clyde is totally blind and relies on another collie, Bonnie, to help him around the dog rescue center in Norfolk, England. Clyde refuses to go anywhere without Bonnie, who stays inches from his side while guiding him on walks or to food and water. She even lets him rest his head on her haunches when he becomes disorientated.

R DANCING CATERPILLARS

Birch sawfly larvae do a group dance routine to put off predators while they are munching through leaves. As many as six caterpillars will rear up with their back legs simultaneously to make themselves look more imposing.

R RAMPANT RABBIT

Benny, a two-year-old giant Flemish buck rabbit owned by Martin and Sharon Heather of Oxfordshire, England, is nearly 3 ft (90 cm) long and tips the scales at over 22 lb (10 kg). His food bill tops $75 a week.

ACTUAL SIZE!

A LITTLE PREY-ER

These other tiny animals also have bizarre ways of protecting themselves.

The Pebble Toad, which lives on the top of the Venezuelan Mountains, has a magnificent method of defense when facing danger. It curls up into a ball, tenses its body and rolls down the side of a mountain, bouncing like a falling pebble.

The River Frog has a bizarre way of defending itself against predators. Instead of running from danger, it will turn over and play dead—its body goes completely limp. Predators would much prefer live food and so leave the "dead" frog alone.

The Goldenrod Spider is able to change colors, like a chameleon, by secreting a yellow liquid onto its body. This is particularly useful for hiding from its predators, and prey, in bright flowers.

The Hagfish is one of the smallest fish in the ocean. When it is in danger, it releases huge amounts of mucus all over its body to make itself slippery. The predator cannot get hold of the fish and suffocates.

Mad Hatterpillar

This Gum Leaf Skeletoniser caterpillar, commonly known in Australia as a Hatterpiller, cleverly defends itself by stacking up its past head cases like hats on top of its head. Found all over New Zealand and Australia, the Hatterpillar molts heads as it grows larger and during this process grows a spike on the top its head. Retaining each head case that falls off, the Hatterpillar is able to stick each one onto the spike, sometimes having as many as six heads (or hats!) on top.

ⓡ FIERCE FROG

A species of frog that lived in Madagascar some 70 million years ago was so big and aggressive that it may even have eaten baby dinosaurs. Larger than any frog living today, *Beelzebufo ampinga* was 16 in (40 cm) long, weighed around 10 lb (4.5 kg) and possessed a very wide mouth and powerful jaws.

ⓡ CLOSE CALL

A tiny chihuahua, weighing about 4 lb (1.8 kg), somehow survived and recovered after being trodden on by her best friend— a 1,980-lb (900-kg) Clydesdale horse. Little Berry was playing with her friend Leroy at their home in Geelong, Victoria, Australia, when the giant horse accidentally stepped on the dog's head.

SNAIL TRAIL

THE GIANT AFRICAN SNAIL IS ONE OF THE WORLD'S MOST DESTRUCTIVE CREATURES AND CAN GROW UP TO 10 IN (25 CM) IN LENGTH. FOUND MOSTLY IN EAST AFRICA, ASIA AND THE CARIBBEAN, THEY GO GLOBAL BY CLIMBING INTO PRODUCE CONTAINERS AND SAILING ALL OVER THE WORLD. IN 1966, A BOY FROM MIAMI, FLORIDA, ACQUIRED THREE OF THESE SNAILS, WHICH HIS GRANDMA RELEASED INTO A GARDEN. SEVEN YEARS LATER, THERE WERE 18,000 OF THEM AND IT TOOK THE FLORIDA AUTHORITIES TEN YEARS AND $1 MILLION TO ERADICATE THEM.

ⓡ FAITHFUL FRIEND

Buddy, a German Shepherd dog, has phoned for help on three separate occasions when his owner, Joe Stalnaker of Scottsdale, Arizona, was incapacitated by seizures. Amazingly, the emergency operators took the calls from the clever hound to save its owner's life.

ⓡ LONG BUG

Chan's megastick, a stick-insect bug discovered on the island of Borneo by a Malaysian naturalist in 1989, measures 22 in (55 cm) long! Its body alone, without the legs, measures a staggering 14 in (35 cm).

ⓡ INSECT COLLECTION

Founded as part of the British Museum in 1756, London's Natural History Museum has nearly nine million butterflies and moths in its collection.

ⓡ SPINY NEWT

The Iberian ribbed newt, found in Morocco, Portugal and Spain, has sharply pointed ribs that it can stick through its sides to protect against predators.

SHARK JUMP

In December 2008, a reef shark at a Bahamas resort jumped from its aquarium, landed on a nearby water slide, slid down to the swimming pool and surprised the staff.

JUNK FOOD

Zeke, a cat owned by the Scarpino family of Cedar Knolls, New Jersey, had surgery to remove more than a year's accumulation of hair ties, ribbon, twist ties and junk from his stomach—which had grown to five times its normal size.

CANINE CASTAWAY

A pet dog that was swept overboard on a sailing trip swam 5 mi (8 km) through shark-infested waters and survived on a remote island for four months by feeding on baby goats. The grey and black cattle dog was reunited with owners Jan and Dave Griffith after being found by rangers on the largely uninhabited St. Bees Island off the coast of Queensland, Australia.

PUSHY PORKER

A pig the size of a Shetland pony terrorized a woman in Murwillumbah, New South Wales, Australia, in 2008. The pig took up residence at the home of Caroline Hayes and refused to leave her alone.

HOPPING MAD

A kangaroo burst through the window of a house and hopped into bed with a startled Australian family in March 2009. Beat Ettlin rescued his children from the kangaroo that stood around 6 ft (1.8 m) tall by wrestling the animal into a headlock and dragging it down the hall and out the front door.

ESCAPE BID

An ingenious orangutan tried to escape from an Australian zoo in May 2009 by short-circuiting an electric fence. Twenty-seven-year-old Karta jammed a stick into wires connected to the fence and then piled up sufficient debris to enable her to scale a concrete and glass wall at Adelaide Zoo. On reaching the top of the fence, she sat there for 30 minutes before changing her mind and returning to the enclosure.

COLOMBIAN MONSTER

An extinct species of snake, which lived in Colombian jungles 58 million years ago, could reach lengths of up to 42 ft (13 m)—that's longer than a bus.

CRANE PURSUIT

Conservationists in Wisconsin help endangered whooping cranes to migrate south for the winter by encouraging them to fly in pursuit of a microlight plane. The hand-reared birds are taught that the microlight, which plays recordings of simulated crane calls, is their parent, so when the aircraft takes off, they dutifully follow for more than 1,250 mi (2,000 km) to the warmth and safety of the west coast of Florida.

CLONED PET

A Florida family paid $155,000 for a clone of their dead dog. Nina Otto from Boca Raton had the DNA of her beloved golden Labrador, Sir Lancelot, collected and frozen five years before his death in 2008. In 2009, the family collected Lancelot Encore, a three-month-old puppy that was an exact genetic replica of their deceased pet.

BOUNCING FISH

A new species of fish has been discovered that bounces on the ocean floor like a rubber ball. The psychedelic dogfish, which was discovered off the coast of Indonesia in 2008, bounces around in a haphazard manner because its tail is off-center and because it propels itself forward jerkily by expelling water from tiny gill openings.

BAY OF PIGS

SWIMMERS OFF THE BIG MAJOR SPOT ISLAND IN THE BAHAMAS ARE AMAZED TO SEE FERAL PIGS ENJOYING THE CRYSTAL CLEAR WATER. THE AREA IS KNOWN LOCALLY AS "PIG BEACH," AND NOBODY IS QUITE SURE HOW THE PIGS GOT THERE. THE ISLAND IS UNINHABITED EXCEPT FOR VISITORS BRINGING SCRAPS FOR THE GROWING PIG POPULATION, WHO PADDLE OUT TO BOATS TO MAKE SURE THEY GET THE FOOD FIRST.

Cow Strange

This six-year-old cow was born with six legs and can be seen in a zoo in Yichang, China. Unsurprisingly, it is a big hit with the visitors. The condition, known as "Polymelia," can affect most animals, and may be caused by a genetic disorder, a deformed twin being partially absorbed in the womb, or environmental issues.

℞ BLOWN AWAY

A Chihuahua swept up into the air and blown away by a 70-mph (110-km/h) gust of wind was eventually found safe and sound more than a mile (1.6 km) away. Weighing 6 lb (2.7 kg), little eight-month-old Tinker Bell was standing on her owners' platform trailer at a flea market in Waterford Township, Michigan, in April 2009 when she was hurled out of sight by the force of the sudden blast of air.

℞ MAGNETIC CROCS

Biologists in Florida tape magnets to the heads of nuisance crocodiles to disrupt their magnetic sense of direction when they relocate the animals.

℞ TV ADDICT

A pet rabbit in Xiamen, China, is so addicted to South Korean TV soap operas that she attacks her owners if they change the channel while she is watching. Every night at 10 p.m., the rabbit, Jia Xiaoyu, climbs between the couple to watch an imported drama, but starts biting the pillow and becoming aggressive if her favorite show, *Ms. Mermaid*, isn't on.

℞ SNAKE BITE

Johannes Swart spent 37 days in a glass box, measuring 16 x 13 ft (5 x 4 m), with 40 highly venomous snakes at a conservation park near Pretoria, South Africa, in September 2009. His stay ended when he was bitten on the foot by a deadly puff adder and had to undergo emergency surgery in the local hospital.

℞ WHISTLING APES

An orangutan at the National Zoo in Washington, D.C. has amazed keepers by learning to whistle. Thirty-two-year-old Bonnie taught herself after listening to keepers whistling while they worked. She is thought to have taught another orangutan at the zoo to whistle, too.

℞ MAN BITES SNAKE

A Kenyan man escaped from a python by biting it after the snake had wrapped him in its coils and dragged him up a tree. During the three-hour struggle, Ben Nyaumbe smothered the snake's head with his shirt to prevent it from swallowing him and then bit the python on the tip of its tail.

Snake Boy

Uorn Sambath from Setbo, Cambodia, has an unusual pet for a boy. He has developed a friendship with a huge 16-ft (4.9-m) python. He gives the serpent hugs and kisses and sometimes sleeps inside the coils of the snake, which weighs over 220 lb (100 kg) and requires three adults to carry. The python first slithered into the boy's bedroom when he was three months old, and now has its own room in the family home.

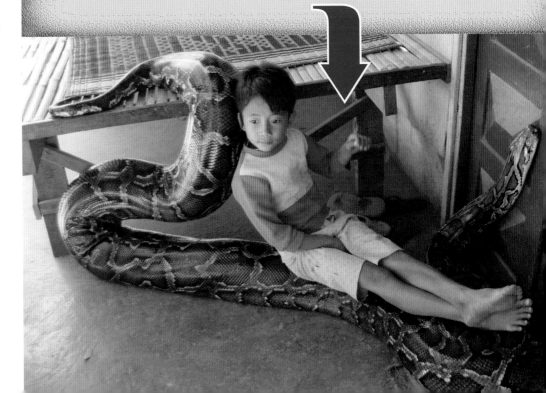

Mad Menagerie

VENICE BEACH FREAKSHOW

Ripley's ask

Why did you create the Freakshow?

I have been a collector of circus, sideshow and Freakshow memorabilia since I was a kid. I started the Freakshow to show kids of all ages the wonders of the universe, to remind them that life is a special gift in all of its amazing forms. When I was a kid, I visited a similar show and was never the same. I loved it! There is nothing in the world like the look of wonder in a kid's eyes when they see a living two-headed animal. It's as though the entire world is new to them. That is why I created the Venice Beach Freakshow, to raise those questions on the mysteries of life and to celebrate the magnificence and majesty of creation with children of all ages.

Todd holding Myrtle and Squirtle, who share the same shell, outside his Venice Beach Freakshow

TODD RAY'S "FREAKSHOW" HOUSES ONE OF THE STRANGEST COLLECTIONS OF LIVE CREATURES ON THE PLANET. TODD ESTABLISHED HIS MENAGERIE OF ANIMALS ON THE BEACH BOARDWALK AT VENICE, CALIFORNIA, AFTER RETIRING FROM A CAREER IN THE MUSIC INDUSTRY. HIS COLLECTION CONTAINS TURTLES, SNAKES AND LIZARDS WITH MULTIPLE HEADS, A DOG WITH FIVE LEGS, AN IGUANA WITH TWO TAILS, A HAIRLESS RAT, ALBINO SNAKES, AND MANY OTHER ODDITIES. INSIDE THE SHOW ARE LESS FORTUNATE FREAKS OF THE NATURAL WORLD, SUCH AS DOUBLE-HEADED COWS, CHICKENS AND EVEN A RACCOON, PRESERVED IN JARS OF FORMALDEHYDE FOR CURIOUS VISITORS TO SEE.

One of the many oddities in Todd's extended collection, a two-faced kitten preserved in formaldehyde

Double- tailed iguana

Cheech and Chong, a turtle with
two heads and six legs

Double- headed
bearded dragon

Rocky the five- legged miniature
pinscher, held by Todd's daughter Asia

Laverne and Shirley
the two- headed
kingsnake

Giant Limb

Motola, a 48-year-old Asian elephant from Thailand, needed a heavyweight solution when she lost part of one of her legs after stepping on a land mine ten years ago. After trying various prototypes, she was recently fitted with a custom-made permanent prosthetic limb strong enough to hold her weight at the Elephant Hospital in North Thailand. The jumbo operation to fit Motola's new leg required enough anesthetic to knock out 70 people.

℞ DOLPHIN RESCUE

In April 2009, thousands of leaping dolphins in the Gulf of Aden prevented Somali pirate speedboats from attacking a flotilla of Chinese merchant ships. When the dolphins, which were swimming next to the Chinese ships, leaped out of the water, the pirates decided to turn back.

℞ SPORTING PENGUINS

In May 2009, New Zealand hosted the world's first sports tournament for penguins. The Penguathlon took place in Orakei, near Auckland, and saw King and Gentoo penguins go beak to beak in five events— football, Frisbee, surfing, swing ball and waddle racing.

℞ ZEBRA RIDE

Former racehorse jockey Bill Turner rides a zebra to his local pub in the town of Sherborne in Dorset, England. He bought the zebra from a game reserve in Holland and learned to ride it in just two weeks.

℞ OCTOPUS STUDY

British marine experts have discovered that instead of eight arms, an octopus really has only six. A new study has revealed that it uses six of its tentacles as arms for eating, but the back two limbs act as legs to help it move across the ocean floor.

℞ METAL CROC

Doug Mader, a veterinarian in Marathon, Florida, used four metal rods and 41 screws to reconstruct the jaw of a crocodile that had its head crushed by a car in December 2008.

℞ DENTAL CARE

Female long-tailed macaque monkeys near Bangkok, Thailand, have been observed teaching their young how to floss their teeth. The adults were seen using strands of hair to clean between their teeth, and this practice became more regular and more elaborate when the females were with their babies, suggesting that they were trying to teach the youngsters the importance of good dental hygiene.

℞ 15,000 FEET

The sunflower starfish grows to a diameter of more than 3 ft (1 m) across and has around 15,000 tube feet on the underside of its body.

Crocodile Man

Chito Loco thinks nothing of frolicking in the water with a 980-lb (445-kg) crocodile. Chito rescued the giant reptile after farmers shot him 20 years ago, and nursed him back to health. The Costa Rican fisherman now puts on a weekly show during which he feeds and even rides the croc, which he named Pocho, who is an impressive 16 ft (5 m) long.

MEAT EATER

INTREPID EXPLORERS HAVE RELEASED DETAILS OF AN AMAZING NEW PLANT SPECIES, CAPABLE OF TRAPPING AND DEVOURING A FULL-SIZE RAT, ON AN ISLAND IN THE PHILIPPINES. IN A QUEST TO FIND THE PLANT, WHICH WAS LAST RECORDED IN 1907, STEWART MCPHERSON'S TEAM CLIMBED A MOUNTAIN IN THE MIDDLE OF A PRISON, GUIDED BY THREE CONVICTED MURDERERS, AND DISCOVERED THE CARNIVOROUS PITCHER PLANTS AT THE SUMMIT. THE PLANTS ARE THE SIZE OF FOOTBALLS AND LINED WITH TENTACLES THAT SECRETE STICKY GLUE TO ENSNARE INSECTS AND RODENTS, BEFORE IT DISSOLVES THEM WITH ITS ACID-LIKE ENZYMES.

Weird Vegetation

Dragon Arum At night the flowers of this plant trap flies attracted by its smell of rotting meat. The plant lets them go free in the morning so they can transfer its pollen.

Mimosa pudica Its name means "shy plant," and if it is touched or exposed to heat its branches shrink away and its leaves curl up.

Hydnora africana This is a parasitic plant with a feces-like odor that attracts dung beetles who then help to pollinate the plant.

Titan Arum One of the largest flowers in the world, it smells like dead animals and only flowers once every six or seven years.

Common Bladderwort This is an aquatic plant capable of trapping and digesting worms, tadpoles and even young fish.

℞ HOT HIPPO
A hippopotamus that decided to escape the South African heat by climbing into a 10-ft-high (3-m) water tower for a long soak found it couldn't get out again. A farm worker realized the animal was stuck, and in a four-hour operation a team from the Mpumalanga Tourism and Parks Association drained the tank and used poles to nudge the hippo into a steel cage before winching it to safety with a hydraulic crane.

℞ PANDA-MONIUM
In June 2009, keepers at Thailand's Ayutthaya Elephant Kraal painted five of their elephants in black and white watercolor paint to make them look like giant pandas! The bizarre move was intended to raise the profile of the elephant—Thailand's national symbol—after the whole country had gone panda-crazy since the birth of a female panda cub at a zoo in Bangkok.

℞ SURPRISE VISITOR
In March 2009, a sick turtle swam directly to the Turtle Hospital—a turtle treatment facility in the Florida Keys! The 73-lb (33-kg) loggerhead turtle was found to be suffering from a bacterial infection.

℞ RAT PACK
White laboratory rats protect official police records in the city of Karnal in the Indian state of Haryana by scaring away mice that would damage paperwork and eat evidence.

℞ BEE SWARM
Employees at a game store in one of the busiest shopping areas of New York City were trapped inside for several hours in May 2009 while thousands of bees swarmed outside in the street. After a passerby managed to lure some of the bees into a box, a specialist arrived in protective gear and used the scent of a queen bee to collect the rest of them.

℞ FROZEN BUG
The Alpine weta of New Zealand, a large, cricket-like insect, can freeze solid for several months without suffering any ill effects.

℞ SEA HUNT
A fugitive sea lion tried to escape from Californian police officers in June 2009 by taking control of their speedboat. The animal, nicknamed Snoopy, was picked up by Orange County sheriffs after reports that he had bitten a boy in Newport Harbor. But once on board the patrol boat, the resourceful sea lion apparently managed to start the throttle, steer the boat and even sound the siren.

Snake Foot

This snake was discovered in China in 2009 with a single clawed foot growing out from its body. The 16-in-long (40-cm) mutant reptile was found by Duan Qiongxiu clinging to the wall of her bedroom in Suining with its talons. Mrs. Duan was so scared that she beat the snake to death with her shoe. Growing a foot is a very rare mutation for a snake—they more frequently grow two heads—and scientists are working to find out if the foot evolved from changes in the snake's environment.

CRUEL TWIST

A dog in China became so attached to two red pandas she had adopted that she rejected her own puppy. The rare pandas were abandoned by their mother shortly after being born at Taiyuan Zoo, but were nursed back to health with love and milk from the dog. However, the dog became convinced that the cubs were its own babies and refused to nurse her own puppy.

SIGN LANGUAGE

A Border collie puppy is learning sign language after it was discovered that she is totally deaf. Pixie is being taught to recognize hand commands by trainer Liz Grewal in Coffs Harbour, New South Wales, Australia.

PRESIDENT'S BEARS

U.S. President Thomas Jefferson received a gift of two grizzly bears in October 1807. He was so delighted that he kept them on the White House lawn for months.

TOILET ORDEAL

A puppy survived being flushed down a lavatory in June 2009 after his four-year-old owner decided that his pet needed a wash. The week-old cocker spaniel was muddy following a walk, so young Daniel Blair of Middlesex, England, decided to wash it by putting it in the toilet and flushing it. The puppy was rescued by plumbers after being trapped in a waste pipe for nearly four hours.

SILK BELL

Europe's water spider spends its entire life underwater and builds a silk diving bell to store oxygen.

BEST FRIENDS

Gerald, a 15-ft-tall (4.5-m) giraffe at Noah's Ark Zoo Farm in Bristol, England, has an unusual best friend—a goat named Eddie. The pair have been inseparable for more than three years, with Gerald letting his little friend climb on his neck and share his bedding. He even chases away the zebras who bully Eddie.

CATERPILLAR INVASION

The President of Liberia declared a state of emergency in January 2009 owing to giant armies of caterpillars. In the worst invasion in 30 years, tens of millions of marching caterpillars swarmed over 80 towns and villages, preventing farmers from reaching their fields and causing others to flee their homes.

CYANIDE GLANDS

The dragon millipede of Thailand has bright pink coloration and glands that produce cyanide poison.

WEDDING GUEST

A dog who saved a woman's life after it found her dying of hypothermia was invited to be guest of honor at her wedding five years later. Zoe Christie had been discovered in November 2004 with severe hypothermia in a field in Devon, England, by John Richards and his boxer dog Boris. Mr. Richards had walked past Zoe's body, but Boris saw her and made such a commotion that his owner turned round and went back to see what the problem was.

HOUSE GUESTS

Lesley Coles of Somerset, England, wondered why her shopping bag was heavy—and when she looked inside she found a 3-ft (90-cm) python curled up in the bottom. The snake was thought to have been secretly living in the cupboard of Mrs. Coles' house for up to six months after crawling in through a hole made for the electrical meter.

GOOD MEMORY

Elephants can recognize groups of people by their specific smell, color and the style of their clothing.

Incy Wincy Spider

The tiny "happy-face" spider can be found in the rainforests of only four islands in the world—Oahu, Molokai, Maui and Hawaii. Measuring around 1/5 in (5 mm), no one really knows why the colorful patterns on the spiders' backs look like happy faces. One theory is that the patterns evolved to confuse their predators—birds—but the species is nevertheless under threat from a growing number of animals that have been introduced to the islands. Perhaps they need to evolve a scary face!

HORSING AROUND

Gracie, an inquisitive young horse from Pullman, West Virginia, had to be cut out of a tree when she got her head stuck inside the trunk in 2008. Neighbor Jason Harschbarger heard the horse's loud whinnying as she was struggling to get out and came to her rescue, eventually freeing her with a chainsaw. Gracie suffered only a few minor injuries and a dislocated jaw, but is now back in full health and steering well clear of trees!

TUNEFUL TOADS

In 2009, fire-bellied toads from Denmark, Germany, Latvia and Sweden croaked it out for the second annual international toad song contest, held in the Schleswig-Holstein area of Germany.

BOXER DOG

Chela, a dog owned by Peru's national police force, has been taught to box. Trainer Cesar Chacaliaza says the German shorthaired pointer wasn't keen on wearing boxing gloves at first, but she has now learned to jab with her front paws while standing up on her hind legs.

TALENTED PIG

Sue, a Kune Kune pig owned by Wendy Scudamore from Herefordshire, England, shakes hands by presenting a trotter on command and can perform agility tests as ably as any dog. In fact, Mrs. Scudamore hopes that one day Sue will be able to herd sheep just like the pig in the movie *Babe*.

LONG REACH

The Giant Pacific octopus has an arm span of more than 14 ft (4 m) across—that's greater than the height of two adult men.

RUBBERY SKELETONS

Sharks, skates and rays have skeletons made of cartilage—the same rubbery substance that gives shape to your ears and the bridge of your nose.

FLYING CHIMP

Bili, a three-month-old bonobo chimpanzee, sat in the cabin with the rest of the passengers for his flight from Birmingham, England, to his new home at Frankfurt Zoo in Germany.

WEASEL'S REVENGE

In 2009, Mr. Zhang of Wuchang, Hubei Province, China, said his family were being harassed by a weasel after he had caught its mate in a trap. Zhang said the male weasel excreted on tables, threw dead mice into the family home and even jumped screaming onto their bed.

SWALLOWED RING

Anne Moon from Yorkshire, England, lost a $2,250 antique diamond engagement ring in August 2009 when it was swallowed by a piglet. She went to pat Ginger, a ten-week-old Kune Kune pig, at a farm but it clamped its teeth around the ring and refused to let go.

FATHER AT 110

In 2009, a tortoise living in Norfolk, England, became a father at age 110. Billy, a spur thigh tortoise, became a father after finally mating with Tammy, a 47-year-old female, who had rejected his advances for 15 years.

ROVING EYE

The flounder is a fish with a migrating eye. At first the fish swim vertically with an eye on each side, but later one eye moves around to join the other and the fish start to swim flat.

FREAKY PIG

A piglet born in Zhejiang Province, China, in 2009 had two mouths and three eyes. The mother was completely normal, as were the other seven piglets in the litter.

CANINE COMMUTERS

Stray dogs in Moscow, Russia, use the subway to travel to the city center in search of food. They board the trains each morning and travel back on the subway to where they live in the evening. If they fall asleep and miss their stop, they get off and take another train back to the center.

Albino Turtle

RESEMBLING AN UNCOOKED CHRISTMAS TURKEY, THIS WHITE BEAST IS IN FACT A RARE ALBINO TURTLE. FOUND ON THE BANKS OF THE YELLOW RIVER IN HENAN PROVINCE, CHINA, IN 2009, IT MEASURES 16 IN (40 CM) IN LENGTH AND WEIGHS 14 LB (6.5 KG). THE MUTANT TURTLE REPORTEDLY ACQUIRED ITS ALL-WHITE SKIN, APART FROM ONE PINK PATCH, THROUGH A GENETIC MUTATION CAUSED BY POLLUTION.

One Pig Race

Cushendun Community Fête, in Northern Ireland, enjoyed a fun-filled pig-racing event complete with colorful woolen jockeys in July 2009. Popular in the U.S.A., the races are usually often a main attraction at county fairs. Only juvenile pigs are allowed to participate and they race around a grass or dirt track and even jump over hurdles.

® THREATENING KISS

In a bid to ward off predators, and to suggest that they are larger than they really are, orangutans make their voices sound deeper by blowing exaggerated kisses. They achieve the sound—called a kiss-squeak—by holding leaves or their hands up to their mouths.

® TURTLE RECALL

A runway at John F. Kennedy International Airport in New York City was shut down briefly in July 2009 after about 80 turtles emerged from nearby Jamaica Bay and crawled onto the tarmac. The invasion by the 8-in-long (20-cm) diamondback terrapins caused flights to be delayed for up to 90 minutes.

® DOG'S DINNER

When their dog Bertie started walking strangely, Mark and Michelle Jewell from Essex, England, took him to a veterinarian who found that nine golf balls were lodged in Bertie's stomach.

® LITERATE DOG

New York animal trainer Lyssa Rosenberg has taught her terrier Willow to read! Willow plays dead when she sees the word "bang," stretches a paw in the air when she sees "wave" and stands on her back feet to beg when she sees the words "sit up." Willow can do 250 different tricks and it took her just six weeks to recognize words and respond to them.

® AGED TORTOISE

Jonathan, a tortoise living on St. Helena Island, is estimated to be over 176 years old. The earliest photo of him, standing beside a Boer War prisoner, dates back more than 100 years.

® DACHSHUND DASH

San Diego, California, is home to the Wienerschnitzel Wiener Nationals—a sprint race created especially for dachshunds.

® SHARK SOUL

To put a male shark in the mood for love, staff at the Sea Life London Aquarium, England, piped the sounds of Barry White and Marvin Gaye into his tank. They hoped that the romantic music would encourage Zorro, a six-year-old zebra shark, to breed with a female, Mazawabee, who had been single for several years.

Monkey Business

Visitors at Knowsley Safari Park, Prescot, England, will need to learn to keep their luggage inside their cars after more than 20 resident baboons completely emptied visitors' suitcases in July 2009. The naughty baboons have cleverly worked out how to break into car roof racks leaving visitors no choice but to helplessly watch their belongings being strewn all over the ground! The incident has occurred so frequently that the Park's General Manager, David Ross, has had to advise cars with cargo cases not to drive through the monkey enclosure.

℞ TRACKING DEVICE

A 6-ft (1.8-m) python that was stolen from a research center near Perth, Western Australia, was traced by its last meal. The snake was snatched shortly after it had eaten a woylie, an endangered marsupial that, unbeknown to the unlucky thieves, had been fitted with a tracking device. The device showed up even from inside the python's stomach, alerting scientists and police to the snake's whereabouts.

℞ FROG FIND

Half a century after last being spotted, a population of rare California mountain yellow-legged frogs was rediscovered in 2009. The elusive amphibians were located in the San Bernardino National Forest by scientists following the same course as a 1908 expedition.

℞ ELEPHANT HANGED

On September 13, 1916, "Murderous Mary," an elephant from Sparks Brothers Circus, was hanged for killing a handler in Erwin, Tennessee. A crowd of 2,500 gathered to watch as the five-ton elephant was hanged by the neck by a chain attached to a 100-ton derrick car.

Short Legs

Fire crews were called out four times to rescue Mayflower, a grey Shetland pony apparently stuck in mud, only to find that the animal simply had short legs! Her unusually short legs and long body mean she is only half the height of other ponies grazing on salt marshes near the River Test in Hampshire, England.

℞ SENIOR DOG

Max, a terrier-cross belonging to Janelle Derouen of New Iberia, Louisiana, celebrated his 26th birthday in 2009—making him a staggering 182 years old in dog years.

℞ FIVE LEGS

Lilly, a Chihuahua puppy, was born in Gastonia, North Carolina, with five legs. The extra leg, which had no feeling, hung down between her two rear legs until it was removed at age seven weeks.

℞ DEEP DOWN

The Hadal snailfish lives at depths of 4.8 mi (7.7 km) under the Pacific Ocean in the Japan Trench, the deepest a fish has ever been filmed.

℞ COOKIE BEAR

A black bear was found sitting on a freezer eating cookies after breaking into a bakery in Tobermory, Ontario, Canada, in July 2009.

℞ TWISTED FLIGHT

When some geese come in to land from a great height, they fly upside down while keeping their head and neck the right way up! The display of contortionism, known as whiffling, enables the birds to release air from their wings and thus reduce their speed prior to landing.

℞ LUCKY STRIKE

A chicken in England has laid an egg shaped like a bowling pin! Natalie Wiltshire said the odd egg was laid by one of the 20 chickens she keeps in Willoughby, Northamptonshire.

℞ SHRINKING SHEEP

A breed of wild sheep in Scotland is shrinking in body size as a result of climate change. Since 1985, Soay sheep on the uninhabited island of Hirta in the St. Kilda archipelago have shrunk by five percent, their legs getting shorter and their body weight decreasing. In the past, only big sheep could survive the harsh winters in the area, but scientists say that because of climate change the winters have become milder and grass is now available for more months of the year, enabling smaller sheep to cope.

Mistaken Identity

Reggie, a 3-ft-long (1-m) kingsnake kept as a pet in West Sussex, England, required emergency surgery after attempting to eat his own tail. He mistook his tail for another snake but was unable to regurgitate it because of his backward-facing teeth. He was prevented from choking to death by veterinary surgeon Bob Reynolds, who pried open the snake's mouth, dislocated its jaw and removed the tail before it had been digested.

℞ TWO HEADS

A cobra with two heads was born in China in 2009. The cobra, which was able to eat by using both of its mouths simultaneously, hatched at the Jiujiang home of rail worker Mr. Liu, who breeds snakes as a hobby.

℞ PAMPERED PET

An Israeli woman paid $32,000 so that her boxer dog Orchuk could travel in business class with her from Paris, France, to Tel Aviv. She paid for an entire compartment to carry her, the dog and a veterinary on the four-hour El Al flight. The Israeli airline had to remove several seats to make way for the dog's cage.

℞ HORSE DRESS

Bavarian designer Hildegard Bergbauer usually creates traditional *dirndl* dresses for women, but now she has branched out and started making them for cats, dogs and even horses, too!

℞ BEAR WITNESS

When naturalist Casey Anderson married actress Missi Pyle in Montana in 2009, his best man was Brutus, a half-ton grizzly bear. Brutus also joined the 85 guests at the reception, where he helped himself to some wedding cake. Having hand-reared the bear from a cub, Casey has forged a close relationship with the 7-ft-8-in-tall (2.3-m) animal. They walk and swim together and Casey has started teaching Brutus to fish.

℞ LIQUID LUNCH

Spiders are unable to eat solid food, so they must liquefy the insides of their prey. They do this by regurgitating digestive juices onto the prey and then crushing it with their jaws and sucking up the juices.

℞ BUTTERFLY HAVEN

There are almost 20,000 known species of butterflies and an amazing 40 percent of these are found in South America.

℞ NUCLEAR HOME

Half of the world's wild two-humped Bactrian camels live in a former nuclear weapons test site in Xinjiang, China.

℞ LOVE DARTS

About one-third of snail species grow "love darts," which they use when mating. The snails shoot the mucus-covered dart, which enhances fertility, into another snail's skin.

℞ BALD CAT

A cat who is bald apart from a mass of chest hair has become a tourist attraction at the Exeter Veterinary Hospital in New Hampshire because of his weird appearance. Eight-year-old Ugly Bat Boy, whose breed is not known, was adopted by Dr. Stephen Bassett shortly after he was born bald, probably as a result of a genetic defect.

℞ SWINGING DOG

Sara, a Labrador-chow cross, loves spending her days on the swings at her local park. She enjoys it so much that her owners, the Lanier family from Boone, North Carolina, take her to the park several times a week.

Cat Nap

Riana with the latest addition to her cat family, baby cheetah Aviva.

BIG-CAT KEEPER RIANA VAN NIEUWENHUIZEN FROM BLOEMFONTEIN, SOUTH AFRICA, SHARES HER HOME WITH NINE CHEETAHS, THREE LEOPARDS, TWO WOLVES, A JAGUAR, A LION AND THREE DOGS. RIANA HAND REARS THE ABANDONED OR ORPHANED ANIMALS AND USES THEM TO RAISE AWARENESS OF ENDANGERED SPECIES IN HER COUNTRY.

Fiela, who shares 55 lb (25 kg) of chicken a day with the other animals, is seen here sitting at the dinner table with her owner Riana.

Riana bought her first cheetah, Fiela, in 2006 at just six weeks old. Fiela is fully house-trained and allowed to roam free in Riana's house.

CHEMICAL ALERT

Argentine ants produce chemicals that alert their nestmates to the fact that they are still alive. Once they stop producing it, they are picked up and carried to a garbage pile by the other ants.

FLAG THIEF

A squirrel was caught stealing small U.S. flags from a cemetery and carrying them up to its nest. Every Memorial Day, volunteers place the flags next to the graves of nearly 1,000 veterans buried at Mount Hope Cemetery in Port Huron, Michigan, but in May 2009, workers noticed several flags had been torn off their wooden staffs. The cheeky squirrel was then spotted detaching a flag and running up a tree with it to the nest.

LEG TWITCH

A harvestman arachnid's legs can twitch for up to an hour after being detached from its body.

PIGEON HONOR

G.I. Joe, a carrier pigeon for the U.S. Army, helped save the lives of 1,000 British soldiers during World War II—and in 1946, London's mayor presented him with an honorary medal for his work.

LARGE APPETITE

Indonesia's komodo dragons, the world's largest lizards, can weigh more than 170 lb (77 kg) and are capable of eating 80 percent of their body weight in a single meal.

NAME CHECK

Smokey the cockatiel was reunited with his owner after saying his own name on the phone. Having escaped from the home of David Edwards, the missing bird had been found in nearby Wrexham, North Wales. To prove that she was the rightful owner, Mrs. Edwards asked for Smokey to be put on the phone and as soon as he heard her voice, he started repeating his name.

WHO'S A CLEVER BOY?

In 2009, the American Red Cross presented an award to Willie the parrot for saving the life of two-year-old Hannah Kuusk at her home in Denver, Colorado. When Hannah started choking on some food, the normally quiet Willie alerted his owner by flapping his wings and repeatedly squawking, "Momma, Baby!"

SWALLOWED WHOLE

An Australian woman was horrified when her pet dog was swallowed whole by a snake in March 2009. Patty Buntine of Katherine, Northern Territory, was worried when Bindi, her three-year-old Maltese terrier cross, went missing. On going outside to investigate, she saw the snake with its belly bulging so much it was unable to move. The dog amounted to around 60 percent of the snake's bodyweight, which meant that the serpent's snack was like a fully grown man swallowing a 16-year-old boy.

EXPLODING GLANDS

Several species of Southeast Asian ants have exploding glands in their heads, allowing them to launch suicidal chemical attacks on enemies.

SYNTHETIC BEAK

A stork with a damaged beak was given a new one in 2009 by a Hungarian bird hospital. The stork, which was thought to have flown into a wall, had its lower beak repaired in an operation, while specialist Tamas Kothay built a new top beak out of synthetic resin.

Snake Attack

A python was caught suffocating an unfortunate cockatoo in Cairns, Australia, in 2008. Artist Cindy Lane was working in her studio when she heard loud squawking, and moving outside she discovered the snake coiling itself around the bird high up in a tree in her backyard. She reported that the python took around two hours to completely swallow its feathered prey.

Flappy Meal

A GOLDEN ORB WEAVER SPIDER
MANAGED TO ENSNARE A
CHESTNUT–BREASTED MANNIKIN
FINCH IN ITS WEB IN A GARDEN
NEAR ATHERTON, AUSTRALIA.
THE GIANT SPIDER WOULD HAVE
THEN PROCEEDED TO INJECT THE
STRUGGLING BIRD WITH VENOM TO
PREPARE IT FOR EATING, AND WRAP
THE CORPSE INTO A FOOD PARCEL,
AS IT WOULD BE TOO MUCH FOR
THE SPIDER TO EAT IN ONE SITTING.
GOLDEN ORB WEAVER SPIDERS
CAN GROW LARGER THAN A HUMAN
HAND AND USUALLY PREY ON LARGE
INSECTS, SO IT IS HIGHLY UNUSUAL
TO SEE ONE CATCHING A BIRD.

ACTUAL SIZE!

HIGH LIFE

The common swift spends most of its life in flight, nests on vertical surfaces and never willingly touches the ground.

DANCING PARROT

The antics of a cockatoo from Indiana on an Internet video-sharing website have convinced scientists that birds really do dance to music. More than two million people viewed Snowball's rhythmic movements online as his dancing feet diligently followed the beat of his favorite Backstreet Boys song, even when the tune was speeded up or slowed down.

FEATHERED CRITICS

By rewarding them with food, Japanese scientists believe that racing pigeons can be trained to study paintings and evaluate them—exactly as you might expect from an art critic. The study shows that, with practice, pigeons can learn to appreciate the color, pattern and texture of paintings.

WOLF DETERRENT

Wolves can be kept at bay using a simple technique of a rope with a red ribbon, or series of red flags, tied to it. The technique is known as fladry and has been used for centuries in Europe.

DARING DIVE

To impress a mate, Anna's hummingbird (named after a 19th-century Italian duchess called Anna Massena) dives through the air at speeds of around 50 mph (80 km/h). Sometimes the dives are aimed at other birds, sometimes at people. Because the bird is typically only 4 in (10 cm) long, its speed is the equivalent of a car traveling at 1,300 mph (2,090 km/h)—that's almost twice the speed of sound. To perform its astonishing dive, the tiny hummingbird—a native of California—must whirl its wings at more than 1,000 beats a minute and burn body fuel some 400 times faster than a human.

ANGRY HIPPOS

A CROCODILE WAS BITTEN TO DEATH AFTER BECOMING TRAPPED AMONG A GANG OF 50 ANGRY HIPPOS ON THE BANKS OF THE GRUMETI RIVER IN THE SERENGETI NATIONAL PARK, TANZANIA. THE CROC GOT TOO CLOSE TO A FEMALE HIPPO AND HER CALVES, AND THE ENTIRE HIPPO GROUP GATHERED IN A CIRCLE TO PROTECT THEM. INSTEAD OF BACKING OFF, THE CROC PANICKED AND TRIED TO ESCAPE ACROSS THE BACKS OF THE HIPPOS, WHO RESPONDED WITH A FRENZIED ATTACK. THE CROC'S ARMOR-PLATED BODY WAS NO MATCH FOR THE HIPPOS' HUGE TEETH, WHICH CAN APPLY SEVERAL TONS OF PRESSURE IN A SINGLE BITE. FIGHTS BETWEEN HIPPOS AND CROCS ARE RARE, AS THEY USUALLY SHOW MUTUAL RESPECT, BUT WHEN A HIPPO HAS YOUNG TO PROTECT, IT BECOMES ONE OF THE MOST AGGRESSIVE CREATURES IN THE ANIMAL KINGDOM.

℞ BEEHIVE FENCE

Farmers in Kenya stop elephants from destroying food crops by using fences of bees to frighten the animals away. The fences are constructed of beehives connected by lengths of wire, and while the elephants manage to avoid the hives, their efforts to force their way through the wire cause the hives to swing violently and the bees to attack. The angry bees swarm around the elephants' eyes and up their trunks and can even kill elephant calves because they have thinner hides than adult elephants.

℞ MANY TEETH

While humans get only two sets of natural teeth to last them their entire life, alligators get between 2,000 and 3,000 teeth during their lifetime.

℞ TALENTED TERRIERS

When dog owner Sun Chien of Shenyang, China, suffered a stroke, he built a shopping cart and trained his two terriers—Pong Pong and Wow Wow—to do his shopping. The dogs push the cart, which has holders for money and shopping lists, to the shops by themselves—and if one gets tired, he hops in and lets the other one do the pushing for a while.

SHARK CESAREAN

When a pregnant shark at an aquarium in Auckland, New Zealand, was bitten in the side by another shark, visitors watched in amazement as four baby sharks swam out through the gaping wound. Staff described the deep gouge as like the mother shark having a cesarean section. The injured shark needed stitches—but only after four more pups were found alive inside her.

℞ BABY SAVED

A dog was believed to have saved the life of an abandoned baby girl in La Plata, Argentina, in 2008 by keeping her warm with her own puppies. Farmer Fabio Anze found the naked baby girl, who was just a few hours old, among his dog China's puppies.

℞ FROG'S LEG

A giant bullfrog that had been attacked by a dog near Johannesburg, South Africa, became the first frog in the world to be fitted with a false leg. In a delicate two-hour operation, the amphibian had his shattered lower leg bone replaced with a one-inch-long (2.5-cm) steel rod.

℞ BARBECUE HORROR

A Chihuahua puppy survived after spending three days with a barbecue fork embedded in his brain. Twelve-week-old Smokey was playing at a family barbecue in London, Kentucky, in 2009 when a fork snapped in half on the grill, flew through the air and impaled itself in his head. The dog ran off into nearby woods but was found cowering in the undergrowth two days later and taken to an animal hospital where the 3-in (8-cm) prongs were removed from his brain.

℞ HOLY COW

A calf born in a remote village in Pursat Province, Cambodia, in August 2009 had thick, dark, scaly skin like a crocodile's. The day after it was born, a three-month drought ended, leading villagers to declare the calf to be holy. The animal lived for only three days, but was given a ceremonial funeral.

℞ BIONIC GOOSE

When a two-week-old gosling was found with a broken leg, veterinarians at Tiggywinkles Wildlife Hospital, Buckinghamshire, England, gave the little bird a bionic limb. She was fitted with tiny steel pins, nuts and bolts to build a leg brace that enabled her to walk again.

In May 2009, Canadian freestyle motocross rider Jeff Fehr completed a massive jump off a ramp over a cowboy ranch in Alberta, Canada, close to the Rocky Mountains. Fehr pulled the tricky "Superman Seat Grab" move at the top of his leap.

BED ROCK

A 1980s' INVENTION ALLOWS MOUNTAIN CLIMBERS WITH PARTICULARLY STRONG NERVES TO SLEEP THOUSANDS OF FEET UP VERTICAL CLIFF FACES. THE PORTALEDGE IS A SMALL PORTABLE TENT, SUSPENDED BY ONLY ROPES AND FABRIC ATTACHED TO TEMPORARY ANCHOR POINTS JAMMED IN ROCK CRACKS. THE TENTS LOOK PERILOUS BUT ARE REPORTED TO BE SURPRISINGLY STABLE; SOME CLIMBERS EVEN TAKE THE RISK OF LIGHTING GAS STOVES INSIDE TO COOK FOOD AND MELT SNOW. IT IS RECOMMENDED THAT PORTALEDGE OCCUPANTS REMAIN HARNESSED TO THE CLIFF FACE WHEN ASLEEP, IN CASE THEY HAVE A HABIT OF FALLING OUT OF BED.

℞ EVEREST MATCH

Two teams of English cricketers trekked nine days to the slopes of Mount Everest in April 2009 to a play a game of cricket at an altitude of 16,945 ft (5,165 m). The challenge was the idea of cricket enthusiast Richard Kirtley who had noticed that Everest's Gorak Shep, the highest plateau of its size in the world, resembled London's famous Oval cricket ground.

℞ PLUCKY PITCHER

Bert Shepard pitched for the Washington Senators Major League baseball team despite having lost a leg as a fighter pilot during World War II.

℞ 36-HOUR GAME

In April 2009, at Bristol, England, two soccer teams played a charity match that lasted 36 hours and produced more than 500 goals. The epic match ended with Leeds Badgers beating Bristol Academy 285 to 255.

℞ UNLUCKY BOUNCE

Chasing a deep fly ball in a game with the Cleveland Indians in 1993, Texas Rangers' baseball star José Canseco lost sight of it as he was crossing the warning track and allowed it to bounce off the top of his head and over the fence for an embarrassing home run. His aberration proved decisive as the Indians went on to win 7–6.

℞ LONG DRIVE

A golf course stretching along 848 mi (1,365 km) of desert highway opened in Australia in 2009. The Nullarbor Links spans two time zones, measures more than the entire length of Britain and has holes at 18 towns and service stations. After finishing a hole, golfers have to drive up to 62 mi (100 km) to the next tee and it takes up to four days to complete a round.

℞ SURPRISE LANDING

In February 2009, a cricket game in Himachal Pradesh, India, came to a halt when a confused pilot landed a helicopter on the field.

Don't Look Down

This picture is the right way up! In the skies over Illinois in 2009, a fearless group of 108 daredevils jumped from a plane at 18,000 ft (5,486 m), reaching speeds of 180 mph (290 km/h) as they plummeted head first toward the ground in tight formation. After 40 seconds of individual free fall, the jumpers made the risky mid-flight maneuvers required to get themselves into position, and held on tight, completing the formation only a few seconds before breaking apart for landing.

℞ DOWNHILL SKIER

Austrian Alpine skier Balthasar Egger traveled approximately 232 mi (374 km) downhill on skis in 24 hours at Heiligenblut, Austria, in March 2009.

℞ GOLF MARATHON

Tom Bucci of Latham, New York, played 1,801 holes of golf in a week at the Albany Country Club in June 2009. Despite losing 75 minutes to a thunderstorm, Bucci played 15 rounds (270 holes) every day, averaging 90 strokes per round, including 32 birdies and his first-ever hole-in-one.

℞ CALORIE BURN

A cyclist competing in the Tour de France can burn up to 10,000 calories during a mountain-stage day—that's more than four times as much as someone walking for 75 minutes a day for an entire week.

℞ BUSY DAY

On August 4, 1982, Texan-born outfielder Joel Youngblood got hits for two different Major League baseball teams in two different cities on the same day. In the afternoon he played for the New York Mets at Wrigley Field, Chicago, Illinois, against the Chicago Cubs. Then, after he had been traded, he appeared in a night game for the Montreal Expos in Philadelphia, Pennsylvania.

℞ LONG ODDS

The odds of a baseball fan being hit by a ball at a Major League game are 300,000 to 1.

℞ GOAL RUSH

During a 2008 Olympic pre-qualifying tournament, the Slovakian women's ice-hockey team defeated Bulgaria 82 goals to 0, scoring at the rate of more than one goal a minute.

℞ REAL GLOBETROTTER

Marques Haynes of the Harlem Globetrotters played basketball for more than 50 years, making his final appearance in 1997 when he was in his early seventies! He played more than 12,000 games in 97 countries, traveling more than four million miles (that's about 160 times around the world). He learned his famously fantastic dribbling skills from his sisters and could dribble the ball six times a second, his hand just a few inches above the floor.

℞ STILETTO SPRINT

At a race in Nanning, Guangxi Province, China, all the runners wear high heels—both men and women! Male runners must wear shoes with heels at least 3 in (8 cm) high, while women have to run in 4-in (10-cm) stilettos because they are more used to wearing high heels.

℞ DIAPER WRAP

Ukrainian heavyweight boxer Vitali Klitschko wraps his hands in his three-year-old son's wet diapers after a bout to keep his fists from swelling up. He says that baby urine is ideal because it is pure, doesn't contain toxins and doesn't smell.

℞ HOOP HOPPER

Thirteen-year-old Anna Schmeissing of Chicago, Illinois, can play basketball while hopping on a pogo stick.

℞ GREAT NATE

Nate Kmic of the Mount Union, Ohio, college football team is the only U.S. college football player to run more than 8,000 rushing yards, which he did during his college career between 2005 and 2008.

℞ SNOW GOLF

An Italian ski resort stages a golf tournament in up to 3 ft (90 cm) of snow and at an altitude of 5,250 ft (1600 m). Players use brightly colored orange balls on the specially built nine-hole course at the Rein resort in Taufers.

℞ HANDICAP GOLFER

Forty-five-year-old former soldier Alan Perrin, who is almost blind and has only one arm, hit a hole-in-one at his local Exminster Golf Club, near Exeter, Devon, England, in April 2009. He and his golfing partner could hardly believe it when, after several minutes of searching, they finally found the yellow ball in the hole.

℞ MALE DOMINATION

Of nearly 300 athletes who took part in the first Winter Olympics, held in Chamonix, France, in 1925, just 13 were women—and they were only allowed to compete in figure skating events.

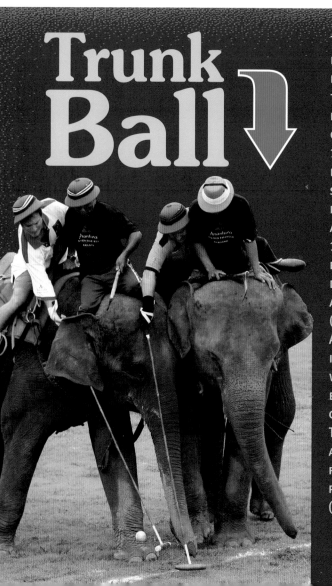

Walking in the Air

In August 2009, aged just eight years old, Tiger Brewer from London, England, stood on the top of a biplane flown by his grandfather at 100 mph (160 km/h). His wing-walking feat took place at a height of 1,000 ft (304 m) above Rendcomb airfield in Gloucestershire, England, and followed a family tradition—Tiger's grandfather, Vic Norman, manages SuperAeroBatics, the world's only formation wing-walking team.

℞ CROWD EJECTED

In June 2009, an umpire at an Iowa high school baseball game ejected the entire crowd of more than a hundred fans for being unruly. Don Briggs took the drastic action during the game between Winfield-Mount Union and West Burlington because he said the fans were yelling and arguing.

℞ YOUNG HUSTLER

Keith O'Dell Jr. of Gloversville, New York State, plays pool for up to three hours a day—even though he is just two years old.

℞ BLIND BOXER

Bashir Ramathan of Kampala, Uganda, has been blind for over a decade but has recently resumed his career as a professional boxer.

Trunk Ball ⬇

THE UNUSUAL SPORT OF ELEPHANT POLO WAS FIRST PLAYED IN INDIA IN THE EARLY 20TH CENTURY, BUT THE MODERN GAME ORIGINATED IN NEPAL IN 1983 WHERE THE GAME IS NOW A REGISTERED OLYMPIC SPORT. TOURNAMENTS, PLAYED IN THAILAND, NEPAL AND SRI LANKA, DRAW IN 12 INTERNATIONAL TEAMS EVERY YEAR FROM FIVE DIFFERENT CONTINENTS AND ARE ORGANIZED BY THE WEPA (WORLD ELEPHANT POLO ASSOCIATION). EACH MATCH INVOLVES 28 ELEPHANTS, EACH WITH TWO PLAYERS ON ITS BACK, AND MAHOUTS (DRIVERS) CONTROLLING THE ELEPHANTS. THE GAME IS PLAYED ON AN AREA THE SIZE OF A FOOTBALL FIELD AND PLAYERS WIELD POLO STICKS THAT ARE 6–9 FT (1.8–2.7 M) IN LENGTH.

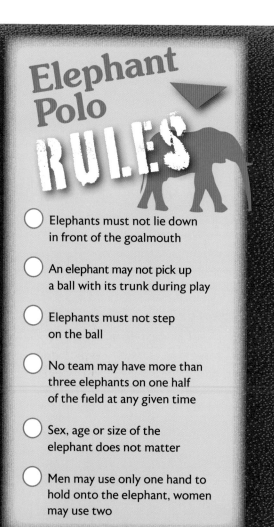

Elephant Polo RULES

- Elephants must not lie down in front of the goalmouth
- An elephant may not pick up a ball with its trunk during play
- Elephants must not step on the ball
- No team may have more than three elephants on one half of the field at any given time
- Sex, age or size of the elephant does not matter
- Men may use only one hand to hold onto the elephant, women may use two

℞ VOLCANO BOARDING

In the new sport of volcano boarding, thrill-seekers race at speeds of up to 50 mph (80 km/h) down the sides of an active volcano. Dressed in protective jumpsuits, kneepads and helmets, competitors hurtle down Nicaragua's 2,382-ft-high (726-m) Cerro Negro mountain—which has erupted 20 times since 1850, the last as recently as 1999—on specially constructed plywood boards.

℞ BASEBALL BUZZ

A 2009 baseball game between the San Diego Padres and the Houston Astros was delayed in the top of the ninth inning when a swarm of bees took over part of left field at Petco Park, San Diego, California. As the bees advanced menacingly, the players fled from the field and fans were cleared out of several sections down the left-field line.

℞ WATER JUMP

In July 2009, 13-year-old Charlotte Wharton from Northamptonshire, England, leaped a distance of nearly 100 ft (30.5 m) on water skis. Charlotte, who had been skiing for just two years, soared nearly 50 ft (15 m) high in the air at 30 mph (48 km/h) as she jumped 98 ft 8 in (30.1 m), which is the equivalent of three standard double-decker buses parked end to end.

It's All Gravy

The World Gravy Wrestling Championships took place in Lancashire, England, in 2009, to raise money for charity. A leading gravy-powder manufacturer provided 440 gallons (2,000 l) of gravy for the contest—the equivalent of 40,000 portions—for the 16 competitors to battle in. The overall winner was "Stone Cold Steve Bisto," aka Joel Hicks, a 30-year-old barrister who was watched by hundreds as he took the crown after having competed for three years in a row.

℞ VETERAN BOWLER

Emma Hendrickson from Morris Plains, New Jersey, took part in the U.S.A.'s Ten-Pin Bowling Championships in April 2009—at 100 years of age! Making her 50th appearance in the competition, the great-great-grandmother rolled 115, 97, and 106 for a 318 total.

℞ CHILL FACTOR

In one of the coldest springs in the history of Major League baseball, the start of the 2007 season found that a cold player hitting a cold baseball with a cold bat proved to be difficult. Home runs and total runs scored sank to their lowest levels since 1993.

℞ REFEREE'S NIGHTMARE

An Italian amateur soccer team drives referees to distraction—because every single player has the same surname, De Feo. What's more, the coach, secretary, doctor and all 12 sponsors of the club are also called De Feo—and the team's ground in Serino is located on Raffaele De Feo street.

℞ BEGINNER'S LUCK

In March 2009, a 62-year-old Norwegian, Unni Haskell, hit a hole-in-one with her first ever swing on a golf course. Mrs. Haskell had received just two months of lessons before taking aim on the 100-yd (91-m) hole in St. Petersburg, Florida.

Keel Walk

English sailor Alex Thomson decided that he wanted to see the sea from a different angle, so he clambered out onto the keel of his 60-ft (18-m) racing yacht when it was fully keeled over and sailing hard off the south coast of England. The experienced ocean racer, who braved the waves in a smart suit provided by his sponsor, said that it was "pretty dangerous but a real buzz."

℞ HIGH TEE
A team from Bay College, Michigan, created a wooden golf tee that was over 26½ft (8 m) tall—80 times bigger than a normal tee. The head measured 35 in (90 cm) in diameter and the whole tee weighed almost a ton.

℞ MAGIC MINK
In 2008, 73-year-old Ken Mink made the basketball team at Roane State Community College in Harriman, Tennessee—52 years after his last college game. The veteran even made two free throws as King College's B team were beaten 93–42.

℞ POLE RACE
Rune Malterud and Stian Aker of Norway skied nearly continuously for 17 days 11 hours to win the Amundsen South Pole Race, crossing Antarctica to reach the South Pole before five other teams.

℞ BALL JUGGLER
In May 2009, at San Marcos, California, Abraham Muñoz of the U.S.A. ran 3,280 ft (1,000 m) in under five minutes while keeping a soccer ball continuously airborne with his feet.

℞ BASKETBALL BEGINNER
Despite never having played basketball before, S. Ramesh Babu of Bangalore, India, scored 243 baskets in an hour—that's an average of just over four baskets a minute.

℞ SEVEN MARATHONS
Richard Donovan from Galway, Ireland, completed seven marathons on seven continents in less than six days. He began his challenge in sub-zero temperatures in Antarctica on January 31, 2009, and after running marathons in South Africa, Dubai, England, Canada and Chile, crossed the finish line in Sydney, Australia, just five days, ten hours and eight minutes later. He ran a total of 183 mi (295 km) in 130 hours, enduring extreme temperatures and sleeping only in the economy-class seats of airplanes on his flights between continents.

℞ TURKEY TRADE
In 1931, Joe Engel, owner of the Chattanooga Lookouts baseball team, traded player Johnny Jones to Charlotte in return for a 25-lb (11-kg) turkey!

℞ HAVING A BALL
Rikki Cunningham played billiards nonstop for 72 hours in Greensboro, North Carolina, in August 2009. During that time, he played 80 different opponents.

Wild Roller

Extreme inline skater Dirk Auer from Germany reached incredible speeds of more than 180 mph (290 km/h) while being dragged behind a high-powered motorbike at a racetrack in Germany. Dirk has also skated on the roof of an airborne plane and down a roller coaster.

℞ MIGHTY MUSTACHE

After winning seven gold medals at the 1972 Munich Olympic Games, U.S. swimmer Mark Spitz jokingly told a Russian swimming coach that his iconic mustache had helped him to swim faster by deflecting water away from his nose. The following year Spitz noted that every male Russian swimmer had a mustache!

℞ SHADOWBOXERS

To celebrate the first anniversary of the Beijing Olympic Games, nearly 34,000 people gathered in the Chinese capital city in August 2009 and simultaneously performed *taiji*, the martial art of shadowboxing.

℞ GREAT CATCH

Fishing on Lake Minnetonka, Minnesota, in 2008, Jeff Kolodzinski caught 1,680 fish in 24 hours.

℞ BASEBALL BASH

Mike Filippone of North Babylon, New York, swung at nearly 7,000 baseball pitches over a period of 13½ hours in August 2009.

℞ WASTED JOURNEY

The first-ever Olympic competitor from the tiny Pacific island nation of Vanuatu, boxer Eduard Paululum, traveled to Seoul, Korea, in 1988—but ate such a hearty breakfast before his weigh-in that he was disqualified for being 1 lb (453 g) overweight. He had to return home without having fought.

GERMAN 13-YEAR-OLD MAIKO KIESEWETTER SCALED A WALL OF REGULAR-SIZED PLAYING DARTS 16 FT (5 M) HIGH IN HIS HOMETOWN OF HAMBURG IN NOVEMBER 2009.

DART WALL

Splash Landing

After his incredible shallow-water plunges were featured in *Ripley's Believe It or Not! Prepare to be Shocked*, daredevil diver Darren Taylor, also known as Professor Splash, from Colorado has now dropped into just 12 in (30 cm) of water from an even greater height of 35 ft 9 in (10.9 m), emerging soaked, but unharmed. Although his "bellyflop" technique might look painful, by stretching as he falls, Professor Splash reduces the impact on his body when he hits the water.

℞ CADDIE TREK

In July 2009, Billy Foster, the caddie for English golfer Lee Westwood, walked the 88 mi (142 km) from the Scottish Open tournament at Loch Lomond to the following week's British Open at Turnberry.

℞ HOME RUN

From 1943 to 1955, the University of Kentucky basketball team had an unbroken 129 home game winning streak.

℞ CHESS MASTER

In February 2009, over a period of 14 hours, Bulgarian grandmaster Kiril Georgiev played 360 games of chess simultaneously. He won 284 games, drew 70 and lost only six.

Giant Leap for Mankind

Who was the first man in space? Believe it or not, it was not an astronaut, it was test pilot Joe Kittinger. In 1960, he was assigned to discover whether an astronaut could survive an aborted mission, even 20 mi (32 km) above the Earth. Kittinger rose to 102,800 ft (31,330 m) by balloon, and then jumped out. He was so high that initially he felt no wind resistance. He fell for 4 minutes 36 seconds, reaching a maximum speed of 614 mph (988 km/h), before opening his parachute at 18,000 ft (5,500 m).

℞ BALL JUGGLER

Dan Magness from Milton Keynes, Buckinghamshire, England, used his feet, legs and head to keep a soccer ball in the air for 24 hours in May 2009.

℞ SOLO TEAM

Bob Holmes of Rumney, New Hampshire, has played almost 17,000 volleyball games as a one-man team—and has beaten police departments, professional sports teams and a team consisting of more than 1,000 people. He has faced over 400,000 opposing players in that time, but has suffered fewer than 400 defeats.

℞ TENNIS ACE

Over a period of five years, Swiss tennis player Roger Federer reached at least the semifinals of more than 20 consecutive Grand Slam tournaments, and from 2005 to 2007 he reached ten consecutive Grand Slam finals. Between his first-round loss at Wimbledon in 2002 and his defeat in the 2008 Wimbledon final, he won 65 matches in a row on grass.

℞ COLOSSAL PUTT

Irish TV and radio presenter Terry Wogan holed an incredible 99-ft (30-m) putt at Gleneagles golf course in Scotland during a BBC pro-celebrity match in 1981.

℞ CRICKET GOD

Indian cricket fans were so grateful to the national team's captain Mahendra Singh Dhoni for restoring the country's cricketing reputation that they announced in 2008 that they wanted to build a temple devoted to him in his home town of Ranchi.

℞ BRAVE SURFER

Aged 18, Bethany Hamilton finished runner-up in the World Junior Women's Surfing Championships in January 2009—despite having lost an arm to a shark five years previously. Bethany was surfing near her home in Hawaii in October 2003 when she was mauled by a 15-ft-long (4.5-m) tiger shark, but within just three weeks she was back on her board.

℞ ONE-ARMED PLAYER

Despite being born without a right hand and forearm, Poland's Natalia Partyka competes in table tennis competitions for able-bodied athletes and even represented her country at the 2008 Beijing Olympics.

Slink or Swim

Amsterdam-based designer Diddo believes wetsuits shouldn't be limited to boring black, and a shark-attack pattern is just one of his designs—for surfers who wish to leave the water looking as if they have been attacked by sharks. His other designs include a muscle model, a whale-shark pattern and a rusted-iron look, evoking the metal diving suits of old.

MAN Vs BEAST

Spanish bull-leapers in Valencia (known as "recortadores") carry on a tradition that goes back to 1500 BC. They face a bull as it charges and, at precisely the right moment, jump over the speeding horns—toes pointed, arms aloft. Spectators watch as the competitors somersault, twirl and twist through the air, for up to four hours at a time, at every moment risking death or serious injury. The bull always remains unharmed.

Only an amazing 22 inches tall!

Born in 1992, Khagendra Thapa Magar from the Baglung District of Nepal is the smallest known man on earth, standing just 22 in (56 cm), barely the height of a toddler.

When Khagendra was born, he didn't weigh much more than a can of soda, and now that he is an adult he tips the scales at 10 lb (4.5 kg), the same weight as a domestic cat. His tiny size means that he only needs to eat around 3½ oz (100 g) of food each day, the equivalent of two chocolate bars. It is likely that Khagendra's diminutive figure is caused by a pituitary gland problem, but otherwise he is completely healthy and very keen on dancing and karate.

BODY ODDITY

R WAR WOUND

More than 60 years after being wounded by a mortar shell in World War II, John Ready of London, England, still had pieces of shrapnel working their way out of his skin.

R TOTALLY TATTOOED

Since his first tattoo of a small juggling club on his hip, Australian entertainer Lucky Diamond Rich has had 100 percent of his body tattooed. He even has tattoos on top of tattoos!

R KNUCKLE CRACK

The sound caused by a person cracking their knuckles comes from gas bubbles forming and collapsing with a snapping noise.

R POWERFUL PERFUME

Thirty-four people were hospitalized in Texas in July 2009—by strong perfume. Employees at a Bank of America call center in Fort Worth felt dizzy, nauseous and short of breath after a coworker sprayed perfume. As panic spread through the building, workers poured on to the sidewalk outside and another 110 people were treated at the scene for chest pains and headaches.

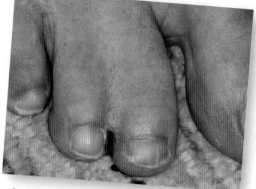

Webbed Wonder

Although normal in birds, reptiles, amphibians and some mammals, syndactyly—or webbed toes—is a rare condition in humans, occurring in about one in 2,500 births. Usually the second and third toes are joined by skin and flexible tissue. The cause in humans is unknown, but it is sometimes hereditary. Famous people with webbed toes include actors Dan Aykroyd and Ashton Kutcher and former Soviet leader Joseph Stalin.

R BABY ALLERGY

Having suffered several blisters and a burning rash after giving birth, Joanne Mackie of Birmingham, England, discovered she was allergic to her own baby. A rare skin disease, *Pemphigoid gestationis*, that developed while she was still pregnant meant that she could not even cuddle baby James or pick him up for the first month of his life because the blisters caused her such pain. To feed him from a bottle, she had to wrap damp towels around her arms.

R LUCKY GIFT

Schoolgirl Sophie Frost of Rayleigh, Essex, England, owed her life to the iPod she was wearing when struck by lightning. She survived the 30,000-volt surge only because it traveled through the gadget's wire, diverting it away from her vital organs. She had been given the iPod just four days earlier as a gift from her grandmother.

Folds of Skin

Arthur Loos, who performed at the Ripley Odditorium in Chicago in 1933, had huge folds of skin hanging down from his face. He suffered from neurofibromatosis, which causes extreme skin abnormalities.

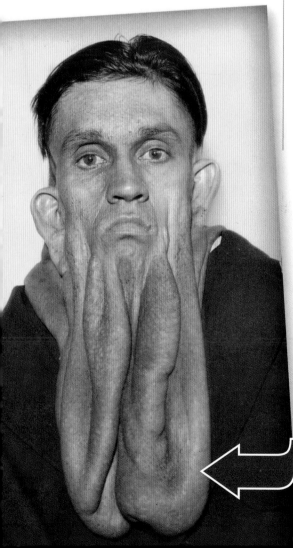

R SLEEP PLUNGE

Marius Purcariu from Arad, Romania, escaped with only minor injuries after falling from a fourth-floor window while he was asleep. He was found wrapped in a curtain on the hood of a car parked beneath his bedroom window. Doctors said that because he was sleepwalking his body was relaxed during the fall, which probably saved his life.

R SEVERED EAR

Doctors in Cologne, Germany, saved a woman's severed ear by stitching it to her buttocks. Julia Schwarz's right ear was bitten off in a fight, but the surgeons' first attempt to sew it back failed because the side of her head had not healed sufficiently. While waiting to carry out a second operation, they made a small incision in her butt and stitched the severed lobe into the pocket, keeping it there until her head had healed.

R LAUGHTER LESSONS

After a study revealed that Germans laugh on average for just six minutes a day, an organization of yoga-laughter therapists was set up in Cologne to teach Germans how to laugh. Laughter is considered healthy and the perfect antidote to aging. There are more than 6,000 laughter clubs around the world on five continents and there is even an annual World Laughter Day.

R STRETCH BRIDE

Suffering from a rare kind of dwarfism, Tiffanie DiDonato of Jacksonville, North Carolina, underwent bone-lengthening procedures so that her body could be stretched an incredible 14 in (35 cm), from 3 ft 8 in to 4 ft 10 in (1.14 m to 1.45 m), in time for her wedding day. Surgeons broke her bones and then inserted a device that slowly pulls them apart. The bone then grows and fills in the gaps so that each day her legs would be stretched another 0.04 in (1 mm). Diastrophic dysplasia (dwarfism) had caused Tiffanie to stop growing at age eight.

R HUMAN LIGHT

Our bodies emit tiny amounts of light a thousand times weaker than the human eye can perceive. The light levels are at their highest in late afternoon and at their lowest late at night, and the brightest light is emitted from the cheeks, forehead and neck. It is the result of bioluminescence, a side effect of metabolic reactions within all creatures.

SHARP FEATURES

Retired bank manager John Lynch of Hertfordshire, England, has over 240 body piercings. He has more than 150 on his head and neck alone and has had to give up flying because he kept setting off airport security scanners. He also has hundreds of tattoos, including an image of Marilyn Monroe that covers most of his torso. He did not get his first piercing until he was in his forties.

MONSTER ARMS

THE IRONICALLY NAMED TINY IRON, FROM LONDON, ENGLAND, HAS ENORMOUS BICEPS THAT MEASURE AN INCREDIBLE 24 IN (61 CM) IN CIRCUMFERENCE—THAT'S BIGGER THAN MOST PEOPLE'S THIGHS—AND CAN SMASH AN EGG WHEN FLEXED! IN THE PAST, TINY PUT HIS MASSIVE ARMS TO USE AS A BODYGUARD, BUT HE IS NOW AN ACTOR AND WRESTLER. IN ORDER TO FUEL HIS 280-LB (127-KG) FRAME, HE EATS A HEAVYWEIGHT DIET OF HIGH-PROTEIN CHICKEN BREASTS FOR BREAKFAST, LUNCH AND DINNER.

ℛ SOLITARY TREE

On vacation in Tenerife, 66-year-old grandmother Maureen Evason from Plymouth, England, was saved from a fatal fall off a 150-ft-high (45-m) volcanic ridge when her head became wedged in the only tree on the mountain. Her head was stuck for three hours between two branches, which provided a natural neck brace to immobilize her body and prevent spinal injuries.

ℛ UNIQUE BONE

The hyoid bone, just above the larynx, anchors the muscles of the tongue and is the only bone in the human body that doesn't touch any other.

ℛ VISION RESTORED

A 70-year-old man who had been "as blind as a bat" for his entire life suddenly acquired perfect vision after suffering a massive stroke. Retired architect Malcolm Darby from Leicestershire, England, had worn thick glasses since the age of two, but when he came to after surgery to clear the blood clot that had caused his stroke, he found that for the first time in his life he could see clearly without them.

ℛ METEORITE HIT

In June 2009, 14-year-old Gerrit Blank survived after being hit by a meteorite that crashed to Earth in Essen, Germany, at 30,000 mph (48,000 km/h). The red-hot piece of rock about the size of a pea appeared as a ball of light before bouncing off his hand and causing a 1-ft-wide (30-cm) crater in the ground. The 100 million-to-one strike knocked him off his feet and left him with a 3-in (7.6-cm) scar on his hand. The noise that followed the flash of light was so loud that his ears were ringing for hours afterward.

ℛ HORSE LEGS

Seattle, Washington State, designer Kim Graham has devised the ultimate accessory for people who want to look taller and more elegant—horse leg extensions. Her Digitigrade Leg Extensions, which are shaped like a horse's leg, are made of steel, cable, foam and rigid plastic and add 14 in (35 cm) of height to the wearer. She says it takes only 15 minutes to learn to walk in them, although the wearer should avoid stairs. The standard legs cost $750—with another $200 for spring-loaded hooves to put an extra bounce in your step.

ℛ THREE GENERATIONS

In August 2009, three generations of the same family were born within 30 minutes of each other in the same hospital in Dublin, Ireland. Family matriarch Eileen McGuinness, 85, was blessed with her 69th grandchild, her 58th great-grandchild and her first great-great-grandchild in startlingly quick succession. Amazingly, none of the three expectant mothers knew the others were in the hospital at the time they were each preparing to give birth.

ℛ BAT BOY

A blind English boy has learned to "see" the world around him for the first time by using echolocation—the technique used by bats and dolphins. By clicking his tongue on the roof of his mouth, Lucas Murray from Dorset, England, can discover where and how big objects are depending on the echoes that bounce back. He uses the method to play basketball, determining which direction the hoop is in and how far away it is before making his shot.

Swollen Nose

Liu Ge has a nose that is nearly 4 in (10 cm) long and 3 in (7.5 cm) wide—an unwelcome side effect of his job as an official brandy taster in Beijing, China. Liu has been drinking up to half a gallon (2 l) of brandy a day for 52 years and it has left him with a condition called rhinophyma, caused by the constant expansion of blood vessels in his nose.

℞ SHARK ATTACK

After a Great White shark bit a chunk out of 13-year-old Hannah Mighall's surfboard and dragged her under the water, the teenager's life was saved by her cousin and fellow surfer, Syb Munday, who swam out to her and began punching the shark on the head. The 16-ft-long (4.9-m) predator, which had attacked off Binalong Bay in Tasmania, Australia, let Hannah go and she survived with bites to her legs that required 200 stitches.

℞ THOUGHT PROCESS

Paralyzed neuroscientist Scott Mackler relies on a computer system that translates thoughts into text, to enable him to continue his work at the University of Pennsylvania. He wears a special cap that picks up the electrical activity of his brain and allows him to select letters just by thinking about them. The computer then turns his sentences into speech.

℞ SWALLOWED PIN

Doctors in China discovered the cause of an eight-year-old boy's constant coughs and colds—a rusty drawing pin stuck in his right lung. Xiao Ming of Mingguang, Anhui Province, had been suffering from the mystery ailments for a year.

℞ STAYIN' ALIVE

A Massachusetts woman revived her husband from cardiac arrest by administering CPR to the funky beat of the Bee Gees' disco classic "Stayin' Alive." After he collapsed during a walk, she remembered a public service announcement by the American Heart Association. It advised people untrained in CPR to help heart attack victims by compressing their chests 100 times a minute and to use "Stayin' Alive," which has 103 beats a minute, as a handy guideline.

℞ MEMORY MAN

Bob Petrella, a television producer in his fifties from Los Angeles, California, can remember almost everything he has done in life since the age of five. He can recall precise details of virtually all his birthdays, along with every New Year's Eve for the last 40 years and all the conversations he has had on most days throughout the last 53 years. He has been diagnosed with the condition hyperthymestia (overdeveloped memory), which has been discovered in just four people around the world.

℞ MIGHTY ATOM

In 2009, at three years of age, Liam Hoekstra from Grand Rapids, Michigan, could shift furniture, lift 5-lb (2.3-kg) weights, do sit-ups and perform incredible gymnastic feats of strength. Although he is smaller than most children his age, he has a rare condition that causes his body to have very little fat and 40 percent more muscle mass. As he has a fast metabolism, he eats up to six meals a day.

℞ PICKLED LEG

Song Weiguo of Jiangyan, China, has preserved his amputated leg in formaldehyde for more than 20 years to warn others of the perils of drunk driving. Having drunk a pint of strong liquor, he lost his left leg in a motorcycle crash in 1989 and now puts the severed limb on display every year on the anniversary of the accident.

Spooky Eyes

Hollywood special-effects artist Kevin Carter creates colored contact lenses, which can make the wearer look as if he or she has been possessed by demons or is an alien visitor from another planet. He spends up to two days hand-painting dye onto each lens with a fine brush, and his scary designs —which also include a shark's open jaws—can sell for up to $750 a pair.

Tiny Teen

Sixteen-year-old Jyoti Amge from Nagpur, India, is one of the smallest teenagers in the world, standing only 23.5 in (60 cm) tall and weighing a little over 11 lb (5 kg). Despite weighing only 9 lb (4 kg) more than she did when she was born, Jyoti says she is no different from other people. She is proud to be smaller, and enjoys all the extra attention she receives. Jyoti travels to the local school on her brother's motorbike along with her sisters. In the classroom she has a custom-made desk next to the other pupils. She has a large collection of dresses like any teenager, and dreams of becoming an actress— she has already starred in a video with Indian pop star Mika Singh.

RIPLEY'S RESEARCH

Jyoti has achondroplasia, a genetic condition and common form of dwarfism that results in shorter bones than normal. An academic study has determined that people with achondroplasia were respected in ancient Egyptian society and often held positions of status and wealth. The tomb of Tutankhamen included a funeral gift depicting a small female person, and the Egyptians worshiped gods that resembled little people.

ACTUAL SIZE!

PREMATURE AGING

Werner Syndrome, a rare genetic disease, causes premature aging—wrinkled skin, baldness, cataracts and muscular atrophy—by the time a person reaches their early thirties.

MADE HIS POINT

To protest a judge's decision that he must sell part of his farm to settle a debt, Orico Silva of Figueira da Foz, Portugal, chopped off his own finger with a butcher's knife on the court desk.

TRAPPED UNDERGROUND

After the Xinqiao coal mine, in southwestern China's Guizhou Province, was flooded in June 2009, three miners survived for 25 days while they were trapped underground by licking water off the walls.

TODDLER CAUGHT

A group of fairgoers in Port Orange, Florida, caught and saved a toddler who was dropped nearly 40 ft (12 m) from a carnival ride in 2008 as her mother dangled helplessly above the crowd. The mother had become trapped when the ride started up unexpectedly just as she and her little girl were getting off it.

SHIPWRECKED FISHERMEN

After their boat sank in heavy seas off the north coast of Australia in December 2008, two Burmese fishermen survived for almost a month drifting on an ice box in shark-infested waters.

NASTY SHOCK

A Chinese boy survived a 10,000-volt shock in March 2009. He Haoyang had been playing with wires in a field in Sichuan Province when they suddenly broke. He escaped with just burns to his hands because he managed to run a few steps away from the accident site, where the grass was left completely burned.

RAIL BIRTH

A baby girl was born in September 2009 on a high-speed train linking Paris, France, and Brussels, Belgium. The baby was delivered by two doctors and two nurses who were on board and answered a call for assistance while the train was traveling at around 185 mph (300 km/h).

ONE VOICE

British researchers have found a 60-year-old woman who can identify only one voice—that of Scottish actor Sir Sean Connery. She suffers from the rare condition phonagnosia, which leaves her unable to identify anyone speaking on the phone or the radio. She doesn't even recognize her own daughter's voice and resorts to a system of codewords to identify friends and relatives who call.

Bare Face

Swiss artist "Dave" created this portrait of President Obama from multiple painted bodies in unison during a performance in Athens, Greece, in 2009. The use of choreography and paint in this way has been described as a new form of art called "fusionism."

BRAIN REWIRED

Even though she has only half a brain, a ten-year-old German girl has near-perfect vision in one eye. Experts were baffled as to how the girl, who was born missing the right side of her brain (which maps the left field of vision) could have excellent left- and right-field vision in one eye, enabling her to see objects on either side. Scans revealed that her brain had rewired itself before she was born. Retinal nerve fibers carrying visual information from the back of the eye that should have gone to the right hemisphere of the brain diverted to the left instead.

TWINS PEAK

The Indian village of Kodinhi, Kerala, has more than 250 sets of twins born to just 2,000 families—six times the global average.

BLACKOUT RAID

Mark Lester from Norwich, England, was spared jail for robbing a supermarket at gunpoint after a court heard that he suffers from a rare medical condition that makes him have blackouts and causes him to forget his actions. After the robbery he told his mother that he had suffered a nightmare about holding up a store with a gun, but when she recognized him from a TV report, she realized it was more than a bad dream.

MAIL BOY

Four-year-old Jakob Strauss got trapped inside a mailbox in Feldkirch, Austria. He wriggled in after mailmen had left the door open, and managed to close the hatch behind him. After passersby heard his cries for help, firefighters used bolt cutters to free him.

GOLFER BOY

After being struck by lightning while playing golf with friends in Cape Cod, Massachusetts, Michael Utley staggered around with smoke pouring out of his mouth, nose and ears. His internal tissues were actually boiling and although his heart stopped, he eventually made an almost full recovery.

MEMORABLE BIRTHDAYS

Thirteen months after giving birth to baby Campbell on August 8, 2008 (08/08/08), Alison Miller of Fayetteville, Arkansas, had a second daughter, Molly Reid, on September 9, 2009 (09/09/09).

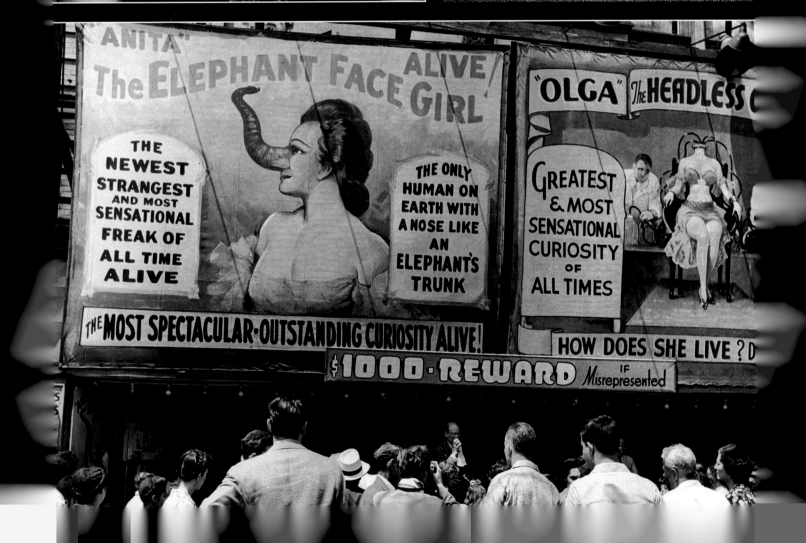

The Elephant Face Girl

ANITA, BILLED AS "THE ONLY HUMAN ON EARTH WITH A NOSE LIKE AN ELEPHANT'S TRUNK," PERFORMED AT THE CONEY ISLAND SIDESHOW IN NEW YORK, IN 1944. DURING THIS TIME, CONEY ISLAND WAS RENOWNED AS THE WORLD CENTER OF THE AMUSEMENT PARK INDUSTRY.

"ANITA" The ELEPHANT FACE GIRL ALIVE!

THE NEWEST STRANGEST AND MOST SENSATIONAL FREAK OF ALL TIME ALIVE

THE ONLY HUMAN ON EARTH WITH A NOSE LIKE AN ELEPHANT'S TRUNK

THE MOST SPECTACULAR·OUTSTANDING CURIOSITY ALIVE!

$1000·REWARD IF Misrepresented

"OLGA" The HEADLESS

GREATEST & MOST SENSATIONAL CURIOSITY OF ALL TIMES

HOW DOES SHE LIVE ?D

Twisted ART

Contortionists defy physical boundaries by twisting their bodies into seemingly impossible, backbreaking positions. Fully grown adults can squeeze their entire body through an unstrung tennis racket that is 10 in (25 cm) in diameter or a toilet seat, or into a glass bottle that is just 2 ft (0.6 m) high. Or they tie their body into intricate knots with their legs wrapped around the back of their neck and touching each other.

The art of contortionism is depicted in ancient Roman, Egyptian and Greek sculptures and has been featured in the Buddhist Tsam dance for centuries. In Mongolia, there are many contortionist schools where children are trained in the art of contortion from as young as five years old. Contortionism is also part of the Hindu discipline of yoga.

In early 20th-century U.S.A., contortionists were popular circus acts. One of the most famous was "Dad" Whitlark, who could still tie his body into pretzel knots and put his face between his ankles at the age of 76. He could also bend over backward and pick up handkerchiefs off the floor with his teeth.

Ethiopian contortionist Kiros Hadgu—alias "The Twisted Kiros"—can dislocate both his arms and his legs and even turn his torso through 180 degrees.

Contortionists are either backbenders or frontbenders, depending on which way their spine is most flexible. A few performers, such as Daniel Browning Smith ("The Rubberboy"), bend both ways (left). He can bend so far backward that the top of his head can touch the seat of his pants and so far forward that he can kiss his own butt!

Frontbending: Frontbenders, like this woman in 1957, twist their bodies into human knots. In this position they can squeeze through small hoops or tight barrels.

DO KNOT TRY THIS AT HOME

Backbending: As demonstrated by this Mongolian contortionist, backbenders can perform while standing, lying on the floor or in a headstand position.

Ripley's Revealed

Balancing Act: Can you work out whose arms and legs belong to whom? A tower of contortionists demonstrate their skills at a show in China.

RIPLEY'S RESEARCH

CONTORTIONISTS ARE OFTEN NATURALLY HIGHLY FLEXIBLE PEOPLE, AND THEY BUILD ON THIS WITH MANY YEARS OF TRAINING. HOWEVER, THE ABILITIES OF MANY CONTORTIONISTS ARE BELIEVED TO BE HEREDITARY. CONTORTIONISTS' VERTEBRAE TEND TO BE SPREAD FURTHER APART THAN A NORMAL SPINE, GIVING THEM EXCEPTIONALLY LONG AND FLEXIBLE LIGAMENTS, WHILE THE COLLAGEN THAT MAKES UP THE LIGAMENTS IS ALSO EXTREMELY SUPPLE. THESE ELEMENTS OF THE SPINE ARE MORE COMMON IN WOMEN, AS FEMALE HORMONES ARE THOUGHT TO HAVE A SOFTENING EFFECT ON COLLAGEN FIBERS. SOME CONTORTIONISTS ARE BORN WITH EHLERS-DANLOS SYNDROME, A CONDITION THAT CAUSES ABNORMAL COLLAGEN PRODUCTION AND CAN THEREFORE INCREASE LIGAMENT ELASTICITY.

Marinelli Bend: Mongolian-born contortionist Iona Luvsandorj can support her entire body weight on her mouth in a backbreaking maneuver. She managed to hold the inverted backbend pose, called the Marinelli bend, for 33 seconds in May 2009, her mouth bearing the weight of her body by biting onto a short post.

Split Apart: Ruby Ring, a U.S. contortionist of the 1940s, called herself "The Mother of the Oversplit"—a split of more than 180 degrees. She stood with her legs on two chairs and then, with nothing to hold on to, slid the chairs apart into an eye-watering oversplit.

Enterology: Enterologists squeeze themselves into tiny boxes or containers, as demonstrated by this contortionist in 1925.

Man in a Bottle: Argentinian contortionist Hugo Zamoratte specialized in squeezing himself into bottles—but he nearly died while practicing his act in a Santiago, Chile, hotel room in 1982. He became stuck in the bottle, the door of which had accidentally locked, and after 40 minutes in a very uncomfortable position he was starting to hallucinate. He was saved by the timely arrival of a bewildered cleaner, who opened the door of the bottle and freed the exhausted contortionist.

Geoff has a coat of arms tattooed on his right foot.

Close-up of bird-of-paradise flowers on Geoff's right thigh.

Sunflowers are depicted in intricate detail on his left thigh.

This elaborate red flower is tattooed on the back of one of Geoff's knees.

Still Live

Retired history teacher Geoff Ostling from Sydney, Australia, is literally a walking work of art. More than 20 years ago, Geoff began working with well-known tattoo artist eX de Merci, choosing the theme of Australian flowers, and they now cover his skin from neck to toe, depicting every flower he could think of. When Geoff dies, he wants to be skinned and the tattoos displayed whole, just as they are on his body, at Australia's National Gallery in Canberra. He has already lined up the help of a taxidermist for when that day comes.

ℛ SINKHOLE HELL

Jeanne Schnepp, 63, spent nearly a week stuck on a raft in a sinkhole on the Wapsipinicon River in Iowa. She had been fishing from the rubber raft when the strong river current swept her downstream and deposited her in the sinkhole, trapping her between a 12-ft (3.6-m) wall of rocks and a logjam she couldn't climb over. After enduring two thunderstorms, hot days and cold nights, she was finally spotted by an angler.

ℛ TATTOO NERD

Computer nerds have been getting their bodies tattooed with images relating to their laptops. Among popular tattoo requests are a USB cable, the Apple logo and various items of software.

ℛ SHRAPNEL DISLODGED

A piece of shrapnel that had been lodged in the jaw of Alf Mann from Birmingham, England, for 65 years suddenly dropped out in 2009. Alf had struggled to speak and eat properly since being injured by an explosion during World War II—but one morning he woke to find blood on his pillow, along with the ¹/₂-in (1.2-cm) piece of shrapnel.

ℛ JEEP ADVENTURE

A three-year-old boy was rescued in July 2009 after riding his toy jeep into the Peace River, British Columbia, Canada, and floating nearly 8 mi (13 km) downstream. He was found still sitting happily in his battery-powered jeep in water that was 15 ft (4.5 m) deep.

ℛ MAGIC TOOTH

After being blind for 12 years following an accident at work, Martin Jones from Yorkshire, England, had his sight restored in 2009 by having a tooth transplanted into his eye. One of his canine teeth was removed and converted into a holder for a special optical lens by drilling a hole in it. Then the tooth was inserted into his cheek for three months to enable it to grow new tissue and blood vessels before, complete with the fitted lens, being inserted into his right eyeball. Two weeks later, his sight returned and for the first time he was able to see his wife Gill, whom he had married in 2005.

ℛ BROKE FALL

A six-year-old boy survived a 70-ft (21-m) fall from an apartment balcony in Gothenburg, Sweden, in September 2009 when a passerby, who had stopped when he saw the boy fall, managed to catch him.

ℛ TWO WOMBS

Sarah Reinfelder of Sault Ste. Marie, Michigan, who has two wombs, gave birth to twin daughters in February 2009—one from each uterus.

ℛ BODY STRENGTH

At age 83, Sidney Williams of Port Elizabeth, South Africa, can lift up to 353 lb (160 kg) even though he himself weighs only 220 lb (100 kg)—that means he can lift 50 percent more than his body weight.

Needlework

Anatomical technician and embalmer W. K. Foster from Winnipeg, Canada, collected more than 30 tattoos that he removed from dead bodies at the medical college where he worked in the 1920s. Robert Ripley dubbed it the "World's Strangest Art Collection" and displayed a selection at the first Ripley Odditorium in Chicago in 1933. The display is now at the Ripley's museum in St. Augustine, Florida.

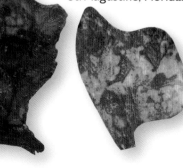

Big Deal

A GERMAN ART COLLECTOR PAID $215,000 TO BUY THIS VIBRANT TATTOO OF THE VIRGIN MARY — EVEN THOUGH IT WAS TATTOOED ON SOMEBODY ELSE'S BACK. THE WORK, BY BELGIAN ARTIST WIM DELVOYE, IS ON THE BACK OF TIM STEINER FROM SWITZERLAND, WHO IS NOW AN EXHIBIT HIMSELF. STEINER HAS TO SHOW THE PIECE THREE TIMES A YEAR, AND IS ALSO BOUND BY AN AGREEMENT THAT MEANS THE TATTOOED SKIN WILL BE RETURNED TO ITS NEW OWNER AFTER HIS DEATH.

IT'S NOT THE FIRST TIME PRIZED TATTOOS BY WIM DELVOYE HAVE BEEN FOR SALE. A FRENCH MAN TRIED TO GIVE A PARIS MUSEUM HIS TATTOO IN HIS WILL, AND A BRITISH MAN ATTEMPTED TO SELL HIS OWN PIECE OF SKIN ART IN AN AUCTION — BOTH HAVE FAILED TO FIND A BUYER SO FAR.

R HOPPING MAD

An 18th-century maidservant from Godalming, England, became a national sensation when she convinced doctors she had given birth to more than 16 rabbits. In 1726, 25-year-old Mary Toft went into apparent labor overseen by John Howard, a male midwife, who recorded that Mary began producing parts of animals, including nine baby rabbits, in one day! Doctors were fascinated by the births, and explained them as "Maternal Impressions," maintaining that her fantasies about rabbits during her pregnancy had created these defects on the human fetus. Mary later admitted staging the births when it was discovered that a porter had smuggled a rabbit into Mary's chamber. The medical profession of the time suffered a great deal of ridicule as a result.

R 16 TOES

A baby was born with 16 toes—eight on each foot—in Leizhou, Guangdong, China, in November 2008.

R PSALM SAVIOR

An Argentinian pastor survived after a book of psalms he was holding deflected a bullet fired at him at close range. Mauricio Zanes Condori was trying to talk two thieves out of robbing his church in Rodeo del Medio in May 2009 when one of the men fired at his chest from a distance of 7 ft (2 m), but the holy book slowed down the bullet and changed its trajectory.

R RARE TWINS

In a one in a million chance, an American mother gave birth to twins who have different fathers. Mia Washington from Dallas, Texas, gave birth to Justin and Jordan within seven minutes of each other, but in a remarkable twist of fate, they turned out to be half-brothers. Miss Washington admitted having an affair and conceived two babies by different men at the same time.

All Fingers and Toes

The chances of having six healthy fingers on both hands, or six healthy toes on both feet, are very slim, but K.V. Subramaniyan from Kerala Province, India, has both! K.V., an acupuncture doctor who was once punished at school for saying that humans have 12 toes and 12 fingers, has a genetic condition known as polydactyly. Usually this means that someone has an extra finger or toe that is just a piece of tissue, occasionally containing bones without joints, but K.V. has fully functioning extra digits on both of his hands and feet, which is extremely rare.

R MID-AIR DEATH

A novice skydiver landed safely in 2009—even though the instructor to whom he was strapped had died of a heart attack in midair. When they jumped out of a plane above Chester, South Carolina, soldier Daniel Pharr was making his first-ever jump, while 49-year-old instructor George Steele was a veteran of more than 8,000 jumps. However, thousands of feet above the ground as they were finishing their free fall and just moments after their parachute had opened, Steele died. Pharr came down about a third of a mile from the intended drop point despite being able to reach only one of the parachute's steering toggles behind the dead man, forcing him to descend in circles.

R SECRET BABY

Doctors in Qingshen, China, discovered that a 92-year-old woman had been carrying an unborn child in her body for more than 60 years. Huang Yijun, of Huangjiaotan, said her baby had died in her womb in 1948, but she could not afford the money to have the dead fetus removed. Her long-standing secret was finally revealed in 2009 after she hurt her stomach and underwent a hospital scan. Doctors were amazed because normally a dead fetus would decay and cause infection, but Huang had stayed healthy all that time.

R TWIN TOWN

Ten percent of children born in Cãndido Godói, Brazil, are twins—and half of them are genetically identical. Twins usually occur in about 1.25 percent of pregnancies.

R SAVED BY DIAPER

Eighteen-month-old Caua Felipe Massaneiro survived a plunge from a third-floor apartment window in Recife, Brazil, in 2008 when his diaper snagged on a security spike, slowing his fall.

Miracle Mother

On the mountains of Rio Talea in southern Mexico, in March 2000, pregnant Inés Ramirez Perez was forced to cut open her own womb to have her baby after suffering for 12 hours with extreme labor pain. With the nearest clinic over 50 mi (80 km) away and no phone to call her husband at the next town, she was completely alone during the procedure. She gulped down rubbing alcohol to numb the pain and then began to cut using a 6-in (15-cm) slaughter knife. She managed to cut away the skin, fat and muscle before pulling out her baby boy, Orlando Ruiz Ramirez. Inés thinks she operated for about an hour before retrieving her baby and passing out. Her six-year-old son, Benito, returned with help several hours later. Inés is believed to be the only woman to have ever performed a cesarian section on herself.

℞ TWO WOMBS

Seeking a hospital diagnosis for a pain in her abdomen, two months' pregnant Lindsay Hasaj of London, England, learned that she had two wombs—a one in a million chance.

℞ GRIZZLY ATTACK

In May 2008, Brent Case of Saanich, British Columbia, Canada, managed to drive more than 15 mi (24 km) to find help after a grizzly bear mauled him so badly that he lost part of his scalp. During the attack, he thought that the bear was literally eating his brains.

℞ SOB STORY

For nearly 20 years, Patricia Webster of Kent, England, suffered from crocodile tears syndrome, a rare medical condition that made her cry uncontrollably whenever she ate food. As a side effect of the condition, nerve fibers that should be used for salivation become damaged and regrow into the lacrimal gland, located under the eye, which controls the flow of tears. So when Patricia chewed and swallowed food, she could not keep herself from crying—until her condition was cured using Botox injections.

℞ KEPT ALIVE

At Oxford, England, in January 2009, a baby girl was kept alive in the womb of her dead mother for two days until she could be born safely. Jayne Soliman collapsed from a brain hemorrhage and although she was declared brain dead, doctors kept her heart beating for 48 hours until they had safely delivered baby Aya prematurely at 25 weeks by cesarean section.

SEEING BLUE

In 2007, Pauly Unstoppable from Canada couldn't resist the chance to have the first ever cosmetic eyeball tattoo. The procedure involved injecting ink into the top layer of his eye with a syringe 40 times, which had the effect of turning the white of Pauly's eye blue. Corneal tattooing is a surgical procedure for patients who have suffered severe eye trauma, but doctors do not recommend having it done for cosmetic reasons.

Arm Lock

Justin Shaw, a professional drummer from Kentucky, takes pride in his exceptionally long arm hair. The longest hair measures a lengthy 5¾ in (14.6 cm), long enough to stretch around a large grapefruit. Justin has always liked the long blond arm tufts, and has never wanted to cut them short. However, since he moved to Miami, Florida, he has recorded a faster growth in his arm hairs—something he puts down to "getting a lot of vitamin D" in the sunshine—yet he still has no desire to cut them.

NEVER WASHES

A man in India who fathered seven daughters has not washed for more than 35 years in an attempt to guarantee that his next child is a boy. Instead of bathing traditionally and brushing his teeth, 63-year-old Kailash Singh, from a village near Varanasi, has a "fire bath" every evening when he stands on one leg beside a bonfire and says prayers. Apparently a seer had once told him that if he did not take a normal bath, he would be blessed with a male child.

KIDNEY STONE

In January 2009, doctors removed a kidney stone that was the size of a coconut from the body of Sandor Sarkadi in Debrecen, Hungary.

SNOWDRIFT

Fifty-five-year-old Donna Molnar of Ancaster, Ontario, Canada, collapsed in a snowdrift in December 2008 and survived three days of sub-zero temperatures and blowing winds until she was rescued. She was eventually found buried in 2 ft (60 cm) of snow, with all but her face and neck covered.

SPAT BULLET

After Richard Jamison of Bridgeton, New Jersey, was shot in the face in February 2009, he spat the bullet out of his mouth, then went looking for help.

CHOPSTICK OP

A Chinese kung-fu master, who accidentally swallowed a chopstick during a training stunt, forgot that it was lodged in his stomach for 20 years until it suddenly started to cause him pain. Forty-year-old Wing Ma finally had the 7-in-long (18-cm) chopstick removed in 2009 during an operation in eastern Wuhan.

FOOD FOR THOUGHT

Researchers in Quebec, Canada, have discovered that thinking too hard can make people fat. Blood tests on student volunteers showed that those who had recently taken an exam ate more because the brain workout sent their glucose and insulin levels haywire, making them hungrier.

FACIAL TUMOR

Fifteen-year-old Lai Thi Dao of Vietnam underwent a 12-hour surgery in April 2008 to remove a tumor that accounted for one-third of her body weight. It started out as little more than a cyst on her tongue when she was three, but grew to weigh over 12 lb (5.4 kg) and consumed the lower half of her face.

EXTRA DIGITS

Kamani Hubbard was born in San Francisco, California, in January 2009 with 24 fingers and toes. The 24 were made up of six digits on each of his hands and feet, and were perfectly formed and fully functioning.

HAND SEVERED

Mr. Shi of Shenzen, China, lost his hand in 2009 when it was pulled off at the wrist during a beach tug-of-war contest. Doctors successfully reattached the severed hand in a five-hour operation.

SELFLESS SURGEON

Italian surgeon Claudio Vitale finished a brain operation on a patient in March 2009 despite suffering a heart attack partway through the procedure. Dr. Vitale realized his patient would never recover if he halted the operation to seek treatment for himself, so he continued for another 30 minutes in the operating theatre at Cardarelli Hospital, Naples, until the patient was out of danger.

ARM RECOVERED

After 11-year-old Devin Funck from Slidell, Louisiana, had his arm bitten off by a huge alligator in a lake near New Orleans in 2008, wildlife officials shot the reptile and recovered the arm largely intact from its stomach.

℞ IMPROVISED DRILL

Rob Carson, a doctor in Maryborough, Victoria, Australia, used a handyman's power drill to bore into a boy's skull and relieve potentially fatal bleeding on his brain. Nicholas Rossi had seriously injured his head falling off his bicycle, but the small hospital did not have neurological drills, so Dr. Carson sent for a household drill from the maintenance room and called a neurosurgeon in Melbourne to talk him through the complex procedure, which he had never previously attempted.

Patient Pinky

Sheng Wang, from Fujian, southern China, left one of his pinky fingernails to grow for 15 years, until it measured an amazing 18 in (46 cm) in length. In 1996, Wang decided to grow the nail for as long as he could to become a more peaceful person and test his patience. He has loved the change so much that he even turned down an offer of nearly $10,000 to remove the nail.

℞ SPECIAL BRANCH

John Nash, a rookie police officer from Rochdale, England, fell while pursuing a suspect, but didn't realize he had impaled his eye socket on the branch of a bush until after he caught and arrested the perpetrator. The 6-in (15-cm) piece of wood snapped off, but it had pierced his eyelid, smashed a cheekbone, forced itself under his eyeball and had come to rest against his brain.

℞ HUMAN TREE

Surgeons operating on a man in Russia in 2009 discovered a tree growing inside his lungs. They think that 28-year-old Artyom Sidorkin had somehow inhaled a seed, which subsequently sprouted inside his lung. The 2-in-long (5-cm) spruce was touching his capillaries and causing him extreme chest pain.

℞ STRONG GIRL

Jacqueline Wickens from Elko, Nevada, deadlifted 308 lb (140 kg) in Anaheim, California, in December 2007—even though she was only 13 years old.

℞ HYPNOTIC DENTIST

In May 2008, Leslie Mason from Essex, England, underwent two hours of root canal work without anesthetic after being hypnotized by his friend John Ridlington. Despite having two upper right molars removed along with their roots, plus two roots from teeth that had been pulled in the 1980s, the patient reported feeling nothing more than "a little sting."

℞ EXTENDED LEAVE

Left unable to walk or talk by a road accident that nearly killed him, computer worker Karl McLennan of Aberdeen, Scotland, returned to his job in 2009 after 12 years of sick leave.

℞ TOO PASSIONATE

In December 2008, a man in Zhuhai, Guangdong, China, kissed his girlfriend so passionately that it popped her eardrum and she went deaf in that ear.

℞ HAIR DETERRENT

Farmers in Malaysia have been gathering sacks of human hair from barber shops to prevent wild boar from destroying their young oil palms. They spread the hair around the crops, and when a boar sniffs the hair, it thinks humans are present and runs off.

Supple Skin

The "girl with the elastic skin" pictured here was famous for the stretchy skin on her cheeks and neck. Etta Lake, who traveled with the King-Franklin Circus in 1889, could pull the skin an amazing 6 in (15 cm) from her cheek.

℞ BIG BABY

In September 2009, an Indonesian woman gave birth to a baby boy weighing a whopping 19.2 lb (8.7 kg). The baby, who is 24.4 in (62 cm) long, was born by cesarean section at a hospital in North Sumatra province.

℞ LUCKY STRIKE

When Nada Acimovich of Sljivovica, Serbia, was struck by lightning, she was saved by her rubber-soled shoes—and the electric jolt cured her deadly heart condition. Her condition, known as arrhythmia, is normally treated with mild electric shocks to reset the heart's rhythm.

℞ LONG STRAND

Brian Peterkin-Vertanesian of Washington, D.C., boasts a single red eyebrow hair that measures an incredible 6 3/8 in (16.2 cm) long. The hair, which he has named Wally, is long enough for him to chew on, although he usually keeps it tucked behind his left ear for safety.

IF YOU WOULD LIKE TO FIND OUT MORE ABOUT THESE ODD WAX CREATIONS, CHECK OUT PAGES 8–9.

Gallery

SARA DISK WEARER OF AFRICA
The Ubangi women of the Sara tribe in Chad, Africa, wear wooden plates in their lips to make them unattractive to raiders.

CROCODILE MAN
Bobby Blackburn from South Africa wears crocodile-teeth dentures, sharp enough to cut through the thickest of meats.

SHOWCASING SOME OF THE MOST BIZARRE AND WEIRD FOLK THAT ROBERT RIPLEY FOUND ON HIS TRAVELS, A VAST MODERN COLLECTION OF WAX HEADS ARE CENTRAL TO THE WORLD OF RIPLEY'S. LOCATED IN RIPLEY MUSEUMS ALL OVER THE WORLD, THE HEADS ARE MADE BY A DEDICATED TEAM OF SCULPTORS, MAKEUP EXPERTS, COSTUME DESIGNERS AND HAIR SPECIALISTS. THE TEAM SPENDS ITS DAYS SURROUNDED BY EXTRAORDINARY ODDITIES IN THE RIPLEY'S ART DEPARTMENT IN FLORIDA. THEY MAKE THE EERILY LIFELIKE HEADS BY PAINSTAKINGLY STICKING EACH STRAND OF HAIR TO THE SCULPTURES AND PAINTING EACH INDIVIDUAL WRINKLE, BELIEVE IT OR NOT!

HUMAN UNICORN
A man named Weng, found by Ripley in Manchuria, China, in 1931, had a 13-in (33-cm) horn growing out of the back of his head.

MAN WITH THE GOLDEN NOSE
Sixteenth-century Danish atronomer Tycho Brahe lost his nose in a sword fight and replaced it with a solid gold replica.

WOLF MAN
Based on the 1931 Lon Chaney movie The Wolf Man, Larry Talbot is bitten by a wolf and gradually and horrifyingly becomes one.

JO-JO THE DOG-FACED MAN
Born in Russia, Fedor Jeftichew suffered from hypertriclosis, or "Werewolf syndrome," and his body was covered with hair up to 8 in (20 cm) long. He became known as Jo-Jo the Dog-faced Man when he became a famous sideshow performer.

EYE-POPPER
Avelino Perez Matos from Baracoa, Cuba, could dislocate his eyes from their sockets whenever he wanted.

LONGEST NOSE IN HISTORY
Thomas Wedders, an 18th-century sideshow entertainer from England, had a nose that measured an incredible 7½ in (19 cm) long.

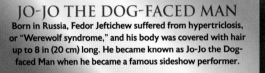

RIPLEY'S HEROES

LIGHTHOUSE MAN
Using a 7-in (18-cm) lighted candle inserted in his head, the Lighthouse Man would act as a human lantern in the unlit alleys of Chunking, China, in the 1930s. He had cut a hole through the bone in his scalp so the candle could be held in place with sealing wax.

GRACE McDANIELS
Billed as the "mule faced woman" during her successful sideshow career, when Grace revealed her face at sideshows, men and women would sometimes faint.

PADAUNG WOMAN OF MYANMAR
The women of the Padaung tribe add a gold ring around their necks annually, to a maximum of 20 rings, which can make their necks 15 in (38 cm) long.

First Steps

Jingle Luis from the Philippines took her first unaided steps at age 15 after doctors at a New York City hospital straightened her severely clubbed feet, which were twisted backward and upside down. Dr. Terry Amaral inserted screws into the bones of her feet and turned the screws bit by bit over a period of six weeks so her feet would rotate, a few degrees at a time, into their correct position.

℞ BAG OF HAIR

Peng Fu, a traveling herbal medicine practitioner from Suining, China, has not cut his hair for over 60 years and carries it around in a bag on his back. When last measured, his hair was 8 ft 10 in (2.7 m) long and weighed nearly 9 lb (4 kg).

℞ TWO-DAY MEMORY

Andy Wray from Essex, England, has a memory that lasts only two days—so if he is parted from his wife or young daughter for 48 hours or more, he can no longer recognize them. He has dissociative amnesia, a condition that effectively wipes his memory clean on a regular basis. Doctors say it is the result of trauma suffered during his time working as a police officer.

℞ ORGANS REVERSED

An Indian man is thought to be the only living person in the world with situs inversus—a condition where his internal organs are back-to-front. Doctors in Mumbai were about to remove a tumor from the kidney of Ashok Shivnani when they realized that most of his chest and abdominal organs, as well as many blood vessels, were in the mirror opposite position of where they should be in his body.

℞ LOUD SNORER

Jenny Chapman from Cambridgeshire, England, snores more loudly than the noise of a jet aircraft. She snores in her sleep at 111.6 decibels—eight decibels louder than the roar of a low-flying jet. She could drown out the sounds of a spinning washing machine, a diesel truck or a speeding express train.

℞ EGYPTIAN MUMMY

Mother-of-three Nileen Namita from Brighton, England, has undergone more than 50 cosmetic procedures to make herself look like the ancient Egyptian Queen Nefertiti. Since 1987, Nileen, who believes she is a reincarnation of Nefertiti, has spent over $300,000 on eight nose jobs, three chin implants, one eyebrow lift, three facelifts, six mini facelifts, two lip surgeries, five eye surgeries and 20 minor facial tweaks—to recreate herself in the image of the "Beauty of the Nile."

℞ MUSCLE BOY

A five-year-old Romanian boy has muscles that are bigger than those of boys over three times his age. Strong boy Giuliano Stroe, who has been training since age two, can perform grueling stunts such as horizontal bar routines, backflips off a table top, and walking on his hands with a weight ball between his legs.

℞ REAL POPEYE

Matthias Schlitte, a German arm wrestler, has a huge right forearm that measures almost 18 in (46 cm) around—over twice the size of his left arm. He is known as the real-life Popeye after the spinach-loving cartoon sailor who has disproportionately muscular forearms.

℞ MIRACLE WALKER

A four-year-old boy who was told by doctors that he would be confined to a wheelchair for the rest of his life has miraculously learned to walk by copying a disabled duckling. Finlay Lomax from Plymouth, England, has cerebral palsy but after his mother took in a day-old duckling with a broken leg, she was amazed to see Finlay standing on his own two feet and mimicking its steps.

℞ TOUGH TEEN

Fifteen-year-old Bobby Natoli of Oswego, New York, did 53 chin-ups in one minute in 2008, surpassing the feat of his father, Robert, who had managed 44 the previous year. Bobby also recorded 209 chin-ups in half an hour when he was just 12 years old.

℞ HAIR SALE

To beat the economic crisis, many women in Spain have started selling their hair. Depending on the length and weight, a ponytail can be worth up to $220 when sold to a company that exports natural hair for wigs and extensions.

℞ CHOPSTICK IMPALEMENT

Doctors in China removed a chopstick that was lodged 0.15 in (4 mm) into the brain of a 14-month-old boy. Li Jingchao, from Shandong Province, was playing with chopsticks when he fell on one and it went up his nose and into his brain.

℞ FLU SHOTS

The University of Central Florida administered 2,527 flu shots to staff, students and local residents in eight hours in September 2009.

℞ SIMPSONS SAVIOR

Choking to death on a sandwich, ten-year-old Alex Hardy from Wakefield, England, was saved by his best friend Aiden Bateman who performed an abdominal thrust maneuver—remembering the technique from an episode of *The Simpsons*.

℞ STRANGER'S DIAGNOSIS

A stranger saved the life of a Spanish bus passenger by telling her that she might be suffering from a rare disease. Montse Ventura was on a bus in Barcelona in 2009, when a woman sitting opposite noticed her unusually shaped hands. She urged Montse to have tests for acromegaly, a disorder caused by a pituitary gland problems that causes abnormal growth of hands and feet. Sure enough, when Montse went to the doctor, a small pituitary gland tumor was found and removed.

℞ VIOLENT SNEEZE

Victoria Kenny from Chichester, England, broke her back—just by sneezing. She sneezed with such force that she ruptured a disk in her spine, leaving her paralyzed for almost two years.

Blood Portrait

A $450,000 self-portrait sculpted by British artist Marc Quinn from his own frozen blood was put on display at London's National Portrait Gallery in 2009. Quinn made his first blood head in 1991, and has subsequently produced a new cast every few years to illustrate how he has aged. He uses 10 pt (4.7 l) of blood for each work, the blood being removed by his doctor, a pint at a time every six weeks.

ICE ORDEAL

LATVIAN ILLUSIONIST GENNADY PALYCHEVSKY WAS ON THE VERGE OF LITERALLY FREEZING TO DEATH AFTER SPENDING MORE THAN 64 HOURS AS A HUMAN ICE CUBE. HE SURVIVED FOR NEARLY THREE DAYS IN THE 6-SQ-FT (0.5-SQ-M) ICE CUBE IN MOSCOW BEFORE SIGNALLING FOR HELP BECAUSE HE WAS SUFFERING FROM SEVERE FROSTBITE. PALYCHEVSKY, WHO HAD TRAINED IN ICE BATHS FOR SIX MONTHS, DID NOT EAT OR DRINK WHILE SEALED INSIDE HIS ICE TOMB.

Lionel The Lion-Faced Man

Born in Poland in 1891 as Stephan Bibrowski, Lionel's entire body was covered in long, thick hair. A very intelligent man who spoke five languages, Bibrowski had a variation of hypertrichosis, known as "werewolf disease." He was famous at Coney during the 1920s and performed his gymnastic act at the Dreamland Circus sideshow.

Zip The Pinhead

Born William Henry Johnson in 1842, Zip is thought to have suffered from a condition called microcephaly, leaving him with an oddly tapered head and an ordinary size face. He performed for over 60 years with the Ringling Brothers at Coney Island, billed initially as a "Wild Man," a missing link from Africa. He later became a comic performer, playing the fiddle so badly that people paid him to stop. He died a wealthy man at the age of 84.

Making a Splash

One of the most famous stunts ever to take place at Coney was an attempt to fly a primitive "airplane" from the top of a 50-ft-high (15-m) ride. The plane simply consisted of a wicker basket with muslin-covered wings hinged to the sides. It had no engine, and the wings were operated by the pilot, a local character called Dutch Charley, who pulled a series of cords and pushed pedals. The contraption was duly hauled to the top of the ride and Charley began pedaling furiously. The cord was then cut, freeing the plane, which promptly plunged into the ocean. Charley had to be rescued by lifeguards.

Jean Carroll, The Tattooed Lady

Believe it or not, Jean started in the sideshows as a bearded lady and finished as a tattooed lady. She fell in love with contortionist John Carson but he couldn't bring himself to marry a woman with a beard. So after a 15-year courtship, she removed her beard using electrolysis and then underwent full body tattooing to maintain her sideshow career.

Violetta, The Limbless Woman

Born in Germany in 1906, Aloisia Wagner entered the world of show business at the age of 15, acquiring the stage name Violetta. Completely self-sufficient despite being born with no arms or legs, she moved around by hopping. Her sideshow performance involved her singing, but also demonstrated her abilities to sew and to light a cigarette using only her mouth.

First Roller Coaster

America's first roller coaster, Switchback Railroad, was opened on Coney Island in 1884. Passengers seated sideways rode a train on undulating tracks over a 600-ft-long (183-m) wooden structure. The train started at a height of 50 ft (15 m) at one end and ran downhill until its momentum ceased. The passengers then got off and attendants pushed the cars over a switch to a higher level. The passengers then returned to their seats and rode back to their original point of departure. Admission was five cents and the ride was so popular that designer LaMarcus Thompson made an average of $600 a day. It had cost him just $1,600 to build.

1829
Coney Island House opens

1876
First carousel built with hand-carved horses and animals, costs five cents a ride

1867
The hot dog is invented at Coney Island!

1879
First horse racing track open

1880
New pier means steamships can ferry passengers from Manhattan

1884
Switchback Railroad, America's first roller coaster, is unveiled

1885
Seven-floor Elephant Hotel opens with 31 rooms

1895
16-acre (6.4 ha) Sea Lion Park opens, North America's first enclosed amusement park

1896
The Elephant Hotel burns down

1897
George Tilyou builds Steeplechase Park

1898
Barnum & Bailey open The Great Water Carnival with clowns, amazing swimmers and log rollers

The Four Legged Woman
Josephene Myrtle Corbin was billed as the "Four-Legged Woman," as she had the lower limbs of her unformed twin growing from her pelvis. However, these legs were too weak to stand on, and her right leg had a clubbed foot, so she could only use one of her four legs. She went on to have five children after marrying Dr. Clinton Bicknell at the age of 19.

Baby in a Jar
A baby was preserved in formaldehyde at a Coney Island sideshow in 1944. Coney Island has a long history of baby exhibits, courtesy of the Infant Incubator, a show where newborn infants were displayed under the care of a corps of trained nurses. The incubator babies were miraculously saved from the fire that swept through the island in 1911.

1983
First Coney Island Mermaid Parade held for contestants in marine costumes

1985
"Sideshows by the Seashore" opened as the only "ten-in-one" sideshow (ten acts for one admission price) in North America

1989
Parachute Jump declared a city landmark

2009
"Sideshows by the Seashore" continues to flourish

Formerly an island but now a peninsula, Coney Island is located in southernmost Brooklyn, New York City. Its popularity as a resort grew in the 1860s when the Coney Island and Brooklyn Railroad started to serve the area, and by 1880 it boasted rides and freak shows. For more than fifty years, until World War II, Coney Island was the biggest amusement area in the US. On just one day in September 1906, no fewer than 200,000 postcards were mailed from Coney Island.

It housed three major amusement parks—Dreamland, Steeplechase Park and Luna Park. Dreamland was illuminated by one million electric lights, and at night its searchlight beamed 50 mi (80 km) out over the Atlantic Ocean. The brain behind Dreamland was Samuel W. Gumpertz, who scoured the globe in search of human oddities to appear at his sideshows. He made five trips to Asia and five to Africa, bringing back little people, bearded ladies and more than 3,000 peculiar performers.

In 1904, Gumpertz created Lilliputia, a miniature city inhabited by little people. The "Midget Village" had a population of 300 Lilliputians and was a tremendous success. For extra effect, he even hired a few giants to wander through its streets.

It was during the early 20th century that many of the sideshows were opened, such as The World Circus Freak Show. The ten-in-one sideshows (offering ten acts for a single admission price) offered a steady career for the performers.

Among the stilt walkers who marched around Coney Island advertising the attractions in the early 1920s was a young Englishman named Archie Leach. He would go on to find fame as Hollywood star Cary Grant.

To cater to the influx of visitors, numerous hotels were built, the most outrageous being one in the shape of an elephant. The Elephant Hotel had a cigar store in one front leg while a spiral staircase in a hind leg led visitors up to a shop and the guest rooms. The animal's head, facing the ocean, offered great views through slits where the eyes were located.

When the nearby Brighton Beach Hotel was threatened by sea erosion in 1888, the entire 500-ft-long (150-m), three-story hotel, weighing 6,000 tons, was jacked up on to 120 rail cars and, with the help of six locomotives, was moved inland 600 ft (180 m)—without breaking a single pane of glass!

After World War II interest in the sideshows declined, nearly putting the organizers and performers out of business. Although most of Coney Island's sideshow performers had become extremely wealthy, there was a clear increase in civilized sensibilities and a growing number of people became concerned about exploitation within the shows.

The sideshow hasn't really died out at Coney Island, but the attention has moved away from "freaks" and oddities of the body and now focuses on performers. "Sideshows by the Seashore," founded by Dick Zigun in 1985, offers such exotic attractions as human blockheads, sword swallowers and fire eaters.

Yet, we can still remember the classic sideshow performers that made Coney Island the sideshow capital of the world…

Elephant Execution The rivalry between the three major parks on Coney Island was fierce. When George Tilyou attracted crowds to Steeplechase Park by beaching an old sailing ship in front of the entrance, the owners of the newly opened Luna Park retaliated by announcing that Topsy, a rogue elephant who had killed three people (including an abusive keeper), would be publicly executed. Opposition from the American Society for the Prevention of Cruelty to Animals ruled out hanging as a method, so it was decided to electrocute her instead. In 1903, an estimated 1,500 people watched as 6,600 volts were sent coursing through the elephant's body, killing her in ten seconds. When Coney Island later burned down, the fire was described as "Topsy's Revenge."

Headless Woman
A performance by an apparently headless woman has been a major attraction at Coney Island sideshows down through the years.

Princess Lola The fattest lady at Coney, Princess Lola claimed to weigh 558 lb (253 kg) in August 1949.

Coney Island Today
"Sideshows by the Seashore" continues the Coney Island tradition of showcasing live bizarre and unusual acts.

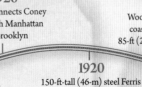
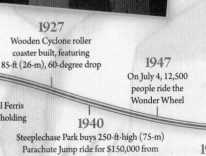

1903
Topsy the killer elephant is executed at Luna Park

1903
Luna Park opens and in just six weeks pays back the $700,000 it cost to build

1904
Dreamland opens, including Lilliputia, a miniature city inhabited by little people

1907
Steeplechase Park, burned down, but it is rebuilt for following season

1911
Huge fire destroys 50 amusement sites, including Dreamland—many animals perish

1917
Fatty Arbuckle and Buster Keaton film the silent comedy movie *Coney Island* at Luna Park

1920
Subway connects Coney Island with Manhattan and Brooklyn

1920
150-ft-tall (46-m) steel Ferris Wonder Wheel opens, holding 144 riders.

1927
Wooden Cyclone roller coaster built, featuring 85-ft (26-m), 60-degree drop

1940
Steeplechase Park buys 250-ft-high (75-m) Parachute Jump ride for $150,000 from New York World's Fair

1947
On July 4, 12,500 people ride the Wonder Wheel

1962
Astroland opens—it closed in 2008.

1964
Steeplechase Park closes

THE CORAL MEN

LIN TIANZHUAN FROM SHUIMEN, SOUTHERN CHINA, FIRST NOTICED THE GROWTHS ON HIS HANDS AND FEET WHEN HE WAS 13, AND OVER THE NEXT 25 YEARS THEY GRADUALLY SPREAD AND HARDENED TO THE POINT WHERE HE COULD NO LONGER BEND HIS ARMS OR LEGS. DUBBED "CORAL BOY" BY FRIENDS AND NEIGHBORS, LIN BECAME A HERMIT, HIDING HIMSELF AWAY AT THE FAMILY HOME. "IF I HAD TO GO OUT I WRAPPED MYSELF UP IN BLANKETS BECAUSE PEOPLE WOULD SCREAM WHEN THEY SAW ME."

"It started with a few hard bumps, so I tried to apply antibiotics and creams but it didn't get better. Instead, it just got worse. They grew and grew and soon they were all over my arms and legs, my back and even my head. It was terrifying. It was as if I was turning to stone."

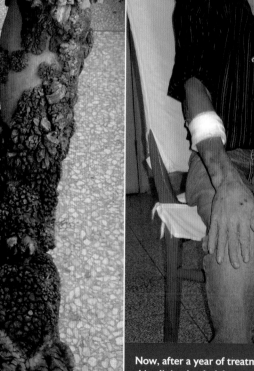

Now, after a year of treatment and surgery at a specialist skin clinic, the dark brown shells have been cut away and he has nothing worse than a few discolored skin patches to remind him of his previous horrific condition.

BEFORE

AFTER

RIPLEY'S RESEARCH

THE CONDITION IS THOUGHT TO BE CAUSED BY THE HUMAN PAPILLOMA VIRUS, A FAIRLY COMMON INFECTION, WHICH USUALLY CAUSES ONLY SMALL WARTS. HOWEVER, IF THE PATIENT SUFFERS FROM A PARTICULAR IMMUNE-SYSTEM DEFICIENCY, THE BODY IS UNABLE TO CONTAIN THE WARTS AND ALLOWS THE VIRUS TO SPREAD AND PRODUCE EXTREME GROWTHS KNOWN AS "CUTANEOUS HORNS." FEWER THAN 200 PEOPLE WORLDWIDE ARE THOUGHT TO SUFFER FROM THIS MYSTERIOUS IMMUNE PROBLEM.

The Root of the Problem

Lin's case is similar to that of Dede Koswara, the Indonesian "tree man." After cutting his knee as a teenager, a small wart developed on his leg and spread uncontrollably so that most of his body was encased in strange treelike growths. The only work he could find was as a sideshow performer and so, when offered the chance of a cure, he was initially reluctant to take it because he would lose his livelihood. Eventually, Dede reconsidered and has undergone nine operations to remove more than 17 lb (8 kg) of gnarled warts from his body.

When interior designer Barend Massow Hemmes from London, England, wanted his work to be noticed outside, he created *Night Shadow*, an extreme motorcycle based on the famous Jaguar car logo and measuring over 7 ft (2.1 m) long. The sleek cruiser is precision-engineered in stainless steel and fiberglass and took three years to build. The black big-cat body is based on a genuine Jaguar car mascot Barend found at a dealership. Many parts of the bike, including the 1200cc engine, were taken from a stripped-down Buell Thunderbolt bike and then fitted to a custom frame. Although Barend designed *Night Shadow* as a work of art, he has ridden the bike at 65 mph (104 km/h) and is sure that it is capable of much faster speeds.

TRAVEL TALES

Lean Machine

In Huai'an City, in East China's Jiangsu Province, a truck driver checks that his bundles of goods are still secure.

℞ IRREGULAR BIKE

Guan Baihua of Qingdao, China, spent 18 months developing a bicycle with odd-shaped wheels. The front wheel is a five-sided pentagon, while the back wheel is a triangle. He says the bike is mainly for fun but adds that riders could use it to lose weight because it takes more effort to pedal.

℞ PUMPKIN HELMETS

After new laws were brought in to force Nigerian motorcyclists to wear helmets, a number of bikers in the northern city of Kano were spotted wearing dried pumpkin shells on their heads.

℞ UNEXPECTED PASSENGER

A delivery man driving a small van near Peddie, Eastern Cape, South Africa, in May 2009 collided with a bull and had to drive around 9 mi (14 km) to a local police station—with the animal still wedged in the vehicle's roof rack.

℞ EMERGENCY LANDING

A small airplane bound for Santa Barbara Airport, California, was hit by three cars after making an emergency landing on a nearby highway. The Piper PA-24 Comanche, with two people on board, touched down a mile from the airport on U.S. Highway 101 after running out of fuel. Although nine people were involved in the accident, nobody was hurt.

℞ TOILET LANDING

A pilot escaped unhurt in May 2009 when his small airplane's crash landing was cushioned by a pile of portable toilets. After taking off from an airfield near Tacoma, Washington State, the Cessna 182's engine failed at a height of about 160 ft (50 m). As it dropped from the sky, it hit a fence, flipped over and landed upside down on top of portable toilets stacked in a storage yard.

℞ REPEAT OFFENDER

A man in Boynton Beach, Florida, received more than 50 traffic citations from police in one day on February 5, 2009.

℞ FARE CHOICE

At Recession Ride Taxi in Essex, Vermont, proprietor Eric Hagen allows his passengers to decide how much they want to pay. Most pay cash, but he has also received a CD from a musician and a $10 supermarket card—and he hasn't been short-changed yet.

Donkey Wreath

Doing all the hard work, a donkey is guided along a road south of Dushanbe, Tajikistan, carrying hundreds of leaves on his back.

℞ KARAOKE CAB

Fan Xiaoming of Changchun, Jilin, China, has fitted out his taxi cab with media players, an amplifier, speakers, LCD screens and a microphone—so his passengers can sing along on their journeys.

℞ UNLUCKY DAY

Former U.S. President Franklin D. Roosevelt was so superstitious that he always avoided travel on the 13th day of each month.

℞ TOWED AWAY

Ruth Ducker of London, England, was told she would have to pay more than $3,000 to reclaim her illegally parked car—after local council workers lifted it up, painted double yellow "no-parking" lines under it and then towed it away.

℞ STILL GOING

Seventy percent of Land Rover all-terrain vehicles—first built in the U.K. in 1948—are still on the road.

Riding Recycler

A woman in Shanghai carries masses of Styrofoam for recycling on the back of her bicycle.

Coco-Nutter

IN MYSORE, INDIA, A COCONUT GATHERER TRANSPORTS HIS
HUSKS TO THE LOCAL MARKET ON HIS THREE-WHEELED RICKSHAW.

Traveling by Air

In Tianjin, China, a cyclist travels under a cloud of bright pink and red helium balloons.

Motor-Hog

Two men in Moung Russey, Cambodia, carry a large pig on the back of their motorbike.

℞ LIFE BAN

In January 2009, a court banned 84-year-old Luba Relic of Warriewood, New South Wales, Australia, from driving until the year 3000.

℞ STRANGE HYBRID

Friends Nicolo Lamberti and Milko Dalla Costa took the chassis of a speedy Ferrari F355 Berlinetta and crossed it with the body of a Citroën 2CV bread van—and created a bread van capable of speeds of 180 mph (290 km/h). After discovering the Citroën in Turate, Italy, the pair spent five years and more than $220,000 putting together their bizarre hybrid.

℞ FOLDING BIKE

Dominic Hargreaves, a graduate from the Royal College of Art in London, England, has devised a bicycle that folds up to be smaller than its own wheels. He sees "the Contortionist" as being the perfect bike for commuters because when folded it can be wheeled along the street by one handlebar.

Fast Fog

This amazing image captures the moment a U.S. Air Force B-2 Spirit Bomber created its own cloud as it approached the speed of sound near Los Angeles in 2009. Despite a wingspan of 172 ft (52 m), the bombers—which cost around $1 billion each when first made in 1989— are designed to be difficult to detect and can travel at 604 mph (972 km/h).

- The first plane to fly faster than the speed of sound was a Bell X-1 piloted by U.S. Air Force Captain Chuck Yeager, which reached a speed of 807 mph (1,299 km/h) in 1947.

- In 1979, Stan Barrett broke the sound barrier in a car. He achieved a speed of 739 mph (1,189 km/h) at Rogers Dry Lake, California, in his jet-powered Budweiser Rocket Car.

RIPLEY'S RESEARCH

THE B-2 SPIRIT BOMBER TRAVELS AT SUCH SPEED THAT A CLOUD OF WATER VAPOR CAN FORM AROUND ITS BODY. THE PHENOMENON IS OFTEN THOUGHT TO BE CAUSED BY THE "SONIC BOOM" HEARD WHEN A PLANE TRAVELS FASTER THAN THE SPEED OF SOUND, BUT ALTHOUGH THE B-2 IS INCREDIBLY QUICK, IT FALLS SHORT OF THE SOUND BARRIER. THE CLOUD IS PROBABLY CAUSED BY RADICAL CHANGES IN AIR PRESSURE WHEN AIRCRAFT APPROACH THE SPEED OF SOUND, WHICH IS ABOUT 760 MPH (1,223 KM/H) AT SEA LEVEL.

R BABY BIKER

A three-year-old boy in India can ride a full-size motorcycle. Shantanu Khan from New Delhi extended the bike's controls so that son Azeem could reach them. Judges were so impressed they issued Azeem a special license to ride the bike around the neighborhood—but not on main roads.

R CHURCH AVOIDANCE

A seven-year-old boy trying to avoid going to church on a Sunday morning took his father's car for a drive around Plain City, Utah. Police officers chased the boy at speeds of 40 mph (65 km/h) before he stopped in a driveway.

R SOLAR FLIGHT

The Cardozo family from Wiltshire, England, traveled 1,242 mi (2,000 km) from Monte Carlo to Morocco in an electric paramotor (a motorized paraglider) powered by the sun. The paramotor was powered by lithium polymer batteries, which were charged in rotation using 12 solar panels on top of a support vehicle. Their journey across the Mediterranean took 15 days and they traveled at altitudes of up to 5,000 ft (1,500 m).

R F1 LIMO

Canadian inventor Michael Pettipas has spent two years building a street-legal Formula-1 stretch limousine racing car with seven seats—six for passengers and one for the driver. The 30-ft-long (9-m) car has an 8-liter engine, can do 0 to 60 mph (0–97 km/h) in five seconds and is capable of reaching speeds of 140 mph (225 km/h).

R PET AIRWAYS

The maiden flight of an airline service that caters solely to pets took off from Farmingdale, New York, in July 2009. With Florida-based Pet Airways, founded by Alysa Binder and Dan Wiesel, pets travel in the airline's main cabin, but owners are not allowed onboard—even in the cargo hold. The company was founded in 2005 and the couple spent the next four years replacing seats with pet carriers in their fleet of five planes. Up to 50 animals at a time are escorted to the airplane by pet attendants, who give the animals a "potty break" just before takeoff and check on them every 15 minutes during the flight. At each of the five U.S. airports it serves, the company has even created a Pet Lounge for its animal passengers—or "pawsengers" as it calls them—where they can wait and sniff before flights.

Flash Cars

English photographers Mark Brown and Marc Cameron have re-created the familiar shapes of well-known sports cars using only flashes of moving light and a camera. This vivid Bugatti Veyron is part of a collection inspired by various iconic cars, which also includes models from Ferrari, Morgan and Aston Martin.

TITANIC TRIBUTE

In London, England, in February 2009, fans of the film *Titanic* donned Victorian costume and sat in old rowing boats as they watched a screening of the blockbuster movie in a swimming pool complete with dry ice and miniature icebergs. The real *Titanic* was an ocean liner that hit an iceberg and sank on its maiden voyage when crossing the Atlantic Ocean on April 14, 1912, with the loss of 1,517 lives.

When the *Titanic* hit an iceberg in 1912, the onboard cinema was showing an early silent film called *The Poseidon Adventure*, which by incredible coincidence tells the story of passengers escaping an ocean liner as it sinks to the bottom of the sea.

℞ FARMING FUNERAL

The coffin of farmer Gordon Hale from Wiltshire, England, was put on a trailer and towed to his grave by the Ford 4000 tractor he had used every day for 38 years. Maintaining the farming theme, mourners wore ribbons of bale twine and the same material was used to form the handles on the coffin.

℞ BIRTHDAY FLIGHTS

On his 16th birthday, Errick Smith of Ocean Springs, Mississippi, flew an airplane and a helicopter solo. Errick, who began taking flying lessons at 14, piloted a Cessna 172 aircraft and two helicopters, an R22 and a Schweitzer.

℞ ECONOMY SALAD

American Airlines saved an estimated $40,000 in 1987 by removing one olive from each salad served to first-class passengers.

℞ DIRTY SEAT

Eighteen-year-old Jack Hyde from Oxfordshire, England, had his driver's test canceled in 2009 because the examiner found crumbs on his car seat.

℞ BIKE STAND

Mr. Liu, a farmer from Jiangxi, China, is able to stand, lie down and even sleep on a motorcycle traveling at high speed. He once drove a motorbike for 3.7 mi (6 km) while standing.

℞ LOW MILEAGE

A Mini car that has been driven only 148 mi (238 km) was worth more in 2009 than it cost its owner in 1989. Ron Frost from Devon, England, paid about £5,800 for the 998cc cherry red Mini 30, but the longest journey it has ever made was 60 mi (96 km). For 20 years he has kept it indoors as part of his private car museum. Its oil has never been changed and it has been washed only twice. The British Mini Club says that the car, which is in pristine condition, would fetch up to £7,000 at auction.

℞ BOND FLYER

German Hermann Ramke has spent nine years developing a James Bond-like jet pack that is powered by high-pressure water. The JetLev-Flyer, which sells for around $140,000, has a top speed of 65 mph (105 km/h), can power the rider to an altitude of 33 ft (10 m) and is able to travel nearly 200 mi (320 km) before it needs refueling. A floating pump powered by a 150-hp four-stroke engine sends water through a 140-ft-long (43-m) hose to a pair of nozzles on the jet pack. The jet leaving the nozzles is powerful enough to propel the rider into the air.

Car Crash Visitors to a square in Berlin, Germany, had to look twice when they encountered a car that appeared to have fallen from the sky and smashed through the pavement. It was actually a convincing sculpture conceived as a publicity stunt by a German website.

BIKE JUMP

In Chicago, Illinois, in July 2009, U.S. freestyle motocross star Ronnie Renner launched into a jump that took him more than 63 ft (19 m) above the ground. Riding his motorbike up a 22-ft-high (6.7-m) quarterpipe, he soared 41 ft 5 in (12.6 m) into the air upside down before landing on a ramp, giving him a total height of 63 ft 5 in (19.33 m).

CENTENARY JUMP

Peggy McAlpine from Stirling, Scotland, celebrated her 100th birthday, in October 2007, by paragliding from the top of a mountain range in Cyprus. Peggy, who is partially sighted and has lived through the reign of five British monarchs and more than 25 prime ministers, leaped from a 2,500-ft (760-m) peak in northern Cyprus for a 15-minute tandem flight.

VARIED JOURNEY

Edwin Shackleton, an 82-year-old retired aircraft engineer from Bristol, England, traveled on 100 types of transport in just over six months. He started on New Year's Day 2009 with a car journey and clocked up number 100 in July 2009 in a hot-air balloon. On his way to his century, he traveled in such diverse modes of transport as a microlight, a fire truck, a garbage truck, a rickshaw, a police car, a chairlift, a quad bike and a sled.

PEDAL POWER

Sam Whittingham of British Columbia, Canada, can reach a speed of over 82 mph (132 km/h)—without an engine. Relying solely on human power, his recumbent bicycle clocked a speed of 82.4 mph (132.6 km/h) on a flat section of road at Battle Mountain, Nevada, in 2009.

HIGH ROLLER

Branden Moyen of Shillington, Pennsylvania, has built a model of a roller coaster 36 ft (11 m) tall and 50 ft (15 m) long from around 40,000 pieces of the construction toy K'NEX. The track measures about 400 ft (122 m) in length and the roller-coaster car travels at speeds up to 70 mph (115 km/h) after being slingshotted to the top of the first hill by 25 rubber bands. His model is a 1:10-scale replica of Klinga Da, a giant steel roller coaster at Six Flags Great Adventure, New Jersey.

SHARP REMINDER

In the 19th century, women traveling alone on trains used to place sharp pins between their lips when entering tunnels in case male strangers attempted to kiss them in the dark.

RODE KILL

CALIFORNIAN HOT-ROD ARTIST JOHN POWERS HAS CREATED "RODE KILL," A UNIQUE, HANDCRAFTED, CUSTOM MOTORCYCLE SEEMINGLY MADE FROM A DECAYING CORPSE. THE BIKE HAS INCREDIBLY DETAILED FEATURES SUCH AS A HEART PROTRUDING FROM AN EXPOSED RIBCAGE THAT HOUSES THE FUEL TANK, AND SUPER-REALISTIC BONES THAT FLEX AT THE ELBOW WITH THE BIKE SUSPENSION.

Maggots!

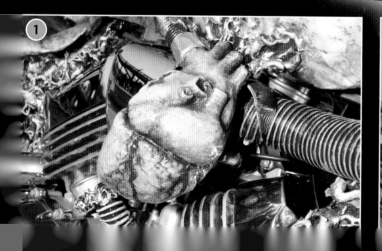

℞ UNDERSEA MAIL

In 2009, a Norwegian mayor sent a letter to an English town through a 725-mi (1,166-km) underwater gas pipeline running beneath the North Sea. Bernard Riksfjord, mayor of Aukra in western Norway, dropped the letter into the Langeled pipeline on August 19, 2009, and five days later the letter, propelled forward by pressurized gas, popped out in the town of Easington, County Durham.

℞ MODEL FLOTILLA

In the course of 75 years, Peter Tamm of Hamburg, Germany, has amassed a collection of 36,000 model ships (each built to 1:1,250 scale), thousands of photographs of ships, a maritime library of more than 100,000 volumes and 15,000 ship menus, some dating back to the 1890s.

℞ ELECTRIC PARADE

More than 200 electric vehicles formed a 2-mi-long (3-km) parade at Bay Harbor, Michigan, in 2009. The line was led by a Milburn Lite electric car dating back to 1920.

℞ DREAM DRIVE

Graham and Eirene Naismith of London, England, sold their house, gave away their furniture and spent ten months driving 31,116 mi (50,076 km) all the way to Australia and then around the entire circumference of the country—with three children under eight. Driving a Toyota Land Cruiser, they traveled through 19 countries and crossed three continents.

℞ SMART BIKE

A bicycle designed to be as intelligent as a computer was unveiled by Britain's former Olympic champion racing cyclist Chris Boardman in 2009. The bike of the future could never be stolen and would feature puncture-proof, self-inflating tires and a mini computer to count the calories as the pedals turned.

℞ LATE FLIGHT

On May 6, 2009, Lillian Gardiner of St. Marys, Ontario, Canada, took her first ever plane ride—at the age of 105.

℞ EPIC VOYAGE

Although paralyzed from the neck down, 37-year-old Hilary Lister from Kent, England, sailed solo around the U.K. in 2009—a distance of 1,500 mi (2,415 km). She operated the 20-ft (6-m) racing yacht by blowing through straws connected to a computer. Her epic voyage took her three months and she covered approximately 60 mi (96 km) a day. Wheelchair-bound since the age of 15, Hilary, who suffers from Reflex Sympathetic Dystrophy, earned a degree in biochemistry at Oxford University despite having to dictate her papers with an epidural drip in her spine.

LOOK CLOSER AND YOU WILL SEE MAGGOTS CRAWLING OVER THE DECAYING FLESH, BLOODSTAINED EXHAUST PIPES, AND HEADLIGHT EYES IN THE SKULL. JOHN WANTED TO GRAPHICALLY DRIVE HOME HOW DANGEROUS POWERFUL MOTORBIKES CAN BE FOR INEXPERIENCED RIDERS— "RODE KILL" WILL REACH SPEEDS OF 140 MPH (225 KM/H).

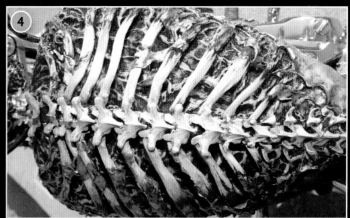

Life in the Skies

To conquer his phobia of flying, Mark Malkoff from New York spent an entire month on an airplane in June 2009. Traveling up to 12 flights a day and 135 in total, he touched down at 38 U.S. airports, spent 267 hours in the air and covered a distance of 111,972 mi (180,201 km) or 4.5 times the circumference of the Earth. Under the rules of the challenge, he was forbidden from actually setting foot in any airport and so had to rest on the plane wings or take a shower on the runway courtesy of a fire truck!

WORK!

REST!

PLAY!

℞ HISTORIC FLIGHT

In 2009, to mark the centenary of French inventor and pilot Louis Bleriot becoming the first person to fly an airplane across the English Channel, another Frenchman, Edmond Salis, repeated the 22-mi (35-km) crossing in a restored Bleriot XI—the same model used by his predecessor on that 1909 flight.

℞ PASSENGER PILOT

Passenger Doug White took over the controls and landed a twin engine plane at Southwest Florida International Airport in April 2009—after the pilot died in mid-flight.

℞ BUSY AIRPORT

The Hartsfield-Jackson International Airport in Atlanta, Georgia, U.S.A., serves 90 million passengers a year—more than the entire population of Germany.

℞ HEROIC REPAIR

In July 2009, after an airplane due to fly from Menorca, Spain, to Glasgow, Scotland, developed an engineering fault, vacationers were spared an eight-hour delay when one of the passengers fixed the plane himself.

℞ PRESERVED WRECK

The HMS *Ontario*, a British warship that sank in Lake Ontario off the coast of New York State, was discovered in 2008 in excellent condition, despite being underwater for 228 years.

℞IPLEY'S ask

Did you eat airplane food all month?
I ate some airplane food. Most of the food was airport food that was brought to me by my crew or people who felt sorry for me. Sometimes I'd go on Twitter and ask for food, which worked very well.

How did you wash?
The plane of course didn't have a shower, so every morning I washed with baby wipes. I washed my hair over the airplane bathroom sink. One time a flight attendant shampooed my hair mid-flight.

Where did you sleep?
I slept alone on the plane in a different row every night. The plane was completely empty. I had my own pillow and sleeping bag. Most nights the cleaning crew had to vacuum around me as I slept.

Did you get bored?
I was never bored. I was constantly meeting people, filming videos, and during flights was keeping in touch with people using Gogo wi-fi.

And finally... did you get over your fear of flying?
After about a week I slowly started to get over my fear of flying by talking to pilots. They really helped me to understand turbulence, which was a huge fear of mine.

℞ FLIGHT RAPPER

U.S. flight attendant David Holmes got so bored with reading out the safety instructions that he decided to rap them. His 80-second rap included: "Before we leave, our advice is, put away your electronic devices. Fasten your seat belt, then put your trays up—press the button and make the seat belt raise up."

℞ HAIR-RAISING

Over 30,000 women and more than 100 long-haired men from Myanmar donated their hair to pay for repairs to a road leading to the remote Buddhist pagoda of Alaungdaw Kathapha. Nearly 1,750 lb (800 kg) of hair was collected, with some locks measuring up to 4 ft (1.2 m) long. The hair was then sold to traders in China for use in wigs or dolls, while the money raised improved access on the pagoda road.

At temperatures of −58°F (−50°C), if a truck falls through the ice and sinks into the water, the driver has less than one minute to get out before freezing to death.

The ice needs to be 40 in (102 cm) thick to withstand the largest 70-ton trucks. Speeds on the frozen road are often limited to below 20 mph (32 km/h) to minimize potential damage as the ice shifts.

EVERY WINTER, HUNDREDS OF TRUCKERS RISK THEIR LIVES BY DRIVING MONSTER 18-WHEELED RIGS WEIGHING OVER 50 TONS ACROSS FROZEN LAKES AND RIVERS, AND EVEN THE FROZEN ARCTIC SEA. THE ICE-ROAD TRUCKERS MAKE AS MANY RUNS AS POSSIBLE (THE "DASH FOR CASH" AS THEY CALL IT), EACH RUN TAKING OVER 20 HOURS. DRIVING HUNDREDS OF MILES AT A TIME, OVER SHEETS OF ICE JUST 28 IN (70 CM) THICK, TRUCKERS DRIVE ON LITTLE SLEEP AND ARE IN CONSTANT FEAR OF THE SOUND OF CRACKING ICE BENEATH THEIR WHEELS, A SOUND THAT COULD SEND THEM PLUNGING TO THEIR DEATH.

RIPLEY'S RESEARCH

THE ICE-ROAD TRUCKERS DELIVER VITAL SUPPLIES TO DIAMOND MINES AND GAS PLANTS IN CANADA'S REMOTE NORTHWEST TERRITORIES. THESE ICE ROADS STRETCH FOR OVER 1,550 MI (2,500 KM) AND ARE ACCESSIBLE FOR ONLY 60 DAYS A YEAR BEFORE THEY START TO MELT. AT THE START OF EACH SEASON, A PROFILER VEHICLE IS SENT OUT TO TEST THE THICKNESS OF THE ICE WITH A RADAR. ONCE THE ROAD IS DECLARED SAFE, PLOWS TAKE TO THE ICE TO CLEAR AWAY THE SNOW.

DRIVING ON THIN ICE

SNOW BRAKES

EXTREME DRIVER AND KEEN SNOWBOARDER Ken Block DROVE HIS $150,000 Subaru RALLY CAR UP ONTO THE SLOPES AT Snowpark, New Zealand, IN 2007. AFTER TOWING SEVERAL SNOWBOARDERS AROUND THE COURSE AT HIGH SPEED, Californian Block RACED PROFESSIONAL BOARDER Torstein Horgmo DOWN A 55-FT (16.8-M) RAMP, SOARING 70 FT (21 M) OVER THE SNOW AND LANDING CLEANLY ON THE OTHER SIDE.

Versatile Craft

Welsh engineers have created a boat that can operate above or below the waves. Above water, the Scubacraft is propelled by a 160-horsepower engine; when submerged, it is powered by electric thrusters and can descend to a depth of nearly 100 ft (30 m). As it is not a pressurized submarine, those on board must wear scuba-diving gear when diving below the water.

℞ RAIL FEARS

British railway pioneer George Stephenson (1781–1848) told public officials that trains would never go faster than 12 mph (19 km/h). This was to allay public fears that speeds of over 12 mph would bring about mental disorders among passengers.

℞ BUS RESCUE

When the driver of a New York City school bus full of children suffered a fatal heart attack while at the wheel, 16-year-old Rachel Guzy took control and brought the vehicle to a halt as it sped toward a busy intersection. Driver Ramon Fernandez collapsed and tumbled out of the moving bus, but Rachel, who does not know how to drive, jumped into his seat and pulled the emergency brake, slowing the bus right down before it gently crashed into a van.

℞ MISSING TRACK

Driving his train along the track in Hungary's Somogy County, Farkas Kolos suddenly realized that the track ahead had completely disappeared. He slammed on the brakes and managed to bring the train to a halt just short of where the track ended. Police confirmed that 2 mi (3.2 km) of track had been stolen.

℞ LOST CAR RESURFACES

A car that had been buried beneath the dangerous mudflats of Brean Beach, Somerset, England, for 36 years suddenly resurfaced in 2009. Terry Hart's Vauxhall Victor sank in the mud in 1973 after he was trapped by the swift incoming tide. Rough weather and choppy seas eventually led to the car's heavily corroded remains being uncovered.

℞ STEAM POWER

A steam car reached an average speed of 139.8 mph (225 km/h) on two runs over a distance of a mile at the Edwards Air Force Base, California, in August 2009—the fastest speed recorded by a steam car in 103 years! The 25-ft-long (7.6-m) British-built car, driven by Charles Burnett III, actually touched 151 mph (243 km/h) on its second run and has been dubbed "the fastest kettle in the world."

℞ FLYING CAR

From 1949 to 1960, Longview, Washington State, engineer Moulton Taylor built six cars that could also fly. His prototype Aerocar had folding wings that allowed the car to be converted into a plane in five minutes by one person. It could drive at 60 mph (96 km/h) and fly at 110 mph (180 km/h).

℞ CORVETTE BURIAL

In 1994, George Swanson of Hempfield, Pennsylvania, was buried in his beloved 1984 Corvette car. His cremated remains still sit in the driver's seat of the Corvette, which is buried in the local cemetery where it occupies 12 contiguous plots.

℞ CYCLING TOUR

Over a period of nine years, Keiichi Iwasaki from Maebashi, Japan, has cycled more than 28,000 mi (45,000 km) through 37 countries. He originally set out on his Raleigh Shopper bicycle in 2001 to tour Japan, but enjoyed himself so much that he caught a ferry to South Korea and has not returned home since.

℞ WRONG SYDNEY

When Dutchman Joannes Rutten and his 15-year-old grandson Nick booked a flight to Sydney, Australia, in 2009, a mix-up caused them to end up in the small former mining town of Sydney, Nova Scotia, Canada. They set off from Amsterdam hoping to visit relatives in Australia, only to touch down on Cape Breton Island, 10,000 mi (16,000 km) from their intended destination.

℞ LONG BIKE

Colin Furze of Lincolnshire, England, spent two months creating a 46-ft-long (14-m) motorbike. He used two Honda 50cc mopeds, which he extended with pieces of aluminum. The elongated bike can travel at speeds of up to 30 mph (48 km/h) but needs six widths of an ordinary road to turn!

DREAM MACHINE

A BROOKLYN-BASED ARTIST COLLABORATIVE—GHOST OF A DREAM (LAUREN WAS AND ADAM ECKSTROM)—CREATED A LIFE-SIZE REPLICA OF A HUMMER H-3 FROM $39,000-WORTH OF LOSING LOTTERY TICKETS. THEIR ARTWORK, TITLED "EASY MONEY, DREAM CAR," FEATURES WINDSHIELD WIPERS, TIRES AND BODY PANELS MADE ENTIRELY FROM LOTTERY TICKETS. THE WHEEL HUBS ARE PLASTIC CASTS OF COIN-COVERED HUBCAPS TO REPRESENT THE TOOL PEOPLE GENERALLY USE TO SCRATCH OFF THE TICKETS.

R MASS ASCENT

In 2009, a total of 326 hot-air balloons took to the skies simultaneously at the Lorraine Mondial Air Balloons rally in eastern France.

R TRUCK SHOWER

A Chinese truck driver was fined in 2009 for having a shower while driving along the country's busy Jinyi expressway. Police officers stopped the truck after spotting water leaking from the cab, but were shocked to see that the driver was soaking wet and had been enjoying a shower from a sprinkler system installed above his head. His wife, sitting in the passenger seat, had been holding up a sheet of plastic to protect the vehicle's instruments from the water.

R MAIL BOAT

The mail boat *J.W. Westcott II*, based in Detroit, Michigan, delivers mail to other vessels that pass along the Detroit River and even has its own postal zip code, 48222.

R MINI MOTOR

Perry Watkins from Buckinghamshire, England, has created a roadworthy car that is only 39 in (1 m) high and 26 in (66 cm) wide. Remembering the children's TV character Postman Pat and his mail delivery van, Watkins bought a Postman Pat coin-in-the-slot children's ride on the Internet, reinforced its fiberglass shell with a steel frame and mounted it onto a mini four-wheeled bike before adding a 150cc engine, mirrors, windshield wipers and lights.

R CROC WALK

A 12-in-long (30-cm) baby crocodile caused panic among passengers on an EgyptAir flight from Abu Dhabi to Cairo in July 2009 when it decided to take a walk down the aisle of the airplane.

R SCHOOL RUN

Having missed his bus one morning in January 2009, a six-year-old boy from Richmond, Virginia, took the keys to his family's Ford Taurus car and decided he would drive to school. He crashed into a utility pole on the way, but escaped with only minor injuries.

R ECO TRAVELERS

Eco-friendly Tom Fewins and Lara Lockwood of Oxfordshire, England, traveled more than 44,000 mi (70,800 km) around the world in 297 days—without once boarding an airplane. They made their way through 19 countries— including Russia, China and the U.S.A., using 78 buses, 61 trains, 34 cars, 18 boats, 6 bicycles, 2 mopeds and 1 elephant. They say they each generated less than 6,600 lb (3,000 kg) of carbon dioxide on their journey, one-third of the amount they would have generated if they had traveled by airplane.

R CARDBOARD CARS

Police in Sibiu County, Romania, use cardboard cutouts of patrol cars on roadsides to frighten speeders into slowing down.

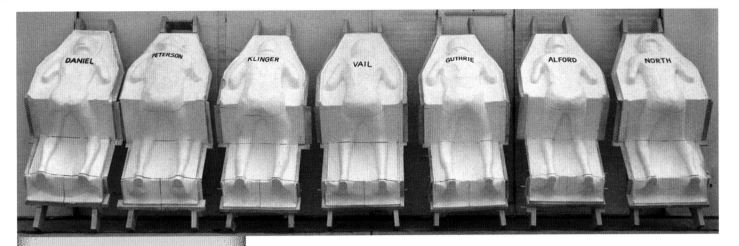

DANIEL PETERSON KLINGER VAIL GUTHRIE ALFORD NORTH

Butt Molds

In the early days of NASA, for reasons of comfort and safety, astronauts on manned space missions sat on couches individually molded to fit their body shape. None of the names on these test seats—pictured at NASA's Langley Research Center at Hampton, Virginia, in 1959—made it aboard the pioneering *Mercury* spacecraft: They belonged to NASA employees.

STUDENT PRANK

Pranksters from the Massachusetts Institute of Technology in Cambridge placed a 25-ft-long (7.6-m) fire truck on top of the school's Great Dome building in 2006. The joke followed a noble tradition. A fiberglass steer from a local restaurant was placed on the dome in 1979, as was a phone booth in 1982, and in 2003 a 45-ft (14-m) replica of the Wright brothers' biplane mysteriously appeared on top of the Great Dome to mark the 100th anniversary of flight.

ROMANTIC ROAD

When it was constructed in 2003, the M6 motorway toll road near Birmingham, England, was paved with 2.5 million pulped Mills-and-Boon romantic novels. The books' paper helps keep the road's tarmac in place and also absorbs noise.

AUDI PARTNER

An Audi car that an elderly woman from Hildesheim, Germany, reported stolen resurfaced two years later buried beneath a layer of dust in her neighbor's garage. She had asked mechanics repairing the car in 2007 to return it to her garage, but they had mistakenly put it in her neighbor's unused garage, where it had remained undetected until the summer of 2009.

HOMEMADE HELICOPTER

Despite having only a basic school education, 20-year-old Wu Zhongyuan of Luoyang, Henan Province, China, in 2009, made his own helicopter, which he claims can fly to a height of 2,625 ft (800 m). It took him nearly three months to build his flying machine, which has a motorcycle engine and wooden blades made from an elm tree.

All Aboard

India has the world's largest rail network. Over 18 million people travel on Indian trains every day—more passengers than any other country—as a result of which trains are often alarmingly overcrowded. Passengers sit on carriage roofs or cling to the sides, with some trains carrying over 3,000 people—twice the intended capacity.

Joe Price from Gloucester, England, was a champion strongman in the 1920s and 1930s, and could bend a solid metal bar between his teeth. He was reported to have had a chest measuring 58 in (147 cm) in circumference and was renowned for the power of his hands. A blacksmith by trade, Price would train with large sledgehammers instead of conventional weights. In 1932, Robert Ripley released a cartoon that showed Price writing successfully with a 50-lb (25-kg) weight attached to his little finger.

Ripley Revealed

PLAYING WITH FIRE

BOTH FIRE-BREATHING AND FIRE-EATING CARRY MAJOR RISKS—SIMPLY INHALING WHILE SWALLOWING FIRE CAN LEAD TO A SEVERELY BURNED MOUTH AND EVEN DEATH. THESE METHODS EACH REQUIRE DIFFERENT SKILLS. A FIRE-BREATHER USES HIS OR HER MOUTH TO SPRAY A FLAMMABLE LIQUID OVER AN OPEN FLAME, CREATING A LARGE, SPECTACULAR BALL OF FIRE FROM THE MOUTH. A FIRE-EATER PLACES FLAMING OBJECTS INTO THE MOUTH AND EXTINGUISHES THEM.

Fire-breathers must avoid highly explosive flammable liquids such as alcohol and spirit-based fuels, and use safer fuels, such as flash point, highly purified lamp oil or paraffin, which is one of the most popular fire-breathing tools. Most of the liquids used by fire-breathers are nontoxic, but inhalations of anything in the lungs other than clean air can potentially lead to fatal conditions.

Dragon's Breath

The fire-breathing trick known as Napalm Dragon's Breath—when the fire-breather removes the fuel or torch and continues to breathe fire—is exceptionally dangerous, as the performer must know how to control his breathing so as not to inhale the flames.

RIPLEY'S RESEARCH

FIRE-EATERS: TAKE A DEEP BREATH AND BEGIN TO EXHALE SLOWLY AS THE LIGHTED TORCH IS LOWERED TOWARD THE MOUTH. THIS KEEPS THE HEAT AWAY FROM THE PERFORMER'S FACE. WITH THE TONGUE WIDE AND FLAT, THE FIRE-EATER PLACES THE WICK OF THE TORCH (WHICH SHOULD BE COOL TO THE TOUCH) ONTO THE TONGUE AND PARTIALLY CLOSES THE LIPS AROUND THE TORCH IN AN "O" SHAPE. TO EXTINGUISH THE FLAME, THE LIPS CAN EITHER BE CLOSED ENTIRELY AROUND THE TORCH, THUS CUTTING OFF THE OXYGEN SUPPLY, OR THE FLAME CAN BE PUT OUT BY MEANS OF A QUICK EXHALING BREATH.

FIRE-BREATHERS: AVOID HIGHLY EXPLOSIVE FLAMMABLE LIQUIDS, SUCH AS ALCOHOL, AND USE SAFER FUELS SUCH AS PARAFFIN. FIRE-BREATHERS ALWAYS CHECK THE WIND DIRECTION BEFORE THEY PERFORM AND CARRY A CLOTH TO WIPE FUEL FROM THE MOUTH IN BETWEEN BREATHING, SO AS NOT TO SET THEMSELVES ON FIRE. BREATHERS WITH BEARDS TAKE EXTRA CARE WHEN WIPING AWAY THE FLAMMABLE SUBSTANCE!

THERE ARE NO REAL TRICKS TO WORKING WITH FIRE. PERFORMERS HAVE TO REMEMBER THAT HEAT TRAVELS UPWARD AND THEY MUST BE PREPARED TO ENDURE PAIN. TOLERATING BLISTERS ON THE TONGUE, THROAT AND LIPS IS ALL PART OF THE JOB.

HISTORY HOT SPOT

Robert Powell was the most famous of the early fire-eaters. He performed in London in the 18th century, charging a shilling for entry to his shows, at which he would eat hot coals and melted sealing wax, and lick a naked flame with his tongue. He also used to take a large bunch of matches, light them and hold them in his mouth until the flame was extinguished, and he sometimes filled his mouth with red-hot charcoal.

A Close Shave

In late-1930s U.S.A., Dr. Mayfield, a popular fire manipulator, came to the forefront of the fire-performing world when he appeared at Ripley's Odditoriums. His act involved shaving himself with a "blazing blowtorch" before putting the torch into his mouth and extinguishing it.

Fire-ing Solo

The following fire-breathing stunts have been developed over the centuries and are known as "One Person Blasts."

45-degree Fire Blast 45-degree up angle, one of the most basic fire-breathing tricks

Camp Fire Flame is directly bounced off the ground

Hell Fire Fireball is breathed straight down and the performer rises as the flames engulf him

Carousel Whilst rotating through a full circle, the performer creates a long horizontal blast

Corkscrew Almost vertical duration blast while the breather spins under it

Popcorn Breather performs three or more short blasts of fire without refueling

Serpent Performer breathes alternative up and down horizontal flames while walking

Moving Fire Breather lights a torch held 3 ft (1 m) from the ignition torch with a sustained blast

SHARK ATTACK

CRAIG CLASEN FROM MISSISSIPPI FOUGHT A TIGER SHARK FOR OVER TWO HOURS IN A FEROCIOUS BATTLE OF LIFE OR DEATH. CRAIG, AN EXPERT SPEAR FISHERMAN, WAS HUNTING BLUEFIN TUNA IN THE GULF OF MEXICO WITH A SMALL GROUP WHEN A 12-FT (4-M) SHARK BEGAN CIRCLING ONE OF THEM. CRAIG INSTINCTIVELY GRABBED HIS SPEARGUN AND STABBED THE SHARK WHEN IT MADE A MOVE TO ATTACK. ONCE HE HAD INJURED THE CREATURE, CRAIG SAID HE FELT A MORAL OBLIGATION TO FINISH THE JOB AND KILL THE SHARK AS HUMANELY AS POSSIBLE. HE SHOT IT SIX TIMES IN THE HEAD WITH HIS SPEARS, BUT SHARKS ARE EXTREMELY RESILIENT AND HE WAS EVENTUALLY FORCED TO KILL IT WITH A BLADE KNIFE THROUGH ITS SKULL. AN EXPERIENCED DIVER AND FISHERMAN, CRAIG HAS COME INTO CONTACT WITH THOUSANDS OF SHARKS IN HIS LIFETIME AND SAID THAT THIS ENCOUNTER WAS RARE AND THE FIRST INCIDENT WHERE HE HAS HAD TO TAKE SERIOUS ACTION TO PROTECT HIMSELF.

℞ HOT RIDER

In summer temperatures of up to 118°F (48°C), Omar Al Mamari, founder President of the Oman Bike Club, rode a motorcycle 1,281 mi (2,062 km)—from Muscat to Salalah and back—in 24 hours in 2009.

℞ FIRE WALL

In March 2009, the Marine Corps Air Station in Yuma, Arizona, created a 15-story-high wall of flame that stretched for 10,173 ft (3,100 m)—that's nearly 2 mi (3.2 km) long. The wall of fire was made up of dynamite, electric blasting caps and 20,000 ft (6,100 m) of detonation cord.

℞ DAPPER DAREDEVIL

Dressed in a tweed jacket, and shirt and tie, dapper daredevil Les Pugh of Gloucestershire, England, abseiled down the side of a 160-ft-high (49-m) office block in the town of Cheltenham in April 2009—at age 93!

℞ ON THE EDGE

In April 2009, 15-year-old Duncan Harris of Normal, Illinois, rode a unicycle on a treacherous 12-mi (19-km) journey along cliff trails at Moab, Utah. He had no brakes except his own legs, no handlebars, and drops of hundreds of feet were just inches away.

℞ SPEEDY WHEELIE

Fifteen-year-old Jake Drummond maintained a bicycle wheelie for over 330 ft (100 m) at Oshkosh, Wisconsin, in July 2009—and covered the distance in just over 15 seconds.

℞ DEATH RACE

Among the competitors in the 2009 Canadian Death Race—run over 78 mi (125 km) of mountainous terrain—was a blind woman, 57-year-old Lorraine Pitt from Peterborough, Ontario. Competitors carry their own supplies in the event, held annually in Grand Cache, Alberta. The race begins and ends on a 4,200-ft-high (1,280-m) plateau, passes over three mountain summits as well as bogs, forests and a river, and includes 17,000 ft (5,180 m) of elevation change.

Mountain Bike

Extreme yoga artist Khiv Raj Gurjar from Jodhpur in Rajasthan, India, balances in extraordinary positions on his bicycle just inches from the edge of rocky outcrops 300 ft (90 m) high. Khiv, who has been practicing and studying yoga since the age of 13, decided to combine both his loves—cycling and yoga—to create this striking discipline in 2006. Now in his sixties, Khiv practices daily for an hour and can perform up to 36 yoga moves balancing on his BMX bike.

℞ SOLO VOYAGE

Sarah Outen from Rutland, England, rowed solo across the Indian Ocean in 2009, making the 4,000-mi (6,400-km) journey from Perth, Australia, to the island of Mauritius, off the east coast of Africa, in 124 days. She spent up to 12 hours a day rowing, often in scorching sun and riding 30-ft (9-m) waves.

R BAR TURNS

In Yerevan, Armenia, in July 2009, Armenian gymnast Davit Fahradyan completed no fewer than 354 turns on a horizontal bar.

R LIMBO SKATER

In July 2009, seven-year-old Abbishek Navale, of Belgaum, India, limbo skated backward under ten multi-utility vehicles (Tata Sumo Jeeps). A few days later, he limbo skated backward a distance of 62 ft (18.8 m), under a series of bars positioned just 8.7 in (22 cm) above the ground. Abbishek, who has also skated 335 mi (540 km) from Bangalore to Belgaum in six days, practices his considerable skills for 2½ hours every day.

R CANADA RIDE

Riding about 185 mi (300 km) a day, Corneliu Dobrin of Abbotsford, British Columbia, Canada, cycled 4,475 mi (7,200 km) across Canada in just 24 days in July 2009. He departed from Vancouver and finished his epic ride in St. John's, Newfoundland.

R KAYAK PLUNGE

Kayaker Tyler Bradt of Missoula, Montana, plunged 186 ft (57 m) in four seconds over the Palouse Falls, Washington State, in July 2009—and emerged with nothing worse than a sprained wrist and a broken paddle. He had visited the spot four times before plucking up the courage to tackle the waterfall, which is so high the spray it generates creates its own rainbow.

R BALANCING ACT

Wearing no harness despite being hundreds of feet up in the air, 24-year-old tightrope walker Samat Hasan, from the Xinjiang region of China, climbed 2,300 ft (700 m) along a high wire spanning a valley in Hunan Province in April 2009. The cable was just 1.2 in (3 cm) wide and had a steep gradient of 39 degrees.

R YOUNG HUNTER

In September 2009, 16-year-old Cammie Colin of Pelion, South Carolina, bagged an alligator 10 ft 5 in (3.2 m) long and weighing 353 lb (160 kg)—in the middle of the night—with a crossbow. Having won a lottery slot for the state's annual public alligator harvest, she shot her prize while out with her family and a guide in an 18-ft (5.4-m) boat on Lake Marion.

R 80 PLUS

Two teams of hockey players—all over the age of 80—took to the ice for a seniors' tournament in Burnaby, British Columbia, Canada in 2009. The oldest player to take part was 87-year-old goaltender Jim Martin.

R FINGER POWER

Kung-fu master Ho Eng Hui pierced four coconuts with just his index finger in a little over 30 seconds in Malacca, Malaysia, in June 2009.

R COURAGEOUS WALK

Phil Packer, a Royal Military Police Officer in the British Army, was so badly injured in a rocket attack in Basra, Iraq, in February 2008 that he was told he would never walk again. Yet a year later he walked the 26.2-mi (42-km) London Marathon on crutches.

R PAPER PLANE

Engineer Takuo Toda, chairman of the Japan Origami Airplane Association, kept a 4-in (10-cm) paper airplane in flight for 27.9 seconds at a competition in Hiroshima Prefecture in April 2009.

R BOTTLE BALANCE

In 2008, Alexander Bendikov of Belarus balanced 18,000 matchsticks horizontally on a bottleneck without using any adhesive.

Dirt Diving

On Pentecost Island in the South Pacific, young men prove their courage by making a 75-ft (25-m) bungee jump headfirst into the earth below. The ritual, known as Naghol (land diving), involves up to 25 men a day jumping from a rickety wooden tower with only vines tying their feet together. Traditionally, between the months of April and May, people would jump to bless the soil for an excellent yam harvest. However, today the ritual is a death-defying act of bravery for young men and boys, some as young as seven or eight years old. Elders tie a vine to each foot while women dance and chant at the sides, hoping the men survive.

Both Mike and his yacht were fitted with the latest hi-tech equipment to survive the harsh conditions.

At home in his cabin—containing bunk, galley, supplies and navigation equipment—Mike catches up on studying for his driving test.

When Mike and his boat were in South Africa for repairs, he met 75-year-old Japanese sailor Minoru Saito, who was in the middle of his eighth circumnavigation of the globe. During his lifetime, Minoru has sailed almost 310,685 mi (500,000 km), the equivalent of sailing to the Moon.

Aged just 17, Mike Perham from Hertfordshire, England, completed a single-handed, round-the-world sailing voyage in August 2009. The intrepid teenager set off from Portsmouth, England, in November 2008—then aged only 16—on board a hi-tech 50-ft (15-m) racing yacht hired especially for the challenge. The circumnavigation took Mike down the west coast of Africa and south of Australia, where damage to the yacht's rudder forced him to wait for repairs before setting off into the treacherous Southern Ocean. Here, the boat battled through freezing seas and 50-ft (15-m) swells. Fifty-knot (57-mph) winds knocked the boat flat to the waves before the heavy keel pulled it upright. Mike was forced to climb the 70-ft (21-m) mast in the middle of the ocean to fix rigging in the knockdown, and had to dive under the boat to cut free snagged ropes. The yacht then sailed up the coast of South America and through the Panama Canal before the final leg of the journey took Mike across the Atlantic, landing at Portsmouth in August: nine months and 24,233 mi (39,000 km) later. The light, hi-speed racing yacht was cramped, noisy and uncomfortable, making it very hard to get rest. Mike slept for about five hours out of every 24, snatching 20-minute naps while the boat was kept on course by an electronic autopilot. With nobody else on deck, there was a danger of colliding with vessels at night and ramming surface hazards such as shipping containers and marine debris. Mike was harnessed to the boat at all times in case he was swept overboard and all of his food was freeze-dried and rationed.

Mike lets off flares to celebrate his return to England after nine months at sea.

The boat rode ocean waves the size of five-story buildings.

WORLD BEATER

Mike had to climb the 70-ft (21-m) mast in the middle of the ocean to carry out repairs.

RIPLEY'S ask

What drove you to start this challenge?
At 14 I became the youngest person to sail solo across the Atlantic. Once I had done that, I knew the next step was to sail around the world alone.

Was the hi-tech boat uncomfortable? How did you sleep?
Totallymoney.com is an Open 50 racing yacht. She is fast, functional and like a racing car...very basic inside. I had a transverse bunk running across the front of the navigation station and the galley consisted of a small sink and single-burner stove. I had to be alert the whole time, even when asleep! I got into the routine of cat-napping for 20 minutes at a time, then checking the boat and adjusting the sails or course. If the motion suddenly changed, my subconscious sensed it immediately and I would wake

up. I also had alarms on the radar, depth sounder and chart plotter that would warn me of anything untoward, though none of these things could identify an iceberg.

What was the toughest part of the trip?
Being away from friends and family. Also, I had to climb the mast three times to make repairs and I don't like heights.

Were you ever worried?
Certainly.

What was the most memorable part of the voyage?
The Southern Ocean without doubt. It was cold and wet down there, but it was certainly exciting. I was surfing along at speeds very close to 30 knots (35 mph) and they were by far the best experiences. I was wearing a grin from ear to ear during those days.

Were you glad to get back on dry land?
It was fantastic to get back and fulfill my dream of becoming the youngest person to sail solo around the world. To get such a big reception and see all my friends and family on the dock was just the icing on the cake. It took a few days to get into the routine of sleeping through the night, but I settled in surprisingly easy and it was fantastic to be back with all my friends.

Do you have any future sailing plans?
The next plan is the *Bounty* boat expedition. In a nutshell, four of us are going to re-enact Capt. William Bligh's 4,000-mi (6,450-km) voyage across the Pacific in an open boat following the story of the *Mutiny on the Bounty*, sailing from Tonga across to Timor!

CHAMPION CRAWLER

The city of Vilnius, Lithuania, stages an annual baby-crawling contest where tiny tots crawl along a 16-ft (5-m) carpeted track, encouraged by their parents waving keys and toys at the finish line. The 2009 winner was eight-month-old Kajus Aukscionis, who completed the course in 18 seconds.

Claws Encounter

INSPIRED BY EDWARD SCISSORHANDS, VALENTINO LOSAURO HAS DEVELOPED FINGERTIP SCISSORS, WHICH ARE MADE FROM ELASTIC AND RAZOR-SHARP STEEL. THEY CUT HAIR TWICE AS FAST AS SCISSORS, CLAIMS LOSAURO, A PIANIST, WHO WANTED TO APPLY THE LIGHT-FINGER TOUCH OF PIANO PLAYING TO STYLING HAIR. "WHEN I CUT HAIR I USE METHODS I CALL 'FLIGHT OF THE BUMBLEBEE,'" HE SAYS, REFERRING TO THE QUICK-FINGER ACTION HE NOW USES AT HIS FLORIDA SALON. "I CAN'T BELIEVE HOW LONG A CUT USED TO TAKE."

Case in Point

It took George Gaspar, from Sherman Oaks, California, just 90 minutes to insert 2,222 toothpicks into his beard.

KISSING FRENZY

Twenty young women lined up in Blackburn, England, in 2009 to give 28-year-old local DJ Paul Winstanley 110 kisses in one minute— that's almost two kisses a second.

DUCK RACE

A staggering 205,000 plastic ducks floated 0.6 mi (1 km) down the River Thames near London, England, in the 2009 Great British Duck Race.

BRICK SMASHER

Using a combination of speed and power, German martial arts expert Bernd Hoehle smashed 12 freestanding bricks in just eight seconds in Hanover, Germany, in 2009.

MOOSE FAN

Al Goddard of Takoma Park, Maryland, has collected more than 1,000 items of moose memorabilia. His collection began in 1975 when he was teaching at a school in Oakton, Virginia, and a student presented him with a stuffed toy moose as a gift.

COFFIN MAKER

During a career spanning more than 30 years, carpenter Herbert Weber from Austria's Salzburg province has built over 700,000 coffins.

PUMPKIN FACES

In October 2008, Stephen Clarke of Havertown, Pennsylvania, carved jack-o'-lantern faces into one ton's worth of pumpkins in 3 hours 33 minutes 49 seconds at Atlantic City, New Jersey.

℞ YOUNG PARAGLIDER

Luan Da Silva from Florianopolis, Brazil, is already an experienced paraglider even though he is just six years old. Both of his parents are paragliding instructors and he made his first flight with his father at age two and his first solo flight a year later. Sitting in a specially weighted harness to stop him from blowing away, Luan loves to leap from the top of a sand dune and soar 65 ft (20 m) into the air.

℞ WEEKLY COLUMN

At age 102, former 1940s pin-up girl Margaret Caldwell was still writing a weekly column, "Memoirs of a Crone," for the *Desert Valley Times* newspaper in Mesquite, Nevada.

℞ TALKATIVE TEEN

Thirteen-year-old Reina Hardesty from Orange County, California, used her cell phone to send 14,528 text messages during the month of December 2008. That worked out at 484 text messages every day—an average of one message every two minutes while she was awake. The online monthly phone-bill statement ran to 440 pages.

℞ GIANT PUZZLE

Indian jigsaw-puzzle enthusiasts created an online jigsaw puzzle with 25,000 pieces in 2009. The challenge attracted over 180,000 participants, each working with 1,000 blocks of 25 pieces to assemble a large image designed by New Zealand jigsaw expert Royce B. McClure. In its physical form, the puzzle measured 36 x 16 ft (11 x 5 m).

℞ ZOMBIE PARTY

In July 2009, a grand total of 3,894 people dressed as zombies for the "Red, White and Dead Zombie Party" event in Seattle, Washington State.

℞ FAMILY RUN

Sixteen brothers and sisters from the Kapral family of Oshkosh, Wisconsin, finished the 2009 Fox Cities Marathon— and all in under six hours. Only two of the family—brothers Vince and Stephen—had completed a full marathon before.

℞ KITE DISPLAY

Some 4,000 Palestinian children flew kites simultaneously for 30 seconds on beaches of the Gaza Strip in July 2009.

℞ YOSEMITE WALK

Without any safety equipment, American Dean Potter walked an unleashed slackline—a rope length that isn't taut—3,200 ft (960 m) above the floor of Yosemite Valley, California. The only things holding him to the rope during his 100-ft (30-m) walk were his size-14 feet.

℞ PIE FIGHT

More than 200 people took part in a mass pie fight on a farm at Genoa, Illinois, in 2009. The fight, organized by farm-owner Molly Holbrook, involved participants hurling chocolate, meringue, pumpkin and custard pies at each other.

℞ MILK DELIVERY

For nearly 100 years, three generations of the Hall family delivered milk to the village of Gunnislake in Cornwall, England, placing an estimated 20 million pints on people's doorsteps. The last in the line, Jo Hall, retired in 2009 after 55 years in the job, during which time she clocked up 176,000 mi (283,245 km) doing her milk delivery round.

℞ FLOWER GARLAND

In May 2009, residents of San Pedro, the Philippines, strung together a *sampaguita lei*—a flower garland—that measured more than 1¼ mi (2 km) long.

A Game of Squash

Austrian artist Willi Dorner is causing a stir across Europe by squeezing bodies into nooks and crannies across the continent. Groups of dancers, climbers and performers, wearing brightly colored clothes, run through busy malls and high streets and suddenly cram themselves into doorways, trees and any gap they can find.

SWORD SWALLOWING

DESPITE VERY REAL DANGERS, SWORD SWALLOWING IS FAR FROM A DYING ART AND A HARDCORE BAND OF ENTHUSIASTS ARE DETERMINED TO KEEP CROWDS THRILLED BY SWALLOWING DOWN A COUPLE OF FEET OF SOLID STEEL FOR THEIR ENTERTAINMENT. BELIEVED TO HAVE ORIGINATED 4,000 YEARS AGO IN INDIA, THE DEADLY FEAT OF SWORD SWALLOWING WAS FEATURED IN THE VERY FIRST RIPLEY'S BELIEVE IT OR NOT! ODDITORIUM IN CHICAGO IN 1933. TODAY THERE ARE NO MORE THAN 100 PROFESSIONAL SWORD SWALLOWERS IN THE WORLD.

Space Cowboy

Chayne "Space Cowboy" Hultgren, a street performer from Australia, is one of the most extreme sword swallowers around. He has swallowed a sword with a 49-lb (22.4-kg) weight suspended from it, and was the first man to swallow a sword underwater—in a tank full of live sharks. Chayne was born with an internal deformation of his digestive system so his stomach sits unusually low. This means that the Space Cowboy can swallow the entire length of a 28½-in (72-cm) sword blade— a blade longer than any other swallower can manage— so that it reaches an inch below his belly button. To conquer the extra long sword, Chayne is able to rearrange his internal organs, elongate his body and change the shape of his stomach.

In 2008, Chayne Hultgren swallowed 27 swords at once, more than anyone had ever done before.

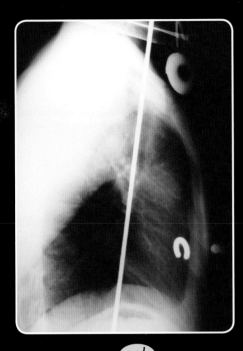

X-ray photographs were taken as Chayne Hultgren swallowed a sword, proving beyond a doubt that there is no illusion involved. He also hammered a 5-in (12.7-cm) nail into his nose at the same time—this is also clearly visible on the X ray.

nail

sword

RIPLEY'S ask

Why did you start sword swallowing? I have been performing street shows since I was eight years old, and as a teenager I began to get tired of the same old traditional circus skills, I wanted to do something more bizarre, more unique and more extreme. Sword swallowing just seemed like the most adventurous skill that I could learn, but I don't think I quite realized how dangerous my new career choice would be.

Was it hard to learn? Yes, it is very hard to learn. I guess I am lucky that I started to force hoses and other objects down my throat at an early age. You need to learn to control muscles that are usually involuntary and this can take many years. I started training for sword swallowing when I was 16 years old.

In the beginning I swallowed a piece of string with a small piece of food tied to the end. I then moved on to forcing hoses down my throat to train the muscles of my esophagus. Every time a person swallows we have circular muscles that retract in our throat. You need to control these muscles so that when you swallow with a blade down your esophagus these muscles stay open and do not get sliced on the blade.

Doesn't it hurt? No, it doesn't hurt, but it is very uncomfortable. Having a foreign object in your throat instantly makes you gag and vomit, and this is just the first obstacle that you need to overcome in order to swallow a sword. I am constantly pushing myself to make the impossible possible, and in order to do this I need to make the pain I experience obsolete. If you want something enough, pain is no longer an issue.

Have you ever had an accident? I was born with an internal deformation of my digestive system that enables me to swallow a sword deeper than any other sword swallower that has ever lived. When I first started swallowing the long sword I was 20 years old, and in a moment of distraction I sliced my stomach lining in a performance. Backstage I started vomiting blood and was rushed to a hospital. To the doctor's amazement I swallowed an endoscope with no anesthetic! I was prescribed serious drugs to stop any infection. It was a lucky escape. It was ten years before I would attempt this swallow again.

Do you train a lot? On days that I am not performing I do need to keep my internal muscles finely tuned, so I use meditation and internal isolation techniques to stay sword-swallowing fit. In my business any mistake is potentially a deadly one!

What are your future ambitions? I love pushing the boundaries of what people think is possible. I regularly perform what is considered by many to be impossible, in the hope that just by seeing these extreme acts people may consider the endless possibilities of what they can achieve.

TURN OVER FOR MORE! ▶

The "Space Cowboy" swallows the entire length of a 2-ft (60-cm) neon glass tube, which is powered by 2,000 volts and filled with deadly mercury gas.

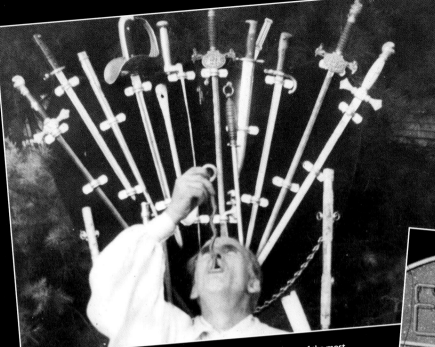

John "Lucky" Ball learnt sword swallowing at the age of 12, becoming one of the most accomplished sword swallowers of his generation. He is pictured here swallowing a corkscrew at a Ripley's Odditorium, a feat more dangerous than a straight sword. "Lucky" Ball could swallow more swords than anyone else at the time, and on one occasion he downed 16.

Accidents do happen...

Sword swallowers often try to swallow objects other than swords, but this is not always a good idea... In 1891, the sword swallower Patrick Mulraney attempted to swallow a violin bow, causing him to vomit blood live on stage. He died soon after. In 1932, after swallowing a watch and chain and then returning it to its owner, professional sword swallower Fred Lowe swallowed a fork, which unfortunately stuck in his throat. It could not be dislodged but eventually dropped down into his stomach. It was surgically removed and Lowe made a full recovery. In 1936, the *Chicago Daily Tribune* reported that experienced sword swallower Bob Roberts died when his trick of swallowing a shotgun barrel and igniting a fuse literally backfired. In 1947, Tony Marnio successfully swallowed 2 ft (60 cm) of neon tubing, which lit up inside him for the audience to see. However, when he attempted to bow, the glass tube shattered and he was rushed to hospital. Francis F. Doran had been swallowing swords for 30 years when a 36-in (91-cm) neon tube exploded before he could remove it from his body in 1969. Surgery was required to remove the glass. Finally, a German sword swallower died after swallowing an umbrella in Bonn, Germany, in 1999. He had accidentally pressed the button that opened the umbrella while it was still inside him.

Ripley's Sword Frights

Sword swallowers have performed at Ripley museums since 1933, when the very first "Odditorium" opened at the Chicago World's Fair. In 1939, Ripley performer Edna Price swallowed electrified neon tubes, and was believed by Robert Ripley to be the first woman to do so, and other entertainers wowed the crowds with their death-defying blade guzzling.

Edna Price, seen here swallowing neon tubes, came from a sword-swallowing family. Her Aunt Maude died in 1920 after swallowing a sword for the King and Queen of England. Edna would swallow up to 12 practice swords at the same time, removing the blades one at a time. She would have her swords chromed each year to protect against nicks and scratches.

Ripley's Sword Swallowing Day

A transatlantic event packed with dangerous stunts took place on February 28, 2009. At precisely 2.28 p.m., 24 sword swallowers swallowed over 100 ft (30 m) of solid steel at Ripley museums from Niagara Falls to London, to mark International Sword Swallowers Awareness Day.

Joseph Grendol swallowed seven swords simultaneously at the Chicago Odditorium in 1934. He could also swallow watches, golf balls and coins before regurgitating them. Probably his greatest stunt was placing a bayonet on the butt of a rifle, swallowing the bayonet up to the rifle butt, and then shooting the rifle!

Alex Linton was originally from Ireland. His father was also a sword swallower. At the climax of his act, Linton would throw his final sword into a block of wood on the stage to make sure the audience knew it was real, and sharp!

®IPLEY'S RESEARCH

DO NOT TRY THIS AT HOME!

IT CAN TAKE YEARS TO LEARN HOW TO SWALLOW FULL-SIZED SWORDS (THOSE WHICH ARE AT LEAST 15 IN (38 CM) LONG). PERFORMERS OFTEN START WITH THEIR OWN FINGERS, OR HOUSEHOLD OBJECTS LIKE SPOONS AND KNITTING NEEDLES, TO TRY AND OVERCOME THE GAG REFLEX THAT PREVENTS US FROM SWALLOWING LARGE, DANGEROUS FOREIGN OBJECTS SUCH AS SWORDS!

SWORD SWALLOWING REQUIRES INTENSE CONTROL OF THE BODY, YET PERFORMERS MUST BE FULLY RELAXED AT THE SAME TIME, A PROBLEM WHEN THE MUSCLES INVOLVED USUALLY RESPOND AUTOMATICALLY IN A REFLEX ACTION. PERFORMERS MUST LEARN TO CONTROL ALL THE CIRCULAR MUSCLES IN THE THROAT THAT SQUEEZE FOOD TOWARD YOUR STOMACH. IT IS INCREDIBLY DANGEROUS TO DISTRACT A SWORD SWALLOWER IN THE MIDDLE OF THEIR ACT, AND ANY DISTRACTION COULD PROVE FATAL, AS THE SWORD MUST PASS VERY CLOSE TO CRITICAL AREAS SUCH AS THE WINDPIPE, VITAL BLOOD VESSELS AND THE HEART. SWALLOWING MULTIPLE SWORDS CAN HAVE A SCISSOR-LIKE EFFECT, GREATLY INCREASING THE DANGER OF CUTS TO THE THROAT.

THE ESOPHAGUS HAS NATURAL CURVES AND KINKS DEPENDING ON THE POSITION OF THE BODY, SO THE SOLID SWORD HAS TO PHYSICALLY STRAIGHTEN THESE OUT AS IT MOVES DOWN. IF THE SWORD IS TOO LONG, OR IF THE PERFORMER LOSES CONTROL, IT CAN DROP INTO THE STOMACH AND CAUSE PERFORATIONS—THIS HAS KILLED MORE THAN ONE SWORD SWALLOWER IN THE PAST.

Revealed . . .

Balloon Burst!

Jemal Tkeshelashvili from Georgia in the former Soviet Union is able to inflate a hot-water bottle extremely quickly until it bursts, using only his nose. He is so fast that he managed to burst one of the bottles in only 13 seconds at an unusual contest in Tbilisi, Georgia. Jemel also competes as a strongman, and can pull a Boeing Airliner with just his bare hands.

Ⓡ FIVE-DAY SPEECH

At the railway station in Perpignan, France, in January 2009, 62-year-old Catalan local-government worker Lluis Colet spoke for five straight days and four nights—a total of 124 hours—about Spanish painter Salvador Dali and Catalan culture.

Ⓡ SUPER SHOOTER

Thirty-four-year-old novice Jim Collins of Cambridgeshire, England, beat experienced rivals from as far afield as the U.S.A., Australia and New Zealand to be crowned world peashooting champion of 2009. The championships, which were started in 1971 by Cambridgeshire school principal John Tyson, who had confiscated a peashooter from a pupil, require competitors to puff peas from a distance of 12 ft (3.6 m) at a 12-in (30-cm) target. Some entrants even use laser-guided peashooters!

Ⓡ GIANT CIGAR

Sixty-five-year-old Cuban Jose Castelar, who has been making cigars since the age of 14, rolled a monster 142-ft-long (43.3-m) cigar in 2009—that's ten times the height of a double-decker bus.

Ⓡ CHANNEL WINGWALK

In July 2009, Tom Lackey, 89, from West Midlands, England, flew across the English Channel at 1,000 ft (305 m) and more than 100 mph (160 km/h) while strapped to the wings of a vintage airplane. The daredevil grandfather performed his amazing wingwalk over a 22-mi (40-km) stretch of water separating France and England on a plane that was just 20 years younger than him.

Ⓡ JET PACK

Using a jet pack powered by hydrogen peroxide, Eric Scott of Denver, Colorado, clocked a speed of 68 mph (109 km/h) at Knockhill Racing Circuit, Scotland, in May 2009. Although Scott's jet pack currently carries only enough fuel to fly him for 30 seconds, it was sufficient for him to beat a Ford Focus RS car driven by British Touring Car champion Gordon Shedden in a drag race.

Ⓡ IPLEY'S ask

What did you eat during your time underwater? For breakfast I ate sausage and cheese. For lunch I had lentil soup, meat balls, chicken and a banana. For dinner I had more lentil soup, sausage, grilled chicken and peach. And once a day I had to have sports food.

How did you actually eat your food? The most important thing while you eat something under the water is to make sure that you do not swallow any water. The best way to eat something is to exhale slowly before pushing something in to the mouth. This requires talent and experience.

How did you manage to get any sleep? Between 1 a.m. and 5 a.m. I slept face downward. And during the day I took naps.

What were the conditions like in the tank? The first two days it was really cold. I took my dry suit off and put on my wet suit (I changed underwater) and then it was OK.

Were you able to communicate with the outside world? The hand signals that I improvised allowed me to communicate with my friends. I also had a full-face mask by Ocean Reef Co. that included a communication device.

Ⓡ MUSCLE MAN

At age 80, Abdurakhman Abdulazizov, from the southern Russian republic of Dagestan, can pull a railway carriage by means of a rope tied to his body and lift an iron girder weighing over 220 lb (100 kg) with his teeth.

Ⓡ SPEEDY JUGGLER

In July 2009, the Czech Republic's Zdenek Bradác, while juggling three balls, made 339 catches in just 60 seconds.

Ⓡ BRIDE PARADE

Sporting full bridal regalia, 110 brides and brides-to-be paraded through Bucharest in June 2009 to promote the institution of marriage in Romania.

Water Home

Cem Karabay, a diver from Turkey, spent five and a half days nonstop living underwater. Surviving on meals put together by an expert nutritionist, and lots of liquids, he managed to eat, sleep, drink and exercise in his tank measuring 16 x 10 x 10 ft (5 x 3 x 3 m), located outside a shopping mall in Istanbul. His diving teacher, Namik Ekin, had previously lived underwater for 124 hours, but Cem's impressive 135 hours and 2 minutes beat his time. After almost a week underwater, Cem had high blood pressure and an eye infection, but he emerged with a greater desire to go back—the next time for ten days!

Ⓡ PRESSING ENGAGEMENT

On January 10, 2009, 86 scuba divers dived 173 ft (52.7 m) to the bottom of a flooded quarry in Monmouthshire, Wales, and ironed clothes on ironing boards at the same time.

Ⓡ BED JUMP

Over a period of 16 hours in May 2009, around 20,000 people in four cities—New York, London, Paris and Shanghai—jumped on four giant beds. The beds, which took a team of 100 people five weeks to build and incorporated over 200,000 nuts and bolts and six tons of steel, measured 49 x 33 ft (15 x 10 m) and were each topped with 30 double mattresses and a huge super-sized duvet that could cover 65 regular double beds.

Jyothi Raj believes he was given the gift of climbing and is happy to teach his skills to anyone who wants to learn, provided they use harnesses.

Real Life
SPIDERMAN

JYOTHI RAJ HAS INCREDIBLE CLIMBING ABILITIES WHEREBY HE IS SEEMINGLY ABLE TO GLUE HIMSELF TO WALLS WITHOUT ANY HARNESSES OR ASSISTANCE, AND EVEN MANAGES TO HANG UPSIDE DOWN USING ONLY HIS FEET! JYOTHI, A CONSTRUCTION WORKER FROM KARNATAKA, INDIA, SPENDS HIS DAYS CLIMBING UP AND DOWN BUILDING SITES USUALLY ON BAMBOO SCAFFOLDING, WHICH CAN BE VERY DANGEROUS. HE STARTED PRACTICING FREE CLIMBING EVERY DAY UNTIL HE WAS ABLE TO CLING TO THE WALLS, USING JUST HIS HANDS, AT 90-DEGREE ANGLES AND EVEN UPSIDE DOWN. HE CLAIMS HE HAS NEVER USED SAFETY EQUIPMENT TO CLIMB AND ISN'T AFRAID OF FALLING. EVERY SUNDAY, JYOTHI COMES TO THE FAMOUS FORT AT CHITRADURGA TO ENTERTAIN HIS FANS. REACHING HEIGHTS OF UP TO 300 FT (90 M), JYOTHI HAS SCALED EVERY WALL POSSIBLE AT THE FORT AND IS READY TO MOVE ON TO BIGGER BUILDINGS AND MOUNTAINS. CLAIMING HE HASN'T HAD AN ACCIDENT IN FOUR YEARS, HIS ULTIMATE GOAL IS TO BE LIKE ALAIN ROBERT, THE FAMOUS FRENCH FREE CLIMBER KNOWN AS THE "HUMAN SPIDER," WHO HAS CLIMBED MANY OF THE WORLD'S TALLEST STRUCTURES, SOME OF THEM OVER 650 FT (200 M) HIGH.

RAISE THE FLAGS

GUINNESS RISHI FROM DELHI, INDIA, WAS FEATURED IN *RIPLEY'S BELIEVE IT OR NOT! SEEING IS BELIEVING* FOR A STOMACH-CHURNING KETCHUP-GUZZLING FEAT. NOW GUINNESS HAS UNDERTAKEN TO GET HIS HEAD, FACE AND BODY PERMANENTLY TATTOOED WITH MORE THAN 200 NATIONAL FLAGS IN FULL COLOR. GUINNESS HAS 24 FLAG TATTOOS ON THE TOP OF HIS HEAD, 25 FLAGS ON HIS FACE AND MORE THAN 150 OTHER FLAGS ON THE REST OF HIS BODY. HE IS NOW WORKING ON TATTOOING A MAP OF THE COUNTRIES OF THE WORLD ON HIS STOMACH.

TATTOOS SO FAR!

℞ CLEVER GIRL

Born in 2006, Karina Oakley of Surrey, England, had an IQ of 160 at just two years old—the same as eminent scientist Stephen Hawking and Microsoft chairman Bill Gates. Karina, whose IQ is 60 points above the British average, was asked to complete a 45-minute test in several different categories, including verbal ability, memory, numbers and shapes.

℞ PADDED BRA

Brazilian Ivonete Pereira's life was saved in April 2009 when a robber's bullet struck a wad of cash hidden in her bra. The 58-year-old had stuffed the bills in her bra because robbery was rife in her local area.

℞ FAT REMOVAL

A half-ton teenager from Houston, Texas, had 70 lb (32 kg) of fat cut off in an operation. Billy Robbins, who at his heaviest weighed 840 lb (380 kg), underwent the radical procedure to prevent his heart from giving out.

℞ NEEDLE REMOVED

Doctors in China removed a syringe needle from 55-year-old Lao Du 31 years after another doctor broke it off in his butt cheek.

℞ SPEARGUN

In March 2009, Emerson de Oliveira Abreu of Brazil accidentally shot himself in the head with a speargun. Despite it going 6 in (15 cm) into his skull, he survived.

℞ FACE TRANSPLANT

Surgeons replaced 80 percent of the face of Connie Culp from Unionport, Ohio, in a 2008 operation, using the bone, muscles, nerves, skin and blood vessels of another person. It was the world's most extensive face transplant surgery ever.

℞ BLOOD LOSS

Named after a French neurologist, "Cotard delusion" is a rare mental disorder in which a person believes he or she is either dead, does not exist, is putrefying or has somehow mislaid his or her blood and internal organs.

℞ WHEELY ODD

Many times world beard champion Elmar Weisser of Baden, Germany, has styled his long beard into designs of Berlin's Brandenburg Gate, London's Tower Bridge and, in 2009, a bicycle. It takes up to five hours to style his beard for each competition.

℞ BIG APPETITE

A former basketball player-turned-street-performer, Zhao Liang, from China's Henan province, stands nearly 8 ft 1 in (2.45 m) tall—and feeds his enormous appetite with a dinner of eight burger-sized steamed buns and three plates of food.

℞ GLASS CHIN

While shaving in 2009, Thomas Entwistle from Bolton, Greater Manchester, England, discovered a piece of glass from a Ford Cortina windshield embedded in his chin 30 years after the accident that put it there.

Sheep Man

"Rham Sam" was a circus sideshow performer in Europe in the 19th century whose body exhibited a mass of sheeplike wooly hair. He is shown here in London in 1890 with lecturer Professor Langdon.

℞ HAIR RAISING

A bullet fired at the head of Briana Bonds of Kansas City, Missouri, in February 2009 was caught in her tightly woven hair weave. The wig saved her life and she escaped unharmed.

℞ BEARD DAY

To mark the 200th anniversary of the birth of evolutionary biologist Charles Darwin, who was born on February 12, 1809, England's Bristol Zoo allowed free admission on February 12, 2009, to anyone sporting a beard—real or fake.

℞ MOVING HEART

When April Pinkard's doctor examined her to treat a rare medical condition, he couldn't find her heartbeat—because her heart had moved to the other side of her chest, occupying an empty space where a damaged lung had once been. Her heart kept floating around her body until April from Live Oak, Florida, was finally given breast implants to keep it in place.

℞ TIMELY TWINS

Twins Tarrance (born 11.51 p.m., December 31, 2008) and Tariq (born 12.17 a.m., January 1, 2009) Griffin of Pontiac, Michigan, were born less than 30 minutes apart but on different days and in different months and years!

℞ DEXTROUS FEET

Forty-nine-year-old Jana Blazova of Presov, Slovakia, learned to use her feet to write and embroider despite being paralyzed by cerebral palsy in childhood.

℞ DELAYED DEATH

Fifty-four-year-old Craig Buford of Fort Worth, Texas, died on December 29, 2008, from complications of a gunshot wound he had sustained 35 years earlier.

℞ GENETIC MIRACLE

In a genetic phenomenon that is at least a one in 500,000 chance, a British couple have given birth to their second set of twins where one daughter is white and the other black. In 2001, when Dean Durrant and Alison Spooner from Hampshire, England, were told they were having twins, they were stunned to discover that one daughter, Lauren, took after her mother with blue eyes and red hair, while her sister Hayleigh resembled her father who is of West Indian origin. Then, in 2008, history repeated itself when Leah was born white like her mother and her twin sister, Miya, had her father's darker skin.

℞ SNAKE WOMAN

In 2009, surgeons in China removed a tumor from a woman's leg that weighed three times more than she does. The non-cancerous growth started out as a birthmark on the body of Wang Houju from Linxi, Shandong Province, but steadily wrapped itself around her leg and up to her waist, earning her the name of "Snake Woman." Eventually, it weighed over 220 lb (100 kg), whereas the rest of her body tipped the scales at just 70 lb (32 kg).

Chad was able to keep two 300-horsepower airplanes grounded on a runway with only his arms for just over one minute.

N393DW

MAN OF STRENGTH

CHAD CAN RIP LICENSE PLATES IN TWO...

WISCONSIN
A 517 394
OCT   TRUCK   06

Chad suffered no ill effects after being pinned to a bed of 12-in (30-cm) nails by 848 lb (385 kg) of concrete until each block was smashed with a sledgehammer on Sixth Avenue, New York.

...AND A PACK OF CARDS!

RIPLEY'S ask

What made you begin breaking ice?
I've been training in the martial arts my entire life. My mom went into labor in one of my dad's martial arts schools and there it began. With years of mental and physical training and conditioning, I have been able to do amazing breaks and feats of strength.

How much training do you do?
What stunt I'm attempting next will determine how I train, but on average I run 2 miles a day and work out for about four or five days a week.

How do you break 16 blocks of ice in one strike?
There is a lot of setup and preparation required when attempting an ice break this large. Unlike concrete, ice starts to sweat and can slide side to side when you hit it. Everything has to be perfect, including the strike, to make a successful break.

Does it hurt?
When I am attempting a record ice break I know it's going to hurt, but I also know there is always enough crushed ice laying around afterward if I need to ice down my wrist.

How do you keep from getting injured?
I have not sustained any major injuries from any stunt I have attempted to date. There is a lot of conditioning, setup and preparation that goes into what I do and that helps minimize the risk.

Do you have any tips for aspiring strength athletes?
My advice to aspiring athletes, or anyone who wants to do something out of the ordinary, is this. "Most people never reach their goals in life because they are afraid of failing and they allow fear to rob them of the potential that they had to be successful. Anything is possible!... Live without fear. Live without limits."

What are your plans for feats of strength in the future?
I am currently training for one of my most extreme stunts yet. I'm going to attempt to hold back a Lamborghini by hand at full throttle for 8 seconds.

ICE BREAKER

CHAD NETHERLAND IS A BLACK-BELT MARTIAL ARTIST WHO SPECIALIZES IN BREAKING HARD OBJECTS WITH HIS BARE HANDS. IN 2009, IN ONE STRIKE, CHAD DESTROYED SIXTEEN 75-LB (34-KG) BLOCKS OF ICE THAT WERE 6 IN (15 CM) THICK, BREAKING A TOTAL OF 1,200 LB (544 KG) OF ICE—ENOUGH FOR A GROUP OF ADULTS TO STAND ON. CHAD, FROM MYRTLE BEACH, SOUTH CAROLINA, LEARNED EVERYTHING HE DOES FROM HIS FATHER, WHO WAS ALSO A WORLD-CLASS MARTIAL-ARTS EXPERT. HE HAS SMASHED 50 BLOCKS OF ICE IN 19 SECONDS LIVE ON TELEVISION AND STOPPED TWO LIGHT AIRCRAFT FROM TAKING OFF FOR OVER A MINUTE WITH ONLY HIS ARMS. IN 2003, HE LAID ON A BED OF 12-IN (30-CM) NAILS WHILE CONCRETE BLOCKS WEIGHING 848 LB (385 KG) WERE SMASHED WITH A SLEDGEHAMMER ON HIS CHEST!

Living the High Life

HEINZ ZAK IS NOT YOUR ORDINARY THRILL-SEEKER OR ADRENALINE JUNKIE. ALTHOUGH HE RISKS HIS LIFE ON A REGULAR BASIS HUNDREDS OF FEET UP IN THE AIR, HEINZ SAYS THAT HE PERFORMS SUCH PERILOUS FEATS TO ACHIEVE A STATE OF INNER PEACE AND TRANQUILITY. "HIGHLINING" IS AN EXTREME FORM OF "SLACKLINING," WHICH INVOLVES A STRIP OF NYLON 1 IN (2.5 CM) THICK STRUNG RELATIVELY LOOSELY HIGH ABOVE WILD TERRAIN OR WATER. THIS MEANS THAT THE LINE FLEXES AND EVEN BOUNCES, MAKING THE SPORT DIFFERENT FROM TRADITIONAL TIGHTROPE WALKING. INTENSE FOCUS ALLOWS HEINZ TO WALK CALMLY ACROSS THE LINE. SINCE THE 1980S, HE HAS TRAVELED THE WORLD SEARCHING FOR THE PERFECT PLACE TO PRACTICE HIS DEATH-DEFYING FEATS.

Bride to Bee

When Li Wenhua and Yan Hongxia, workers at Nanhu forestry commission in Ning'an, China, decided to tie the knot, they made sure they invited some of their coworkers—in the form of tens of thousands of honeybees. A carefully placed queen bee attracted the entire swarm, forming living-insect material for an alternative pair of wedding outfits. The number of people stung at the wedding is unknown.

ARCTIC MARATHON

Wearing only shorts and a pair of sandals, Dutchman Wim Hof completed a 2009 marathon in sub-zero temperatures 200 mi (322 km) north of the Arctic Circle. His body was exposed to temperatures of −13°F (−25°C) as he finished the 26-mi (42-km) trek in 5 hours 25 minutes.

AROUND BRITAIN

Starting and finishing in London, English comedian Eddie Izzard ran 1,105 mi (1,778 km) around Britain from July 26 to September 15, 2009—the equivalent of running 43 marathons in 51 days.

WORM CHARMERS

Ten-year-old Sophie Smith of Cheshire, England, coaxed 567 worms up from the ground in 30 minutes to win Britain's 2009 World Worm Charming Championships. Techniques used to encourage worms to the surface included a man playing the xylophone with bottles and a woman who tap-danced to the theme from *Star Wars*.

MICHIGAN SWIM

By completing a 26-hour, 34-mi (55-km) swim across Lake Michigan in 2009, Paula Stephanson of Belleville, Ontario, Canada, became only the second person to swim across all five Great Lakes. Her first Great Lake swim was across Lake Ontario in 1996 at age 17.

IRON MAN

Japanese athlete Keizo Yamada, known as the "Iron Man," ran three marathons in 2009—at 81 years of age. He completed the Tokyo marathon in 5 hours 34 minutes 50 seconds and kept fit by jogging 12 mi (20 km) every day.

BRIDGE FLIP

Australian motorcycle stunt rider Robbie Maddison performed a no-handed backflip while jumping the 25-ft (7.6-m) gap between the raised spans of London's Tower Bridge in July 2009. He raced up one side of the raised bridge, flew through the air 100 ft (30 m) above the water and made the backflip before landing on the south side of the bridge.

BASKETBALL SPIN

Cheshire Jets basketball team from Chester, England, gathered more than 100 people to spin basketballs on their fingers simultaneously in July 2009.

ELVIS WARDROBE

Vince Everett of London, England, owned more than 3,000 items of Elvis Presley memorabilia, including 14 of Elvis' jackets.

STRAIT CROSSING

Ben Morrison-Jack and James Weight kite-surfed across the Bass Strait in September 2009 from Tasmania to mainland Australia—a distance of 155 mi (250 km).

ROPE TRICK

Damian Cooksey of East Bay, California, landed a frontflip on a 1-in-thick (2.5-cm) slackline—a rope that is not taut. In 2007, in Munich, Germany, he walked 506 ft (154 m) on a slackline without falling off.

FEMALE FORMATION

Jumping from nine planes at an altitude of 17,000 ft (5,180 m), 181 female skydivers from 31 countries joined together in formation above Perris, California, in September 2009.

PIE FIGHT

More than 250 people turned up to take part in a mass custard-pie fight at Colchester, Essex, England, in 2009. Around 650 pies—filled with 53 gal (200 l) of custard—were thrown during the battle.

GROUP SHOWER

One hundred and fifty strangers in swimsuits showered together in a specially constructed 40,000-sq-ft (3,716-sq-m) structure at Gurnee, Illinois, in 2009. The huge shower, designed to hold around 600 people elbow to elbow, had 40 shower nozzles and took 7½ hours to build.

Heat Seeker

As unusual hobbies go, it's a dangerous choice. Keith Malcolm from Aberdeen, Scotland, dresses in several layers of flame-retardant clothing before he's doused in gasoline and set alight like a human torch. He then runs as far as he can before the flames overwhelm him and firefighters put him out. In 2009, Malcolm sped 259 ft (79 m) in aid of charity.

Gallery

SANDOW

Eugene Sandow, real name Friedrich Muller, was born in 1867 in Konigsberg, Prussia. He was the first popular male strongman. Performing mostly in circuses and sideshows, he was famous for his bulging muscles and for breaking chains around his chest until his death in 1925. He notoriously wore a skimpy costume.

SANDWINA

Sandwina was known as "The Strongest and Most Beautiful Woman in the World." She would bend rods and straighten horseshoes to the delight of large audiences who saw her perform with the Ringling Bros. and Barnum & Bailey Circus in the early 20th century. She was born Katie Brumbach, one of 14 children, and performed with her parents Philippe and Johanna Brumbach. Her father would offer 100 marks to any man who could defeat her in wrestling—no one ever won the prize! Sandwina defeated the strongman Eugene Sandow (left) by lifting a 300-lb (135-kg) weight over her head— Sandow only managed to lift it to his chest. It was after beating Sandow that Katie adopted her stage name, "Sandwina."

FROM THE MID-19TH CENTURY, BECOMING A PROFESSIONAL STRONGMAN WAS CONSIDERED TO BE A GOOD TRADE. STRONGMEN, AND SOMETIMES WOMEN, USUALLY STARTED OUT BY DEMONSTRATING THEIR STRENGTH AT COUNTY FAIRS AND LOCAL THEATERS, LIFTING EXTREMELY HEAVY WEIGHTS AND PULLING OBJECTS SUCH AS PLANES AND BUSES. BELIEVE IT OR NOT, SOME USED PARTS OF THEIR BODIES OTHER THAN THEIR ARMS, SUCH AS THEIR TONGUES, TEETH AND EARS, TO PROVE THEIR STRENGTH.

KNUCKLE BUSTER

Mick Gooch must have the strongest fingers in the world. The martial arts expert from Kent, England, is capable of 17 one-armed, single-finger push-ups on the head of a nail. Mick was inspired by the two-finger push-ups performed by kung-fu legend Bruce Lee, and decided to go one incredible step further, a feat that took years of dedication—and broken knuckles—to master.

EAR ACHE

Rakesh Sharma from India strains as he lifts 105 lb (48 kg) with his ears in Punjab, India, in October 2009. He attaches straps and a wooden clamp to his ears before slowly lifting the weights from the ground.

PLANE CRAZY

In perhaps the greatest feat of strength ever, Rev. Kevin Fast from Cobourg, Ontario, Canada, successfully pulled a giant Globemaster airplane weighing 416,000 lb (188,694 kg)—the weight of more than 50 African elephants—for 29 ft (8.8 m) across the runway at an airbase in Trenton, Canada, in 2009.

GOING STRONG

HAIR RAISING

Zhang Tingting, a Chinese strongwoman, successfully pulls six cars a distance of 165 ft (50 m) in Beijing in 2009, using her hair.

EYE-CATCHING

Yang Guanghe has a painstaking talent for using his eyelids to move heavy objects. In Guangzhou, China, in 2009, he dragged a car using ropes attached to his lower eyelids.

STRONG TONGUE

Habu, known as the "Man with the Iron Tongue," was a 1930s strongman from India who was able to lift up to 105 lb (48 kg) by hooking the weight to his tongue and lifting it from above.

TOTEM TEETH

Strongman Al Fraser from New York is seen in this photograph, taken in 1939, lifting three tables and a chair, all stacked on top of one another and weighing a total of 150 lb (68 kg), with his mouth and teeth.

ON THE BALL

RIPLEY'S LOVED THE GIANT RUBBER-BAND BALL MADE BY JOEL WAUL SO MUCH THAT IT BOUGHT IT. THE PROBLEM WAS GETTING THE GIANT BALL, MADE FROM 780,000 RUBBER BANDS, TO RIPLEY'S ORLANDO WAREHOUSE FOR STORAGE. AT 9,400 LB (4,264 KG) AND 7 FT (2.1 M) TALL, THE BALL IS NOT EASY TO MANEUVER AND CAN BE DANGEROUS— RIPLEY'S PREVIOUSLY REPORTED THAT, WHEN THE BALL WAS JUST 400 LB (181 KG), IT ROLLED OVER AND SPRAINED WAUL'S HAND. IN OCTOBER 2009, A RIPLEY'S TEAM ARRIVED AT WAUL'S LAUDERHILL, FLORIDA, HOME WITH A TRANSPORTER TRUCK AND CRANE. THE BALL WAS CAREFULLY HAULED UP FROM WAUL'S DRIVE (IT SMELLS TOO BAD TO HAVE BEEN KEPT IN HIS HOUSE) AND LOADED ONTO THE TRUCK, BEFORE MAKING A SLOW JOURNEY TO THE WAREHOUSE. ITS PERMANENT HOME WILL BE THE RIPLEY'S MUSEUM IN HOLLYWOOD, CALIFORNIA, WHICH IS TEMPORARILY WITHOUT A ROOF, SO THAT IT CAN BE LOWERED IN. IT IS TOO BIG TO ROLL THROUGH A DOOR, AND ONLY JUST MADE IT INTO THE WAREHOUSE!

RIPLEY REVISITED

Up in Flames

In 2009, 17 people were each completely engulfed in fire without oxygen supplies at the same time in South Russell, Ohio. The group, led by local man Ted Batchelor, walked around Bell Road with their bodies in flames for an amazing 43.9 seconds. The team prepared for eight months for the event in their burn suits, and not one person sustained even a minor injury as the feat took place.

In the warehouse!

℞ TOILET LINE

In an event organized by the United Nations' children's agency UNICEF to raise awareness for the need for clean water, 756 people lined up to visit a toilet in Brussels, Belgium, in March 2009.

℞ BOOK TOWER

In June 2009, John Evans of Derbyshire, England, balanced 204 books on his head in a pyramid-shaped tower that was 4 ft (1.2 m) high and weighed 284 lb (129 kg). The contents of a can of hairspray were used to stop the books from slipping off his head.

℞ NONAGENARIAN SKYDIVER

In April 2009, George Moyse of Dorset, England, went skydiving for the first time—at age 97. Strapped to an instructor, he jumped out of an airplane at 10,000 ft (3,048 m) above Salisbury Plain, Wiltshire, and carried out a free fall for the first 5,000 ft (1,525 m) at speeds of nearly 120 mph (193 km/h).

℞ HUMAN WHEELBARROWS

In Singapore in April 2009, no fewer than 1,378 students from Temasek Polytechnic took part in a mass human wheelbarrow race. At the same event, students formed an unbroken human wheelbarrow chain comprising 74 people.

℞ PAPER BALL

To illustrate the importance of recycling and the enormity of waste, Enrique Miramontes and Ricardo Granados—two friends from San Diego, California—have spent more than six years creating a giant ball of discarded paper that weighs 200 lb (91 kg) and is 3 ft (1 m) high. In that time Miramontes alone has spent over $3,000 on masking tape and over 2,000 hours layering the pieces of paper on top of each other. He had the idea as a 16-year-old high school student when a friend threw a rolled up ball of paper at him in biology class.

℞ MELON SMASH

At the 2009 Chinchilla Melon Festival, held in Queensland, Australia, local melon picker John Allwood smashed 47 watermelons with his head in one minute.

℞ TREE PLANTERS

On a single day in July 2009, a team of 300 volunteers planted more than half a million mangrove trees in the Indus River delta region of Sindh province, in southern Pakistan.

℞ MASS KISS

On Valentine's Day 2009, nearly 40,000 people (20,000 couples) gathered in Mexico City's main square and kissed for 10 seconds.

℞ REVERSE WALK

In 2008, Bill Kathan of Vernon, Vermont, walked backward from one rim of the Grand Canyon, down to the basin and back up the other side in 15 hours.

℞ YOUNG CLIMBER

Six-year-old Tom Fryers from South Yorkshire, England, has already climbed 214 peaks in England's Lake District—the equivalent of climbing five Mount Everests. Tom scaled his first peak when he was just three and has since covered 480 mi (772 km) and climbed more than 150,000 ft (45,720 m), including the two highest mountains in England—3,209-ft (978-m) Scafell Pike and 3,162-ft (964-m) Sca Fell.

In 1917, 16-year-old Elsie Wright, from Bradford, England, photographed tiny "fairies" dancing for her cousin, Frances Griffiths. The photographs came to the attention of Sir Arthur Conan Doyle, author of the Sherlock Holmes novels, who published the girl's pictures with an article on fairies. The pictures became famous and many thought the fairies to be genuine. It was not until 1982 that Elsie and Frances admitted that they had fabricated the photographs with cardboard fairies.

BIZARRE MYSTERIES

For over 200 years, treasure hunters have tried to get to the bottom of the so-called "money pit" on Oak Island, Nova Scotia, Canada. The 200-ft-deep (60-m) pit was first discovered by Daniel McGinnis in 1795 but flooding, collapse, and a series of booby traps have since made it impenetrable. Six treasure hunters have been killed in the quest, believing the pit to contain a valuable haul of treasure. Theories as to the exact nature of the treasure include it being a pirates' booty, the French crown jewels, the treasures of King Solomon's temple, or even the Holy Grail.

NAZCA LINES

Across a plain 50 mi (80 km) long and 15 mi (24 km) wide on Peru's arid Nazca Desert sit a series of around 900 huge geometric shapes, ranging from simple lines to complex drawings depicting animals, plants and birds. They include a spider, a hummingbird, a whale, and a 1000-ft-long (300-m) pelican. One of the straight lines is 9 mi (15 km) long. The forms are so difficult to spot from the ground that they were not discovered until the 1930s when a plane flew over the plateau.

SPRING-HEELED JACK

A seemingly respectable man walked into a London police station in 1837 and recounted how his daughter had been attacked by a cloaked figure who had blue and white flames shooting from his mouth and metallic claws. Renowned for his ability to leap remarkable heights, the mysterious character known as Spring-Heeled Jack continued to fascinate and terrify Victorian London for years and was even reported as far afield as Liverpool and Scotland.

MARY CELESTE

Built in Nova Scotia, Canada, the 282-ton merchant ship *Mary Celeste* sailed from New York in November 1872 bound for Genoa, Italy, with a cargo of 1,701 barrels of alcohol—yet when it was discovered off Portugal on December 4, the ten people on board had completely vanished and were never heard from again. There was no sign of a struggle, the cargo was largely intact, the ship was in excellent condition, the weather was calm and the crew were experienced. Although the ship's lifeboat was missing, all the belongings of the crew and passengers had all been left onboard.

FEATURELESS FACE

IF VISITORS TO THE CHIESA DELLA SANTA CHURCH IN BOLOGNA, ITALY, GAZE LONG ENOUGH INTO A GRATED OPENING IN THE CHURCH WALL, A STRANGE, DARK, ALMOST FEATURELESS FACE WILL STARE BACK AT THEM. THE SPOOKY APPARITION IS THE MUMMIFIED RELIC OF ST. CATHERINE OF BOLOGNA. SHE DIED IN 1475, BUT AFTER A SERIES OF MIRACLES, HER BODY, INEXPLICABLY SHOWING LITTLE SIGN OF DECAY, WAS EXHUMED BY NUNS. A FEW YEARS LATER, CATHERINE APPEARED TO ONE OF THE NUNS IN A VISION, ASKING TO BE PLACED IN THE SMALL CHAPEL, SITTING UPRIGHT. SO THEY DRESSED HER IN NUN'S CLOTHING, PLACED A GOLDEN CROSS IN HER HAND AND SAT HER IN A GOLDEN CHAIR, WHERE SHE HAS REMAINED FOR MORE THAN 500 YEARS.

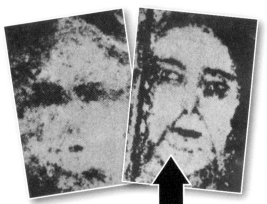

Floor Faces

Maria Gomez Pereira was startled to see an image of a man's face suddenly appear on the kitchen floor of her house in Belmez, Spain, in 1971. She had the floor pulled up and relaid, but the face reappeared in the exact same spot within a week. It was discovered that the house was built on a graveyard, and excavations beneath the floor revealed human remains, which were duly removed. A new floor was then laid, but within two weeks a series of faces began appearing again.

℞ MOUNTAIN LIGHTS

For more than 800 years, mysterious groups of lights have been observed on Brown Mountain, North Carolina. The lights are usually white, but have also been known to turn red, blue or yellow. One theory is that they are the result of swamp gas released by decaying animal and plant matter, but there are no swamps in the area. Others suggest the illuminations could be ball lightning.

Masked Man

For a century it was believed that in 1908 adventurer Harry Bensley had set off from London on a six-year trek around the world, wearing an iron mask and pushing a pram to win a $100,000 bet with eccentric American millionaire J. Pierpont Morgan. However, far from reaching China and Japan as he had claimed, there is now doubt that Bensley ever left Britain. His family can find no evidence of him venturing abroad, and when he resurfaced he showed no signs of wealth, even though his supposed winnings were the equivalent of over $2 million today. So the mysterious case of Harry Bensley remains unsolved.

℞ WHITE RIVER MONSTER

Fishing on the White River at Newport, Arkansas, in 1971, Cloyce Warren and his friends saw a huge spout of water rise skyward. Moments later a 30-ft-long (9-m) creature with a spiny backbone briefly surfaced before disappearing back into the depths. Although Warren managed to take a photo of it, the White River Monster has never been identified.

℞ STONE STATUES

Nearly 900 giant stone statues, at least 400 years old, with elongated human heads and torsos, are scattered across Easter Island in the South Pacific—but nobody knows why the islanders built them or how they transported them into position. The statues—or *moai*—are an average 13 ft (4 m) high and weigh 14 tons (although some weigh more than 80 tons), and it is estimated that up to 150 people would have been needed to drag each one across the countryside on wooden sleds.

℞ KILLER EAGLE

Research in 2009 showed that a huge man-eating bird of prey from ancient Maori legend really did exist. The Maoris of New Zealand told of a massive bird that would swoop down on people in the mountains and kill children. Scientists have known about a giant eagle for more than a century, based on excavated bones, but new studies of its behavior indicate a truly fearsome predator weighing up to 40 lb (18 kg) that probably did attack humans.

℞ ELTANIN ANTENNA

In 1964, the U.S. polar research vessel *Eltanin* found a strange antenna at the bottom of the Atlantic Ocean, 1,000 mi (1,600 km) south of Cape Horn. It was a pole with 12 spokes radiating from it. The spokes were at an angle of 15 degrees from one another and each had a spherical shape on the end. Some experts thought it was a new marine life form; others believed it to be a relic of an ancient civilization.

£21,000.
THE BIGGEST WAGER
ON RECORD!

This amount will be won if the gentleman accomplishes the feat of WALKING ROUND THE WORLD adhering to the conditions.

Light Show

Thousands of people saw a mysterious giant spiral of light appear in the sky over Norway on the morning of December 9, 2009. It began as a spinning circle of white light centered around a bright moonlike star and then spread out, sending a blue-green beam down to Earth. The eerie phenomenon, which was visible for hundreds of miles, was in the sky for several minutes. Theories included it being a misfired Russian missile, a meteor fireball or a previously unseen variation of *aurora borealis*, the northern lights.

® LAKE WORTH MONSTER

On November 5, 1969, a 7-ft-tall (2.1-m) biped covered in short white fur, with a white goatlike beard, was spotted by many witnesses around Lake Worth, Texas. When someone tried to approach it, the beast howled, threw a car tire some 500 ft (150 m) at the crowd and fled. Although people discovered footprints 16 in (40-cm) long, no one ever found the Lake Worth Monster.

® STRANGE FOOTPRINTS

Members of a British expedition climbing the north face of Mount Everest in the Himalayas in 1921 spotted a group of dark figures moving around on a snowfield above them. When the climbers reached the spot—at around 21,000 ft (6,400 m)— there was no sign of the creatures; instead, there were huge, humanlike footprints in the snow. Local sherpas said they were the tracks of the elusive Abominable Snowman, or Yeti.

® SKULL RIDDLE

A yellowing skull uncovered near Featherston on New Zealand's North Island in 2004 was identified by forensic pathologists as having belonged to a European woman who lived around 270 years ago—a century before the first known arrival of white settlers in the country.

®IPLEY'S RESEARCH

THE LEGEND OF THE YETI DATES BACK TO 1832 WHEN HIMALAYAN GUIDES SPOTTED A TALL, DARK, HAIRY CREATURE WALKING UPRIGHT ON TWO LEGS LIKE A HUMAN. SINCE THEN, THERE HAVE BEEN NUMEROUS EXPEDITIONS IN SEARCH OF THE YETI (OR ABOMINABLE SNOWMAN). HOWEVER, ALTHOUGH THERE HAVE BEEN OCCASIONAL SIGHTINGS, AND STRANGE FOOTPRINTS HAVE BEEN DISCOVERED IN THE SNOW, THE BEAST'S TRUE IDENTITY HAS NEVER BEEN REVEALED. EXPERTS HAVE SUGGESTED IT COULD BE AN ORANGUTAN, A BEAR, A LANGUR MONKEY OR, MOST INTRIGUINGLY, AN UNKNOWN SPECIES.

® DEATH ROAD

In the first 12 months after a new section of highway opened between the German towns of Bremen and Bremerhaven in 1929, there were over 100 crashes close to a small roadside kilometer marker known as marker 239— even though the section of road was straight and flat. On one clear day in September 1930, nine cars left the road here. A local man said an underground stream was generating a strong magnetic current that caused the crashes, so he buried a copper-filled copper box there, after which the accidents stopped.

Legend of the Yeti

U.S. TV-show host Josh Gates displays a cast of what may be footprints of the elusive Yeti, an apelike creature whose existence has been shrouded in mystery for nearly 200 years. The tracks—measuring about 13 in (33 cm) long—were found in 2007 at an altitude of 9,350 ft (2,850 m) near Mount Everest in Nepal.

Vampires

SHOULD YOU DARE TO TURN THE PAGE, YOU HAD BEST DO IT IN DAYTIME, FOR VAMPIRES LURK BETWEEN SUNSET AND SUNRISE...

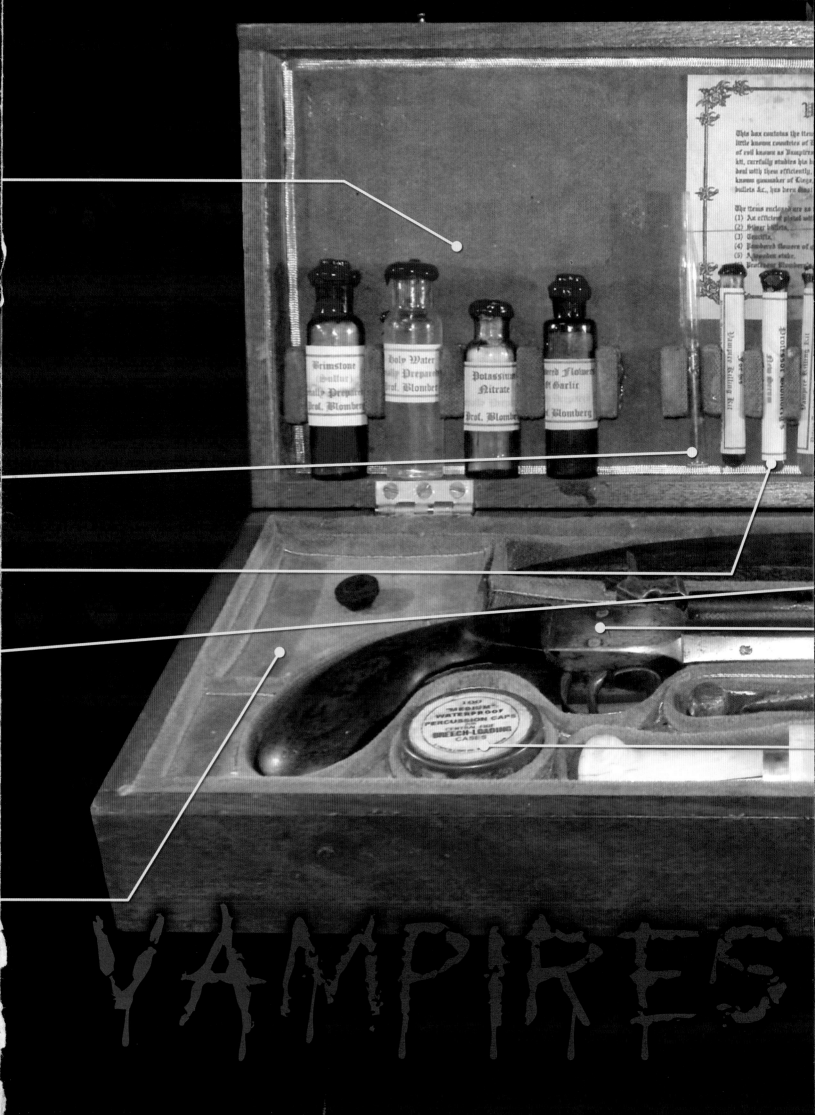

VAMPIRES

Vampire kits first appeared toward the end of the 19th century. Many of them stated their express purpose on the label inside the lid: "This box contains the items considered necessary for the protection of persons who travel into certain little known countries of Eastern Europe where the populace are plagued with a peculiar manifestation of evil, known as vampires." Many of the kits were said to be made by a Belgian gunmaker called Nicolas Plomdeur, and were sold by Professor Ernst Blomberg (1821–1903) of Lubeck, Germany.

This kit is one of over 30 such kits owned by the Ripley collection. Collectors around the world compete to own such kits, and have paid as much as $24,000 for one. This particular kit contains several must-have items:

1 WAX-SEALED VIALS

(containing powdered flowers of garlic, holy water, brimstone, and potassium nitrate)

Each vial is labeled with its contents and says "Specially prepared by Prof. Blomberg." Brimstone and potassium nitrate are components of gunpowder, which could be sprinkled around the grave of a possible vampire or, if a hunter was feeling brave, placed inside the nose, ears and eyes of the body, and then ignited. Garlic has an ancient tradition of having healing qualities, and a reputation of purity much like silver. In ancient times, anyone who didn't like the stuff was condemned as a vampire. It has also been hung outside doorways to protect the home, and handed around in churches to check that the congregation was entirely human. Holy water (ordinary water blessed by a religious figure) will burn the skin of a vampire and cause extreme pain, though is unlikely to kill the creature.

2 GLASS SYRINGE

Most probably used in conjunction with Professor Blomberg's serum.

3 PROFESSOR BLOMBERG'S SERUM

These vials state that a patent was applied for in London, but the exact contents of the serum are unknown. It is speculated that it contains holy water, garlic extract, honey and salt.

4 CRUCIFIX

A ready-made cross can be held up to protect an individual from an oncoming vampire. Other items in the kit are embellished with additional crosses for protection. It may help also to wear a crucifix on a chain around your neck. A strong religious faith can also serve to help the bearer of the crucifix in battle with a demonic force. The form of a cross was believed to drain a vampire of its strength, drive it away, and if touched, burn the vampire's undead flesh. A crucifix—a cross bearing the figure of Christ on it—is considered to be a stronger tool than any other ordinary cross.

5 SILVER BULLETS *(not visible)*

A hidden pocket in the box contains silver bullets. Silver is renowned for its purity, hence the belief that it can finish off evil creatures such as vampires and werewolves. There is much debate about the validity of this claim, as vampire folklore predates guns with bullets. Many vampire experts accept that modern writers have introduced this aspect of vampire hunting, but also add that silver crosses, daggers, and silver nails in a coffin are effective against candidates for vampirism.

This well-stocked kit is complemented by rosary beads and a Holy Bible.

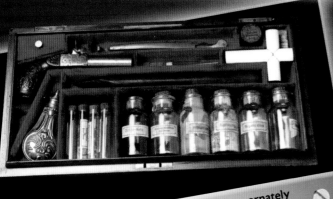

This French kit from the 1890s features an ornately carved pistol and powder flask.

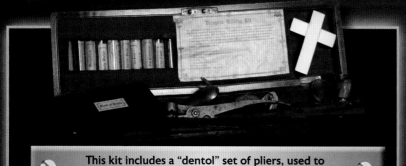

This kit includes a "dentol" set of pliers, used to remove the fangs of vampires.

Vampires, unnaturally pale and apparently frail, are actually freakishly strong, agile and fast. Said to sleep during the daytime, they reveal their true nature at night, seeking victims to quench their thirst for blood. Their fanglike teeth sink into the necks of unsuspecting human prey and drink their fill, topping up their superhuman strength and sucking the life from the body. Occasionally, they will leave a person alive, but the infection they spread transforms any such victim into the next of this undead creed. It's said that death is preferable to an eternity of immortality of the most tortuous kind...

Tales of vampires can be traced back thousands of years to ancient Mesopotamia, but most modern vampire stories have their basis in the folk tales of Eastern Europe. In the 18th and 19th centuries, Gothic horror stories became increasingly popular. Preying on the doubts and fears of a fascinated readership, vampires were a credible explanation for the spread of disease, plague and death. As travelers ventured forth into the far reaches of Europe, they armed themselves with the items thought to safeguard anyone against a vampire encounter. Garlic, crosses, holy water and special bullets were said to target a vampire's weaknesses, and specially made vampire killing kits were also available.

WORLD VAMPIRE WATCH!

YARA-MA-YHA-WHO – Australian aboriginal creature with blood-sucking tentacles

LOOGAROO – Caribbean vampire spirit with no flesh to cover its body

RAKSHASA – Indian blood-sucking demon with venomous fingernails

MANDURUGO – Long-tongued winged vampire from the Philippines

PENANGGALAN – Fanged head from Malaysia that flies at night

IMPUNDULU – Fearsome blood-sucking bird from South Africa

VOLKODLAK – Slavic werewolf that can turn into a vampire

YUKI-ONNA – Japanese snow-woman who drinks blood

BAOBHAN SITH – Ghostly Gaelic vampire-woman

ASANBOSAM – Iron-toothed vampire from Ghana

STRIGOI – Romanian vampire, risen from the grave

JÉ-ROUGES – Haitian vampire werewolf

ADLET – Inuit vampire dog

The aristocratic cloaked vampire as we know him today was made famous by Bram Stoker's 1897 novel Dracula. Films such as Dracula (1931) and Nosferatu (1922)—seen here with Max Schreck in the leading role of Count Orlok—helped whip up enthusiasm and a passion for vampires. Bela Lugosi, who starred in the 1931 film, actually fainted at the sight of blood!

The Düsseldorf Vampire

In the early 1900s, newspapers named a German serial killer "the Vampire of Düsseldorf." Peter Kürten had a violent upbringing and committed many crimes, culminating in several murders. The newspapers reported that he drank the blood of his victims, leading to his grisly nickname. After his trial and execution, his head was dissected to allow a scientific examination of his brain. It was suggested that he suffered from the rare condition known as Renfield's Syndrome, or clinical vampirism, a mental disorder that involves an obsession with drinking blood. Kürten's mummified head is on display in the Ripley's Believe It or Not! museum in Wisconsin.

Bricked Up

This 16th-century woman's skull was found in an archeological dig near Venice, northern Italy, in 2006. The object in her mouth is a brick, placed there after death to prevent her rising from the grave and drinking blood.

Vampire P[...]

In past centuries, plague killed off vast numbers of people, who were then buried in mass graves. These graves were left open for more bodies, and people were able to see the decomposition process—a body's lips shrinking back and revealing the teeth, blood seeping from the mouth, and an increasingly shrunken, pale look. This fitted the vampire stories they had been told, and as more people died it simply proved what they believed about vampires. The older bodies, through natural processes, began to bloat and look as if they had regained their living form through feeding on the blood of living victims.

FEBRUARY 1970

Man Hunts Vampire

Witnesses have told police that they have been frightened by mysterious ghostly figures in the vicinity of Highgate Cemetery, North London. Sean Manchester, vampire hunter, has stated that demonic disturbances are present and should be exorcised. He believes that it is a possessed corpse of a nobleman brought in a coffin to Highgate in the 18th century.

AUGUST 1970

The Dracula Business

As reported by this paper in February of this year, vampire hunter Sean Manchester performed an exorcism on the tomb suspected of containing the Highgate Vampire, after sightings of dark figures and bodies removed from graves in the area created a panic around the cemetery. Manchester stopped short of staking the creature, and the hauntings continued. The vampire hunter now reports that his colleagues have further pursued the cause of the contagion to a mansion in nearby Crouch End, and carried out a full and proper exorcism, resulting in the burning of the vampire, which Manchester believed to be a European nobleman transported to London in a coffin.

Mercy Me

The Brown family of Exeter, Rhode Island, caught tuberculosis in 1892. The mother and then the sister, Mercy, died. When her brother Edwin was also taken ill, villagers were sure a vampire was to blame. Mercy's body was dug up and looked flush, as if her heart was still alive: a sign she was a vampire. Her heart was burnt and the ashes given as medicine to her brother—who was not cured.

MERCY L.
daughter of
GEORGE T. & MARY E.
BROWN,
Died Jan. 17, 1892,
Aged 19 Years.

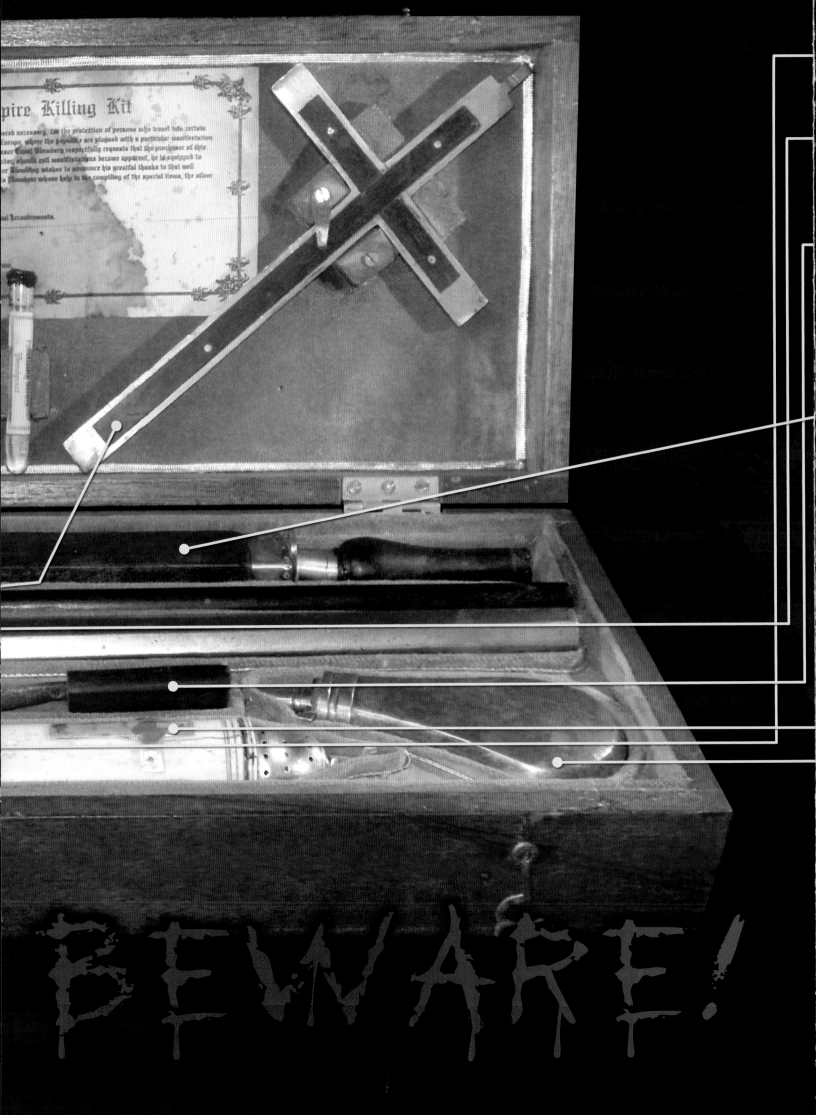

pire Killing Kit

...red necessary, for the protection of persons who travel into certain
...urope, where the peasants are plagued with a particular manifestation
...ssor Ernst Blomberg respectfully requests that the purchaser of this
...ber, should evil manifestations become apparent, he is equipped to
...er Blomberg wishes to announce his greatful thanks to that well
...s Blomberg whose help in the compiling of the special items, the silver

...cal Instruments.

BEWARE!

6 PERCUSSION CAPS

This tin stores 100 medium waterproof percussion caps, which enabled muzzle-loading firearms to fire in any weather.

7 PISTOL

The lower part of the case contains several pieces needed to maintain and fire a pistol, such as a powder stick, a bullet mold and a powder flask.

8 POWDER STICK

This was used to pack the gunpowder in the barrel of the pistol.

9 IVORY INCENSOR

Decorated with a silver cross, the incensor was used to burn incense during worship and ward off evil vampires with its divine powers.

10 WOODEN STAKE

Traditionally, a stake through the heart is the best way to finish off a vampire. This stake has a built-in dagger for good measure. Typical woods used are ash and aspen, believed to have powerful anti-vampire qualities. Many medieval bodies were staked through the heart before burial if the corpse was believed to be at a high risk of becoming a vampire—having died through disease or wicked deeds, for example.

11 BRASS AND COPPER POWDER FLASK

Used to hold the gunpowder needed for the pistol.

Other vampire kits also contained a mallet to help drive a stake through the vampire's heart, rosary beads, and icons from various cultures or religions around the world. Shorter-barreled pistols were common, and some were formed in the shape of a crucifix.

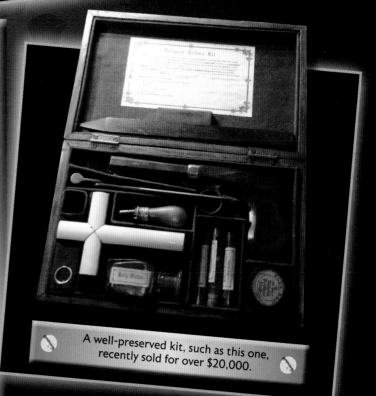

Cunningly disguised as a book, this kit afforded the owner an element of surprise.

A well-preserved kit, such as this one, recently sold for over $20,000.

TIPS FOR VAMPIRE HUNTERS

It's worth noting a vampire's dislike of daylight. In extreme cases, it can destroy the monster, and it disintegrates into dust. Sometimes it simply strips it of its strength or power.

† A vampire prefers to live and feed in darkness. Bear this in mind: if you can maneuver into sunlight, you may be safe.

† A vampire cannot be killed, technically, as it is already dead. But it can be sent back to its grave and kept there.

† Burning is a good technique for dealing with a vampire—be sure that the entire body and organs are burned, though.

† A vampire has an amazing capacity to self-heal and gradually restore strength and bodily form. It may take a long time—but it has centuries of immortality to play with.

† Slicing a vampire in two might finish it off—especially if the head is severed from the body.

† Historically, suspected vampires were staked, their heart removed and burned, and their head chopped off. They were then buried again.

DRACULA DID EXIST!

Vlad Draculea III was Prince of Wallachia, in southern Romania, in the late 15th century. Also known as "Vlad the Impaler," thanks to his habit of capturing enemies and impaling their heads on stakes, he was a fierce warrior and tyrannical leader who killed many thousands of men in battle. The name "Dracula" comes from the old Romanian for devil or dragon, and is thought to have given the author Bram Stoker his inspiration for the title of his most famous fictional character.

Vlad Draculea's many victims were impaled on poles. According to a German pamphlet published in 1488, a few years after Vlad's death, a nobleman visitor found Vlad among a "mighty forest" of impaled bodies. When the nobleman complained of the smell, Vlad "had him impaled high up so that the smell of the others would not bother him."

BLOOD RELATIVES

Doctors in the 1920s could find no reason for a nine-year-old Haitian girl's poor health and suggested she had a wasting disease. A native doctor was not convinced, and upon searching the girl's body found a tiny pin-prick incision on her big toe. The girl's aunt, Anastasie Dieudonne, confessed to drugging her niece and sucking her blood over a period of nine months.

TIME TO KILL

Even in the 21st century, vampire tales abound. In 2004, in Wallachia, Romania (home of Vlad Draculea), a corpse was exhumed and destroyed to prevent it from emerging and drinking the blood of living people. The body had a stake driven through the heart, which was then cut from the chest and burnt.

BLOOD BATH-ORY

Countess Elizabeth Bathory was no fictional character, but a real-life noble woman who was known as "The Blood Countess." Driven by the desire for eternal youth, she is said to have captured and killed as many as 600 Hungarian girls so that she could drink and bathe in their blood. She was walled up in her own castle as a punishment until her death.

Crystal Skull Mystery

AT LEAST 13 BEAUTIFUL CRYSTAL SKULLS—FOUND AT VARIOUS LOCATIONS IN MEXICO, CENTRAL AND SOUTH AMERICA—WERE PRESENTED TO MUSEUMS AND COLLECTORS DURING THE 19TH AND EARLY 20TH CENTURIES. HOWEVER, DESPITE EXTENSIVE TESTS, NOBODY CAN BE SURE HOW AND WHEN THEY WERE ACTUALLY MADE. THE SKULLS ARE SAID TO BE MYSTICAL PRE-COLUMBIAN ARTIFACTS FROM THE MAYAN OR AZTEC CIVILIZATIONS AND TO POSSESS SPIRITUAL POWERS THAT CAN PRODUCE VISIONS, CURE ILLNESS OR EVEN CAUSE DEATH.

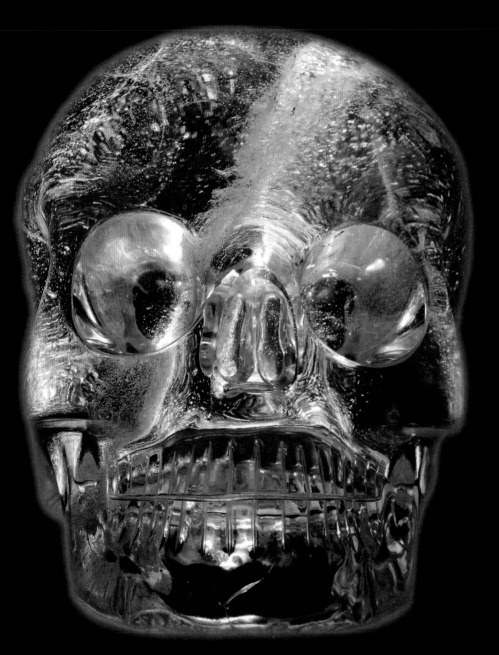

ⓡIPLEY'S RESEARCH

LEGEND LINKS THE CRYSTAL SKULLS TO THE ANCIENT MAYAN CIVILIZATION WHOSE CALENDAR ENDS ON DECEMBER 21, 2012. IT IS BELIEVED THAT IF THE 13 SKULLS ARE REUNITED, IT WILL PREVENT AN APOCALYPTIC CATASTROPHE FROM OCCURRING ON THAT DATE. OTHERS CLAIM THAT THE SKULLS ARE RELICS OF THE LOST WORLD OF ATLANTIS OR ARE THE EQUIVALENT OF ANCIENT COMPUTERS, HELPING US TO LOOK INTO THE PAST, PRESENT AND FUTURE. ANALYSIS OF ONE OF THE SKULLS SHOWED THAT IT HAD BEEN CARVED FROM A SINGLE PIECE OF ROCK CRYSTAL—POSSIBLY BY USING DIAMONDS. HOWEVER, FOR ANCIENT PEOPLES TO HAVE HAND-CARVED SUCH AN INTRICATE SKULL IN THIS WAY WOULD HAVE TAKEN AN ESTIMATED 300 YEARS IN MAN-HOURS. MANY EXPERTS DISMISS THE THEORY THAT THE SKULLS ARE THOUSANDS OF YEARS OLD AND SUGGEST THAT THEY WERE MADE IN THE 19TH CENTURY WITH MODERN TOOLS. NEVERTHELESS, UNTIL SOMEONE COMES UP WITH A DEFINITIVE EXPLANATION, A MYSTICAL AURA WILL CONTINUE TO SURROUND THESE STRANGE AND WONDERFUL CRYSTAL SKULLS.

Crystal Skull

This crystal skull, which stands 4⅓ in (11 cm) high, was presented to a Paris museum by explorer Alphonse Pinart in 1878. There is a prism at the back of the skull, so that any ray of light that strikes the eye-sockets is reflected there and anyone looking into the eye-sockets can see the whole room reflected. The skull is reputed to depict an ancient goddess of the dead and could be as much as 35,000 years old, but its actual origins remain a baffling mystery.

An Italian museum offered up some bizarre fare for visitors in 2008, including chocolate-covered locusts. The Natural Science Museum in Bergamo held the event to promote "entomophagy," the practice of eating insects, which is common in many cultures around the world. A variety of bug salads were also on the menu, made from crickets, worms and other insects.

Tasty Treats

From smoked rattlesnake to creamed armadillo, there is some crazy canned food available around the world for those with adventurous taste buds. From popular foods, such as cheeseburgers, to more gruesome offerings, such as the cockroaches (shown here) or ants' eggs, there is something to suit everyone—you can even buy a whole chicken in a can, complete with bones and skin!

R MANY BEERS

Over 5,000 different types of beer are brewed in Germany. There are about 1,300 breweries in the country, and the Weihenstephan Abbey Brewery in Bavaria has been making beer for nearly a thousand years—since 1040.

R ROTTEN STENCH

In May 2009, rotten food in a refrigerator released odors so vile that hundreds of people were evacuated from a building in San José, California, and seven others were sent to the hospital. One of the few people who didn't need treatment was the office worker who was cleaning out the fridge at the time—suffering from allergies, luckily she couldn't smell a thing.

R POISON ROOT

Cassava root, a common tropical food source, contains cyanide and can poison a person if it is not prepared correctly.

R GLOWING JELLO

By including food-safe quinine as an ingredient, gastronomes Sam Bompas and Harry Parr from London, England, have created a jello that glows blue in the dark.

R MARS CROP

NASA scientists say that the soil on Mars would be good enough to grow asparagus and turnips, but unfortunately not fertile enough for strawberries.

R ROMANTIC CHEESE

In the 12th century, Blanche of Navarre tried to win the heart of French King Philippe Auguste by sending him 200 cheeses every year.

R COSTLY CURRY

To coincide with the DVD release of Oscar-winning movie *Slumdog Millionaire* in June 2009, Bombay Brasserie restaurant in London, England, prepared a curry that cost $3,000 a portion. The dish, called the Samundari Khazana, or Seafood Treasure, contained Devon crab, white truffle, Beluga caviar, quails' eggs, sea snails, and a Scottish lobster coated in edible gold leaf.

R SNAKE BITE

Until health authorities stepped in to stop the practice in 2009, a prized delicacy on the menus of restaurants in the southern Chinese province of Guangdong was meat from a chicken that had been bitten to death by a poisonous snake.

R SUPER SANDWICH

In June 2009, the Bradley County Chamber of Commerce made a 168-ft-long (51-m) BLT (bacon, lettuce and tomato) sandwich at the 53rd Annual Bradley County Pink Tomato Festival in Warren, Arkansas. The sandwich, which took nearly two hours to build, used 300 lb (136 kg) of bacon, 80 lb (36 kg) of lettuce and 60 lb (27 kg) of tomatoes, and oozed 220 fl oz (6.5 l) of mayonnaise.

R CHICKEN FEED

The average meat-eater consumes 1,200 chickens per person during his or her lifetime—that's 3,970 lb (1,800 kg) of chicken meat, the equivalent of eating a four-year-old elephant.

R CRAZY CRAVINGS

Thirty-seven-year-old Rakesh "Cobra" Narayan, of Moala, Fiji, will eat just about anything—including floor tiles, pieces of concrete, clothes, shoes, furniture and even a lawn mower. His crazy cravings started when he was ten and chewed some chicken wire. Then, because he was still feeling peckish, he ate a raw chicken. Now he eats nuts and bolts, insects, lizards, grass, grease and his favorite, broken fluorescent-tube lights. At first the sharp objects used to cut the inside of his cheeks but since he learned to cope with the diverse materials in his mouth, he claims to have never suffered any ill effects.

R INSECT DIET

A mountain hiker survived five days after a bad fall on a mountain by eating centipedes, ants and even a poisonous wolf spider. Derek Mamoyac from Philomath, Oregon, was descending 12,300-ft (3,750-m) Mount Adams in Washington State in October 2008 when he fell and broke his ankle. Despite his injury, he continued his descent by crawling or, if that became too painful, shuffling on his backside. When his food supplies ran out, he ate insects to keep his strength up.

R GARLIC BALLS

American First Lady Eleanor Roosevelt used to eat three chocolate-covered garlic balls every morning. They were prescribed by her doctor to improve her memory.

R LETTUCE EUPHORIA

Lettuce has the same effect on rabbits as opium has on humans. Lettuce contains lactucarium, which has been used as a sedative in sleeping draughts and can cause a sense of mild euphoria in rabbits.

CREAM TEA

In May 2009, Anne Tattersall from Devon, England, created an enormous cream tea, featuring a scone that weighed 99 lb (45 kg) and measured 3 ft (1 m) in diameter. The scone was baked by Nick, Amy and Mary Lovering and Simon Clarke and was filled with 20 lb (9 kg) of jelly and 35 lb (16 kg) of clotted cream.

BILLION FROGS

Up to one billion frogs are eaten by people around the world each year.

RAW TALENT

JIA JEM DECIDED TO MAKE THIS STYLISH DRESS OUT OF RAW MEATS WHEN SHE HAD NOTHING TO WEAR TO A FRIEND'S PARTY. JIA, FROM CHICAGO, ILLINOIS, MADE THE DRESS OUT OF SALAMI BECAUSE IT'S THIN AND STAYS IN ONE PIECE, AND BACON BECAUSE IT LOOKS MEATY. SHE STARTED WITH A BASIC THICK COTTON DRESS, LAYERED THE MEAT ON TOP THEN COVERED IT WITH A CLEAR VINYL. THE DRESS TOOK HER SIX HOURS TO MAKE AND WAS REFRIGERATED UNTIL IT WAS TIME FOR THE PARTY.

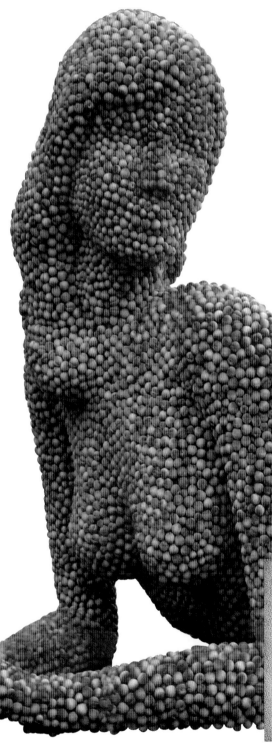

WORM CANDY

Annie Munoz of Panama City, Panama, makes candies filled with grasshoppers and mealworms, and lollipops with worms inside.

TASTY JAIL

Inmates at Parappana Agrahara prison in Bangalore, India, refused to apply for bail because the jail food was so good. Juvenile offenders even lied about their age to get in. It may be no coincidence that the prison recently housed 4,700 inmates—more than twice its capacity.

CHOWDER CROWD

At the 28th annual Chowderfest held in Boston, Massachusetts, in July 2009, 2,000 gal (7,570 l) of New England's signature dish of clams, cream and potatoes were served to a crowd of around 10,000 people.

FISH MADNESS

Some herbivorous fish can cause a form of food poisoning that can bring on severe hallucinations when eaten.

Soft as a Peach

Using 24,000 peaches, this sculpture of Australian actress Jolene Anderson was made and displayed in Sydney's First Fleet Park, Australia, in 2008. An advertising agency constructed the 39-ft (12-m) model to promote a skincare range. With the key slogan "Skin good enough to eat," the work was intended to remind Australian women that their skin is soft and fragile, like a peach. What a shame the peaches will eventually rot!

TOMATO FORCE

In Guiyang, China in 2009, hundreds of people hurled tomatoes at each other at a bizarre promotional event organized by a local shopping center. Inspired by the famous Tomatina festival in Spain, the juicy battle required a massive haul of tomatoes weighing more than 20 family cars and costing almost $15,000.

℞ PRECIOUS PARMESAN

At some banks in the Emilia-Romagna region of central Italy, a deposit of Parmesan cheese can be used to guarantee a loan. An 88-lb (40-kg) round of Parmesan is worth more than $400, and if the borrower defaults on repayments, the banks recover their losses by selling the cheeses. One bank holds over 400,000 rounds of Parmesan.

Holy Cannoli

Speed eater Kevin Basso devoured 17 whole cannoli at the 2009 Little Italy Cannoli Eating Competition in New York City. Kevin finished third, with winner 'Crazy Legs' Conti gulping down 20½ of the traditional Italian desert pastries in just six minutes.

℞ RAW BLOOD

A restaurant in Hanoi, Vietnam, serves customers a bowl of raw pig or duck blood at 75 cents each. Equally popular is a frozen pudding made from the fresh blood of the same animals.

℞ RIB FEAST

Pat "Deep Dish" Bertoletti of Chicago, Illinois, ate 5 lb 12 oz (2.6 kg) of ribs in 12 minutes at the Best in the West Nugget World Rib Eating Championship in Sparks, Nevada, in September 2009.

℞ GIANT DOG

More than 2,000 people ate a 660-ft-long (200-m) hot dog in Santa Marta, Colombia. Twelve of the city's leading fast-food cooks used 220 lb (100 kg) of bread, 275 lb (125 kg) of sausages, 250 bottles of sauce and tons of vegetables and cheese to make the dog.

℞ DINOSAUR CAFÉ

At the T-Rex Café in Kansas City, Kansas, customers can eat with dinosaurs. The diner's prehistoric environment features life-size animatronics dinosaurs and bubbling geysers, and the chance to dig up dinosaur fossils.

℞ MASS CRUNCH

More than 39,000 baseball fans ate potato chips simultaneously in the middle of the second inning of a game between the New York Mets and the Cincinnati Reds at Citi Field, New York, in July 2009. The crunch could be heard all over the ballpark.

R ROBOT CHEFS

A restaurant in China serves meals cooked by robot chefs. Hundreds of recipes for traditional Chinese dishes have been stored in the databases of the computers that control the movements of the two robots at the I Robot restaurant in Nanning, Guangxi Province. Human involvement is limited to preparing the ingredients.

R DOGGY ICES

A company from North Yorkshire, England, has devised a range of luxury ice creams—for dogs. The frozen yogurt treats come in three flavors and contain hidden dog biscuits as well as yucca extract to reduce the unpleasant odors from flatulence!

R MINCE DISH

The town of Ehden, Lebanon, produced a giant circular kibbeh—a dish of minced meat and cracked wheat—that covered an area of 215 sq ft (20 sq m). The dish required 265 lb (120 kg) of mince, 21 gal (80 l) of olive oil, 175 lb (80 kg) of cracked wheat, 11 lb (5 kg) of salt and 2 lb (1 kg) of pepper.

R CHAMP CHESTNUT

Joey Chestnut of San Jose, California, swallowed 68 hot dogs in ten minutes to capture his third straight Fourth of July hot-dog eating contest at Coney Island in 2009. His winning technique is to grab two hot dogs at a time, force them into his mouth and, with a minimal number of chews, gulp them down. He then dips the buns in water and simply lets them slide down his throat.

Hopping Mad

Pan-fried grasshopper is considered a delicacy in Korea and other parts of Asia. Insect gourmets say it tastes best seasoned with lime or salt, or dipped in garlic butter.

R WHOLE LOTTA SHAKIN'

In May 2009, Chris Raph of Minneapolis, Minnesota, bar manager at the Shout House Dueling Pianos bar, poured 662 cocktails in an hour, averaging over ten cocktails per minute.

R FAST FOOD

The first American-style fast-food restaurant in North Korea opened in June 2009. The Samtaesong restaurant in Pyongyang serves up such traditional American fare as burgers, French fries, waffles and draft beer.

R VALUABLE NOSE

Cheese tester Nigel Pooley from Somerset, England, has insured his nose for $8 million. He uses his refined sense of smell to select more than 12,000 tons of Cheddar cheese every year.

R INFLAMMABLE WATER

In early 2009, the tap water to some residents of Fort Lupton, Colorado, contained so much dissolved natural gas that it was combustible.

R CAMEL CHOCS

Dubai-based company Al Nassma specializes in making camel-milk chocolates. It has 3,000 camels, which produce enough milk to make 100 tons of low-fat chocolate a year.

R CARRIED THE CAN

At his retirement ceremony in 2009, U.S. Army Colonel Henry A. Moak Jr. finally opened a 40-year-old military-issued can of pound cake. Moak was given the can in 1969 when he was a Marine helicopter pilot, but vowed to keep it unopened until the day he retired.

What's Your Poison?

In Laos, drinkers can buy a bottle of snake wine—with a real dead snake inside. The poison of venomous snakes is dissolved in the liquor, which is then used for medicinal purposes. Snake products help treat a range of ailments, including arthritis, fever and whooping cough.

COCA-COLA ADDICT

For years, Jason Morgan, a 32-year-old truck driver from Neath, South Wales, drank more than 20 pt (10 l) of Coca-Cola every day. He would drink five 64-fl-oz (2-l) bottles daily—equivalent to 26 cans!

NEW YEAR CAKE

In December 2008, bakers in Bucharest, Romania, made a cake that weighed an amazing 619 lb (280 kg). The tiered cake was covered with fruit and whipped cream and decorated with the Romanian and European flags, along with the words "Happy New Year 2009."

GIANT JAMBALAYA

More than 50 volunteers from Gonzales, Louisiana, teamed up in June 2009 to cook a giant jambalaya in a pot that measured nearly 8 ft (2.4 m) in diameter. The pot was so big that it had to be transported by forklift and placed in a specially dug trench. Several people had to stir the dish simultaneously, using 9-ft-long (2.7-m) paddles. The recipe contained 1,200 lb (545 kg) of pork and sausage, 300 lb (135 kg) of onions, 16 cups of red and black pepper, 20 lb (9 kg) of garlic and 100 gal (378 l) of water.

FLOATING APPLES

The reason that apples float when dropped in water is because they are 25 percent air.

HOT STUFF

In April 2009, Anandita Dutta Tamuly of Jorhat, Assam, India, ate 51 ghost peppers—one of the world's spiciest chilis—in two minutes. She has been hooked on hot peppers since the age of five when chili paste was smeared on her tongue by her mother to cure an infection.

TAKE THAT

When thieves attempted to rob pizza delivery man Eric Lopez Devictoria of Miramar, Florida, in December 2008, he threw a piping hot, large pepperoni pizza at the gunman and made his escape.

RICH FOOD

Fifteen gourmands paid $30,000 a head for a special meal prepared by the world's top chefs at a hotel in Bangkok, Thailand, in 2007. The banquet featured ingredients flown in from 35 cities around the world, including lobsters from Maine and oysters from France.

INCREDIBLE INEDIBLE

Pierre Girard of Golden Valley, Minnesota, has a fruit cake that was baked in 1911—a few months before the *Titanic* sank. The alcohol in which the cake was soaked has acted as a preservative, preventing it from disintegrating.

BUFFALO-GUM ⬆

USING ONLY CHEWED BUBBLEGUM, MAURIZIO SAVINI CREATES BEAUTIFUL SCULPTURES SUCH AS THIS PINK LIFE-SIZE BUFFALO MADE FROM THOUSANDS OF PIECES OF GUM. SINCE "AMERICAN GUM" ARRIVED IN HIS HOME COUNTRY, ITALY, MAURIZIO HAS BEEN CREATING VARIOUS PIECES OF EDIBLE ART USING THE COLORFUL GUMS. HIS WORKS, SUCH AS HIS COLLECTION OF SUITED BUSINESSMEN SUSPENDED IN GYMNASTIC POSES, HAVE SOLD ALL OVER THE WORLD FOR AS MUCH AS $65,000 EACH.

A Slice of Life

A bakery in St. Petersburg, Russia, makes amazing intricate and realistic cakes of anything you can imagine. The famous bakery, Zhanna, creates sponge-based masterpieces of such subjects as a treasure chest with flowing jewels to a construction site with bricks and cranes, ensuring every tiny detail is re-created in icing. The cakes are completely edible and not one piece of plastic is involved.

® POPCORN BALL
In 2009, hundreds of volunteers from Sac City, Iowa, used 1,500 lb (680 kg) of popcorn, 2,400 lb (1 ton) of sugar and 1,100 lb (500 kg) of syrup mix to build an enormous popcorn ball weighing around 5,000 lb (2.2 tons). Even though it has a population of just 2,300, Sac City calls itself the "Popcorn Capital of the World" and produces nearly 5 million lb (2.27 million kg) of popcorn every year.

® THE EATER
Salim "El Akoul" (The Eater) Haini of Ain Defla, Algeria, eats lightbulbs, candles, nails, newspapers and sawdust. He once ate a staggering 1,500 boiled eggs in under three hours and on another occasion consumed an entire roasted lamb, weighing 77 lb (35 kg), in one sitting.

® WALK-IN COCKTAIL
The Alcoholic Architecture bar in London, England, pumps out an intoxicating vapor of gin and tonic to leave visitors feeling slightly merry without even having a drink. Customers don protective suits to avoid smelling like a distillery, and to create the impression that they are actually inside the drink, the bar is decorated with giant limes and massive straws while a soundtrack carries the noise of liquid being poured over ice cubes.

® CHEESE ADDICTION
Kate Silk from Manchester, England, is addicted to cheese. She has eaten cheese every single day for over 35 years—since she was two—and cheese is one of only six foods that don't make her sick.

® WHISKY GALORE
Over a period of 35 years, Brazilian whisky enthusiast Claive Vidiz built up a collection of 3,384 different bottles of whisky. Among the many rare bottles he owned was a Strathmill single malt made to celebrate a Scottish distillery's centenary, which was one of only 69 such bottles ever produced.

® MONSTER MUNCH
At Doha, Qatar, in March 2009, a sandwich was made that stretched 5,676 ft (1,730 m)—more than a mile. It contained 1,102 lb (500 kg) of salami and mortadella, 2,205 lb (1,000 kg) of coleslaw, 440 lb (200 kg) of mozzarella cheese, plus lesser amounts of mushroom, onion, garlic and spices.

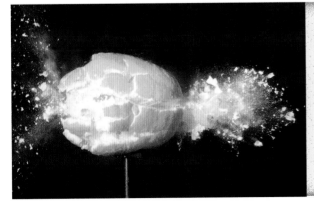

Lemon Crush

Andrew Davidhazy, a high-speed photographer from Rochester, New York City, captured the exact moment a high-powered bullet hit a lemon. Andrew, a professor of imaging and photographic technology at Rochester Institute of Technology, photographed the exploding fruit using a 400-speed film, and a precise burst of light from the electronic flash. The flash lasts just 2 millionths of a second and was perfectly synchronized to the firing of the rifle by an electronic circuit.

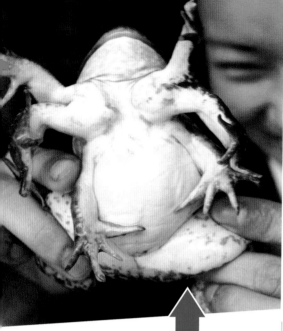

Freed Frog

In 2007, an eight-legged frog was saved from the cooking pot at a restaurant in Quanzhou, southeast China. The one-of-a-kind frog was close to contributing its legs to one of the restaurant's famous frogs' legs dishes, but compassionate staff decided to keep the animal instead of cooking it!

R LOBSTER ROLL

Using 48 lb (22 kg) of lobster meat and 4 gal (15 l) of Miracle Whip, the city of Portland, Maine, in June 2009 baked a lobster roll that measured 61 ft 9½ in (18.8 m) long.

R COLD COMFORT

Immigration officials in Llandudno, Wales, found a Chinese chef living in a freezer inside a restaurant where he was employed.

R PURPLE PEARL

A Florida couple stumbled across a potential fortune in their seafood dinner. George and Leslie Brock were eating steamed clams at a restaurant in Lake Worth when Mr. Brock bit on something hard—a rare, perfectly round purple pearl. Purple pearls are most commonly found in large New England quahogs—clams known for violet coloring on the insides of their shells—and the finest specimens can be worth as much as $25,000.

R STURDY TOASTER

Joan Lopes of Suffolk, England, regularly uses an electric pop-up toaster that is nearly 60 years old. She bought the silver toaster as a wedding anniversary gift for her parents in 1951.

R TURKEY TREAT

A farm in Devon, England, created a roast dinner consisting of a huge turkey stuffed with 11 smaller birds—a goose, a chicken, a pheasant and eight young ducks. Weighing 56 lb (25 kg), the True Love Roast was big enough to feed 125 people.

R POTATO DIET

Joanne Adams from Cleveland, England, used to live on 16 bags of potato chips a day. For some 20 years she ate hardly anything but potatoes, and as a result she kept breaking fingers and her hair grew so slowly she needed to wear extensions.

R PIZZA DELIVERY

In November 2004, Lucy Clough from Sussex, England, hand-delivered a pizza from London to Melbourne, Australia—a journey of 30 hours and a distance of 10,532 mi (16,950 km).

R CALAMARI KING

Patrick Bertoletti of Chicago, Illinois, ate 6 lb 10 oz (3 kg) of deep-fried calamari in ten minutes at Mallie's Sports Grill World Calamari Eating Championship, held in Southgate, Michigan, in May 2009.

DUCKLING DELICACY

DUCKLING EMBRYOS THAT ARE ALMOST READY TO HATCH ARE A CULINARY TREAT IN THE PHILIPPINES. KNOWN AS BALUT, THE POPULAR DELICACY IS SOLD BY STREET VENDORS ACROSS THE COUNTRY. GETTING THE BALUT EGGS TO THIS STAGE IS A PAINSTAKING PROCESS, AS THEY HAVE TO BE CAREFULLY INCUBATED FOR 17 TO 20 DAYS—UNTIL THE DUCKLINGS ARE ALMOST READY TO HATCH—BEFORE THEY ARE PART-BOILED AND SOLD. BALUT HAS BECOME SO POPULAR YOU CAN EVEN GET BOTTLED BALUT, PICKLED BALUT AND BALUT OMELET.

PECKING POINTERS
Balut etiquette

Balut should be eaten in a certain way to get the most from the egg's contents.

First, tap the shell to make an opening large enough to get the fetus broth, or soup.

Drink this soup, which tastes light and quite sweet, through the hole before peeling the shell to reveal the yolk and pre-developed duckling.

Everything inside the egg can be eaten, although most people add some salt and pepper or chili to the fetus before chewing!

Goodbye Rocco by Jorge Perruorria is a 1950s fridge made to look like a brightly colored coffin.

OLIVE THEFT

One morning in May 2008, olive grower Quentin von Essen from the Hunter Valley, New South Wales, Australia, woke to discover that all but two of his 400 olive trees had been stripped overnight by thieves. Apart from the two untouched trees, which were spotlit, the thieves did not leave a single olive on any tree or on the ground—and some of the trees were 11 ft 6 in (3.5 m) tall.

PIZZA LINE

In May 2009, Scott Van Duzer and nine other cooks prepared more than 1,800 pizzas to form a pizza line measuring 1,777 ft (540 m) around an entire city block in Fort Pierce, Florida. It took 1,250 lb (570 kg) of flour, 600 lb (270 kg) of mozzarella cheese, 70 gallons (265 l) of tomato sauce and 400 tables to form the line.

POLICE BALL

A 267-lb (120-kg) matzo ball was unveiled on the streets of New York City in August 2009. Baked by Noah's Ark Original Deli, it was 3 ft (1 m) high and made from 1,000 eggs, 80 lb (36 kg) of margarine, 200 lb (90 kg) of matzo meal and 20 lb (9 kg) of chicken base. The ball was transported in a 24-ft (7-m) freightliner with a police escort.

ENORMOUS ECLAIR

In February 2009, the Swallow Bakery of Chichester, West Sussex in England, made a chocolate eclair that was nearly 12 ft (3.6 m) long. The monster eclair contained 2.2 lb (1 kg) of chocolate and 8 pt (3.8 l) of double cream. It took bakers Lou Allen and Michaela Heard four hours to construct the pastry, followed by another hour filling it with cream before spreading the chocolate on top.

TASTY ORGANS

A restaurant in Tokyo, Japan, serves up sushi body parts hidden inside an edible human "corpse." The corpse, which has a dough "skin" and "blood" sauce, is wheeled into the restaurant on a hospital gurney and placed on a table. The hostess begins by cutting into the "body" with a scalpel, after which the patrons also dig in, opening up the flesh to reveal edible "organs" made of sushi.

HIDDEN ENTRANCE

Evening visitors to The Safe House restaurant in Milwaukee, Wisconsin, are asked for a password to gain admission to the spy-themed eatery and bar, which has a hidden entrance and a secret exit.

PANCAKE BLAST

With their pancake-in-a-can product, workers from the Batter Blaster company made an amazing 76,382 pancakes in eight hours at Atlanta, Georgia, in May 2009. The team used more than 30 grills on the challenge.

Fridge-tastic

An unusual art exhibition in Paris, France, entitled "Energy-Devouring Monsters" featured more than 50 refrigerators. Transformed into colorful works of art by Cuban artists Mario Miguel Gonzalez (known as Mayito) and Roberto Fabelo, the fridges are all classic 1950s models, which were commonplace in Cuban homes until the country replaced all high-energy consuming appliances during an energy crisis in the 1990s. These fridges were saved from the scrapheap and now enjoy a new lease on life in this unique display of icons from Cuba's past.

Fast Food by Luis Enrique Camejo marries a fridge with the front of a 1950s American car in a comment on the consumerism of that era.

TASTY DE-LIGHT

CONSTRUCTED BY CALIFORNIA-BASED ARTIST YA YA CHOU, THIS AMAZING GUMMI BEAR CHANDELIER IS MADE ENTIRELY FROM THE FAMOUS CANDY BEARS AND CAN REMAIN FRESH AND ON DISPLAY FOR UP TO TWO YEARS! FORMED BY STRINGING HUNDREDS OF DIFFERENT FLAVORED GUMMIES TOGETHER WITH BEADS AND STRING, THE CHANDELIER IS JUST ONE OF THE PIECES IN A SERIES OF GUMMI-BEAR SCULPTURES, WHICH ALSO INCLUDE A BEARSKIN RUG AND A DEER.

ℝ MOON PIE
To celebrate the 40th anniversary of the first lunar landing, NASA created a giant moon pie in 2009. The special pie—consisting of marshmallow dipped in chocolate—measured 40 in (101 cm) in diameter, 6 in (15 cm) high and weighed 55 lb (25 kg).

ℝ SMILING PEPPER
When Nigel Hollingsworth from Somerset, England, sliced open a homegrown jalapeno pepper, he was amazed to be greeted by a smiling face! The two halves of the pepper appeared to have a pair of eyes—complete with eyebrows—a nose and a grinning mouth.

ℝ NUGGET DROP
To welcome in the New Year in 2009, a chicken restaurant in McDonough, Georgia, dropped a plaster chicken nugget 6 ft 6 in (2 m) tall and weighing 795 lb (360 kg) into a giant vat of fake dipping sauce.

ℝ PASTA BOWL
In March 2009, a restaurant in Doha, Qatar, dished up a bowl of pasta measuring 20 ft (6 m) long and 6 ft 6 in (2 m) wide and weighing 9,480 lb (4,300 kg).

ℝ EXPENSIVE TASTE
Gennaro Pelliccia, a London-based Italian coffee taster with more than 18 years of experience, has had his tongue insured for nearly $14 million. His job is to test every batch of raw beans before they leave the firm's roastery and he is banned from eating curry within two days of tasting sessions in case the spices dull his sensitivity.

ℝ ORANGE MONEY
Chinese college student Wu Xiaobin paid for his 2009 course fees and living expenses with five tons of oranges. He drove two truckloads of mandarin oranges more than 130 mi (210 km) from the family farm in Quzhou to the city of Hangzhou, where he sold the fruit to fellow students so that he could continue his studies at Zhejiang University of Media and Communications.

ℝ BEER LAKE
A beer lake was formed in the German city of Kassel in December 2008 after a truck carrying 12 tons of freshly brewed beer lost its load while taking a sharp turn. Some 1,600 bottles smashed as they hit the road but their contents quickly froze in temperatures of around 25°F (–4°C).

ℝ PERFECT CHEESE
With the help of scientists from England's Bristol University, West Country Farmhouse Cheesemakers have devised what they claim is the mathematical formula for the perfect cheese sandwich. The formula contains nine algebraic variables, covering such essentials as the thickness of the Cheddar cheese, the thickness of the bread, the dough flavor modifier, the amount of mayonnaise, the thickness of tomato and the depth of pickle.

ℝ HUGE FUDGE
In June 2009, Lansing Community College, Michigan, created a slab of chocolate fudge that weighed 5,500 lb (2,496 kg). The slab was made from 2,800 lb (1,270 kg) of chocolate, 705 lb (320 kg) of butter and 305 gal (1,155 l) of condensed milk.

ℝ UNDERWATER RESTAURANT
Seating 14 people and entered via a spiral staircase at the end of a jetty, the Ithaa restaurant in the Maldives is situated underwater, 16 ft (5 m) below sea level, offering customers a 180-degree panoramic view of the coral reef that surrounds it. Made mostly from acrylic, the 175-ton restaurant was lowered into the water and secured with concrete to four steel piles that had been hammered into the seabed.

Half and Half

This half-red and half-green golden delicious apple truly is a one of a kind. Grown in the village of Colaton Raleigh in Devon, England, by retired painter Ken Morrish, the apple's colors are thought to have appeared owing to a random genetic mutation that has a million-to-one chance of occurring. People were desperate to see the half-and-half apple and even lined up outside Ken's house to take pictures of it!

Pear of Buddhas

After more than six years of work, Gao Xianzhang from Hebei, China, has managed to modify a crop of pears to look like little Buddhas. In 2009, after a lot of effort and rotten fruit, he perfected a technique and was able to mold 10,000 pears into edible Buddha-shaped fruit. Selling them for $10 each, the pears, which resemble baby Buddhas, are grown in special plastic molds on the tree branches from an early stage.

FROZEN FEAST

For the last 15 years of his life, eccentric U.S. movie producer Howard Hughes (1905–76) existed almost solely on a diet of ice cream. He usually ate the same flavor until every supplier in the district had run out.

CHOPSTICK CHALLENGE

In March 2009, Ashrita Furman of New York City ate 40 M&Ms in a minute—with chopsticks.

CHOCOLATE LOVER

Peggy Griffiths from Devon, England, eats 30 bars of chocolate a week—and in 2009 she celebrated her 100th birthday. She has eaten an estimated 70,000 Cadbury's Dairy Milk bars in her lifetime, amounting to an incredible 4 tons of chocolate. Chocoholic Peggy used to run a candy store in the 1930s, but it closed down because she ate all the profits.

Giant Gummi

Derek Lawson makes giant gummi bears at Popalop's Candy Shop in Raleigh, North Carolina. Each one weighs a massive 5 lb (2 kg) and measures a whopping 9 x 5½ x 3½ in (23 x 14 x 9 cm), which is 1,400 times the size of an ordinary gummi bear. It takes nine hours to create each bear and make them taste exactly like the original smaller version. The bears are available in a variety of different flavors including blue raspberry, cola, grape and green apple.

Mice Kebab

After being killed in the fields of Malawi, mice are boiled, dried, salted and sold by children as lunch to passing travelers. For easy handling, half a dozen of the sun-dried rodent carcasses are inserted in a piece of split bamboo. The heads are left on, so the customer eats everything—including the mouse's hair, bones, teeth, tail and toenails.

® RUDENESS PAYS

A bar in the Spanish resort of Cullera offered free beer and tapas in 2009 to customers who insulted its bartenders. The owners of Caso Pocho said the gimmick was designed to relieve stress among its recession-weary clientele, but added that the free alcohol and snacks would go only to those who came up with truly original insults.

® HOSPITAL FOOD

Hospitalis, a restaurant in Riga, Latvia, is hospital-themed with waitresses dressed as nurses, food served in flasks, cocktails served in test tubes and beakers, and medical implements for cutlery.

® EGG-STREME DIET

To build up their body weight for the 2010 Commonwealth Games, India's rugby players were ordered to eat seven meals and at least 15 eggs a day for over a year.

® PIZZA RUSH

Dennis Tran of Silver Springs, Maryland, made three large pizzas in just over 46 seconds in 2008—that's an average of around 15 seconds per pizza. He had to hand-stretch the fresh dough, apply pizza sauce and top the three pizzas—one pepperoni, one mushroom and one cheese.

® SAUSAGE SUPPER

In 2009, cooks from Vinkovci, Croatia, used a vast 8-ft (2.5-m) pan to prepare a sausage that was 1,740 ft (530 m) long and fed around 3,000 people. The sausage was made with 880 lb (400 kg) of pork (from 28 pigs), 88 lb (40 kg) of paprika, 22 lb (10 kg) of salt, 11 lb (5 kg) of garlic and 5 lb 8 oz (2.5 kg) of spices.

® PANCAKE STACK

Sean McGinlay and Natalie King of the Hilton Grosvenor Hotel, Glasgow, Scotland, took 22 hours to build a pancake stack that stood 29½ in (75 cm) high. The tower of 672 pancakes used 100 eggs, more than 17 pt (8 l) of milk, 11 lb (5 kg) of flour and 6½ lb (3 kg) of butter.

® SPACE PEE

The International Space Station has a $250-million water regeneration system that changes urine into drinkable water.

® RICH CAKE

In July 2009, 170 Palestinian bakers from ten pastry shops in Nablus on the West Bank created a giant syrupy Kunafa cheesecake that measured 243 ft (74 m) long, weighed 3,883 lb (1,765 kg) and was big enough to feed more than 100,000 people. The bakers used 1,540 lb (700 kg) of semolina flour, the same amount of cheese and 660 lb (300 kg) of sugar to produce the cake at a cost of around $15,000.

® CHILI GRENADES

To control rioters and fight insurgents, Indian security forces have been conducting trials using hand grenades that contain red-hot chili powder. The grenades use Bhut Jolokia chilis, which are 200 times hotter than the average jalapeno, to choke rioters' respiratory tracts and cause their eyes to water.

® LONG SERVICE

At age 95, Angelo Cammarata retired following over 75 years as a bartender at his family's café in Pittsburgh, Pennsylvania. He served his first drink as a 19-year-old just minutes after Prohibition ended in 1933 and, except for a 30-month break during World War II, he tended the bar right up until 2009.

® KING CABBAGE

Steve Hubacek of Wasilla, Alaska, submitted a cabbage at the Alaska State Fair in 2009 that weighed over 125 lb (57 kg). The head of the cabbage measured about 21 in (53 cm) across and the leaves spanned around 5 ft (1.5 m).

Bug Cuisine

What's bugging you? Taiwanese water bugs on a bed of Japanese udon noodles are a traditional dish in Tokyo.

RED HOT

Brave contestants devour red hot chili peppers in a speed-eating competition in Guizhou, China. Chili peppers are measured in Scoville Heat Units (SHU), which relate to the number of times a chili extract must be diluted in water to lose its heat. The naga morich chili pepper from Bangladesh measures a tongue-numbing 1,500,000 SHU, making it no less than 50 times hotter than cayenne pepper.

Bela Borsodi can make weird and wonderful faces out of any old clothes. The Austrian-born artist, based in New York, has developed a style of intricate fabric origami, folding leather jackets, jeans, shirts and other items so that they form individual quirky faces.

ARTISTIC LICENSE

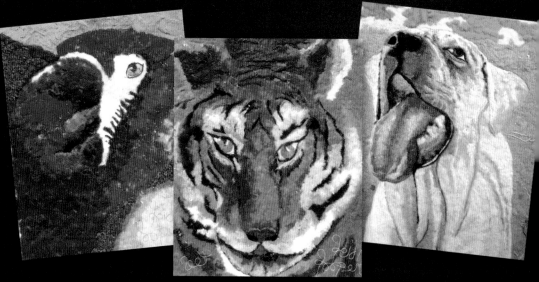

Lint Lady

Heidi Hooper, from Massachusetts, uses dryer lint to create images of animals. The lint is taken from the cotton fiber in towels, chenille from throw blankets and feathers from down comforters that have been through the dryer. Unfortunately, the lint cannot be dyed to a specific color, as it is basically dust, so it can be a difficult task creating a color palette. Heidi will sometimes buy towels in the colors she wants to make her work a little easier.

℞ FRY ART

Ocean City, New Jersey, stages an annual French fry sculpting contest. Competitors take paper plates full of deep-fried potatoes and mash or arrange them together to create oily, high-carbonate models of everything from crabs to log cabins.

℞ COIN FLAG

Inspired by the realization that people don't bother to pick up small-currency 10-won coins on the streets of Korea, Jin Jeong-gun decided to collect as many coins as possible and turn them into a giant mosaic of the Korean national flag. Over a period of 14 years he collected 110,000 coins and then spent four months arranging them into a flag measuring 20 x 13 ft (6 x 4 m). Jin had previously made a pagoda from 2,000 discarded 10-won coins.

Crafty Castle

WHEN WATARU ITOU BECAME BORED DURING HIS UNIVERSITY ENTRANCE EXAMS IN 2005, HE DECIDED TO BUILD A PAPER CITY USING JUST PAPER, A KNIFE AND GLUE. NOW A STUDENT AT TOKYO UNIVERSITY OF THE ARTS, WATARU SPENT FOUR YEARS FOLDING, CUTTING AND STICKING HUNDREDS OF PAGES OF CRAFT PAPER TOGETHER TO CREATE THIS 7.9 x 5.9 FT (2.4 x 1.8 M) MASTERPIECE, WHICH INCLUDES A CASTLE, A CATHEDRAL, AN AIRPORT AND A THEME PARK. WATARU BIZARRELY PLANS TO SET FIRE TO IT EVENTUALLY!

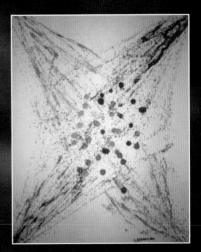

Leandro Granato can achieve amazing symmetry and precision when creating a work by squirting paint from his eye.

Eye Opener

Leandro Granato, an artist from Buenos Aries, Argentina, paints pieces of art using only his eye as a paintbrush. First, he puts the paint into his nose, next he forces the paint up through his eye and finally he squirts it onto a canvas. Leandro achieves this by using his nose sinus cavities, which empty into the eye through small vents. When Leandro puts pressure on his nose, the paint can escape into his eye. Leandro is lucky it doesn't take the other possible exit— through his ears!

℞ SHOE TUBS

A new collection of bathtubs designed to look like women's shoes has been created by Italian designer Massimiliano Della Monaca. Water flows from a jet at the heel of the shoe for hair washing, while the plug is located down at the toe end. One of the tubs was styled on a pair of heels worn by the doll Barbie, who celebrated her 50th birthday in 2009.

℞ BYRON'S JOKE

English romantic poet Lord Byron (1788– 1824) received numerous fan letters from women enclosing locks of their hair—but the hair clippings he sent back for them to swoon over were not from his own head, but from his pet Newfoundland dog.

℞ FASHION RATWALK

For 2009 London Fashion Week, French designer Charlie Le Mindu created a headdress made from dozens of real mice and rat carcasses. The headdress covered the entire face—leaving just a gap for the wearer's eyes—and was adorned with dead rats' tails hanging down the front.

℞ ELEPHANT HEDGE

After falling in love with wildlife on a safari in Kenya, Gavin Hogg decided to transform the box hedgerow of his home near Brecon, Wales, into a herd of elephants. Using a trimmer, shears and a pair of scissors, he painstakingly carved out seven adults and three babies in a 100-ft-long (30-m) trail of green elephants.

℞ HAIR WEAR

Ioana Cioanca from Bistrita Nasaud, Romania, has made an entire wardrobe of clothes from her own hair. Now 72, she grew her hair from the age of 16 until it reached a length of 40 in (1 m) and could be woven. She has already turned her hair into a hat, a shawl, a skirt, a blouse, a raincoat, a pair of gloves, a purse and a handbag.

℞ ICE FIGURES

In an attempt to draw attention to global warming, Brazilian artist Nele Azevedo carved 1,000 miniature figures out of ice and displayed them on the steps of the Concert Hall in Berlin, Germany, in September 2009. He then watched as they quickly melted in temperatures of 73°F (23°C).

R VETERAN CARTOONIST

In 2009, Martin Filchock of Williamson County, Tennessee, was still working as a cartoonist at age 97. He was still producing and selling his work in his 75th year of cartooning.

R SAND ARTIST

Ukrainian artist Kseniya Simonova draws powerful images of World War II in sand. Drawing with her fingers, she uses an illuminated sand table to show how ordinary people in her country were affected by the German invasion.

R HIDDEN PIG

The hidden image of a butchered pig in a Dutch artwork was discovered by a U.S. restorer in 2009— 350 years after the artwork was painted. *Barn Interior*, a 17th-century painting by Egbert van der Poel, was presented to Calvin College in Michigan in 2007 and they in turn sent it to Chicago, Illinois, conservator Barry Bauman for cleaning. Bauman noticed that a ladder on the left side of the painting had been heavily painted over and that the paint was flaking. Underneath he found the pig, hanging dead from the ladder.

Art Angel

See if you recognize any favorite toys in this statue made entirely out of plastic playthings. Artist Robert Bradford, who lives in Cornwall, England, collects thousands of discarded toys and uses them to create life-size action figures. "Toy Angel" stands 6 ft 6 in (2 m) tall and took two months to complete. The artist has also modeled a toy soldier of a similar size, as well as buildings and various animals.

R IMITATION OF LIFE

New York artist Alyssa Monks creates amazingly detailed paintings that look just like photographs. She takes about 1,000 photos—usually of people she knows—for a small series of paintings, using the images to play with the color and make the result look as realistic as possible. She employs no tricks, just intricate brushwork, and for a painting of a woman in a shower, she even re-created the steam effect and the droplets of water by hand.

R MULTI-TALENTED

Kim Noble from London, England, paints in the style of as many as 20 different people. She suffers from a rare personality disorder called Dissociative Identity Disorder (DID), as a result of which 20 people live inside her, ranging from an anorexic teenager called Judy to a man named Ken. Many of her personalities paint and each has its own individual style of painting. In just two years, Kim's personalities produced more than 200 canvasses.

R PRINCIPAL'S PORTRAIT

Fifty-five years after being kicked out of school and told he would never amount to much, a successful artist was commissioned to paint a portrait of the principal who expelled him. David Ingham was thrown out of Ermysted's Grammar School, North Yorkshire, England, as a 12-year-old by Marcelus Forster. However, in 2008 he was approached by the school to paint him.

R FINGER PAINTS

In August 2009, 6,000 children in Belfast, Northern Ireland, used finger paints to decorate a 22,496-sq-ft (2,090-sq-m) canvas with the picture of a house.

R VIRTUAL TRAVELER

Artist Bill Guffey paints stunning pictures of locations around the world—without visiting any of them. Instead, Guffey from Burkesville, Kentucky, uses Google Street View. He has spent hundreds of hours traveling thousands of virtual miles to take in beautiful scenes in every state in the U.S.A. and most of Europe before sitting down to paint them at his home studio. His paintings, which sell for up to $2,500, include a lonely house in Scotland, a canal boat in Amsterdam and a yellow taxi in New York City.

Ⓡ HUMBLE COLLECTORS

Herb and Dorothy Vogel have amassed a world-class art collection comprising nearly 5,000 pieces—on ordinary working-class salaries. A postal worker and librarian respectively, they live in a one-bedroom Manhattan apartment, but their collection, which is worth millions of dollars, is so important that it was accepted as a gift by the National Gallery of Art in Washington, D.C.

Ⓡ RAPID TAPPER

Tap dancer Jo Scanlan of Swindon, England, can perform more than 780 taps in one minute—that's over 13 taps a second!

Ⓡ REGENCY TRAIL

In September 2009, more than 400 fans of 19th-century English novelist Jane Austen walked through the streets of Bath, England, wearing Regency period costume.

Green Piece

Artist Tim Knowles from London, England, has an unlikely assistant—he lets trees do the work for him. With an easel set up under the tree and pens attached to the branches, the paintings take shape of their own accord when the wind blows. According to Knowles, each different species of tree has a distinctive style—hawthorn produces spiky shapes, while the weeping willow makes softer sweeps across the paper.

Ⓡ REVERSE GRAFFITI

A British street artist known as Moose has pioneered a new art form called "reverse graffiti." He uses scrapers, pressure washers and scrub brushes to create clean designs in dirt-covered canvasses, such as tunnel walls and city sidewalks.

Ⓡ GHOSTLY GALLERY

Green-Wood cemetery in Brooklyn, New York City, has a collection of art painted by some of the 600,000 people buried there. Works on display include an 1820s portrait of politician DeWitt Clinton by George Catlin, both of whom are buried at Green-Wood.

Tree People

DEEP IN A NATURAL EUCALYPTUS FOREST IN VICTORIA, AUSTRALIA, A SCULPTOR SPENT 59 YEARS CREATING MORE THAN 90 AMAZING ARTWORKS IN THE TREES. WILLIAM RICKETTS STARTED HIS INCREDIBLE PROJECT IN 1934 AND WORKED ON IT UNTIL HIS DEATH IN 1993, CARVING MYSTERIOUS FIGURES THAT SEEM TO NATURALLY OCCUR IN TREES AND ROCK, BUT ARE ACTUALLY CERAMIC SCULPTURES BLENDED INTO THEIR SURROUNDINGS. THE LOCAL AUTHORITIES EVENTUALLY PROTECTED THE LAND FOR THE PUBLIC AND RICKETTS LIVED IN THE FOREST WELL INTO HIS NINETIES.

Horse Guards Parade, London, England

CHINESE ARTIST LIU BOLIN USES ONLY PAINT AND A SETTING OF HIS CHOICE TO CREATE THESE STUNNING PIECES OF ART. KNOWN AS THE "INVISIBLE MAN," LIU MANAGES TO CAMOUFLAGE HIMSELF COMPLETELY INTO THE BACKGROUND BY PAINTING THE PRECISE COLORS AND DETAILS THAT HE SEES ONTO HIS CLOTHES, WITHOUT ANY DIGITAL TRICKERY. USING HUNDREDS OF DIFFERENT SETTINGS IN CITIES ALL OVER THE WORLD, LIU IS SO EXPERT AT CAMOUFLAGING HIMSELF THAT PASSERSBY NORMALLY DON'T EVEN NOTICE HE IS THERE. AN ASSISTANT HELPS LIU TO PAINT HIS BODY—HE MUST STAND COMPLETELY STILL THROUGHOUT—AND IT CAN TAKE UP TO TEN HOURS TO GET EACH IMAGE PERFECT.

A rare image of the artist himself. Liu Bolin.

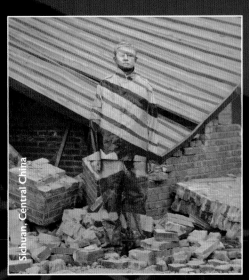

Sichuan, Central China

London, England

Beijing, China

MASTER OF LIGHT AND SHADE

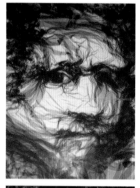

ARTIST BENJAMIN SHINE IN LONDON, ENGLAND, CREATED THIS PORTRAIT OF DUTCH MASTER REMBRANDT VAN RIJN USING JUST ONE PIECE OF BLACK TULLE FABRIC MEASURING 26 x 10 FT (8 x 3 M). BENJAMIN USED A TECHNIQUE OF INTRICATE PLEATING AND PRESSING OF THE MATERIAL, AND TOOK MORE THAN 200 HOURS TO ACHIEVE THE FINAL RESULT. REMBRANDT, KNOWN AS THE MASTER OF LIGHT AND SHADE, WAS A PERFECT SUBJECT FOR BENJAMIN AS HE, TOO, DISPLAYED VARYING TONES OF LIGHT AND SHADE IN HIS PORTRAIT THROUGH THE TULLE FABRIC.

® "THRILLER" STEPS

To mark what would have been Michael Jackson's 51st birthday, on August 29, 2009, more than 12,000 people gathered in Mexico City to retrace the dance steps from his 1983 video "Thriller."

® SHOCK WAVES

As part of his show "Let There Be More Light," London, England, artist Paul Fryer designed a pair of two, fully functioning, 16-ft-high (5-m), aluminum tuning forks, which, vibrating at 72 Hertz, sent shock waves through visitors' bodies.

® ORIGAMI GIRAFFE

Himanshu Agrawal of Mumbai, India, spent 12 hours folding a sheet of paper 35 x 35 ft (10.6 x 10.6 m) into the shape of a 20-ft-high (6-m) origami giraffe. The giraffe, designed by American origamist John Montroll, required over 100 moves and 70 creases in the paper, and the finished article was mounted on a bamboo structure.

® DJ MARATHON

A German DJ broadcast nonstop for more than a week in April 2009. Dominik Schollmayer presented his morning show on Hit-Radio Antenne in Hanover for 169 consecutive hours.

® PAPER DRESS

In September 2009, a woman got married in Kunming, Yunnan Province, China, wearing a dress made entirely out of paper. Designer Zhu Zhu took two and a half months to make the cotton paper dress for the bride, her best friend Sha Sha.

® LONG NOTE

Vocal coach, songwriter and music producer Richard Fink IV of Bergen, New York State, held a single vocal music note for a breathtaking 1 minute 43 seconds in September 2009. He prepared for the challenge by doing regular yoga exercises and extra running.

® TWITTER OPERA

In 2009, London's Royal Opera House staged an opera written by members of the public on Twitter. People were invited to form the libretto by submitting online tweets in the form of messages of up to 140 characters. The words were then set to music, which consisted of original work by composer Helen Porter plus some well-known opera tunes.

Erika Simmons creates a cassette-tape replica of British singer-songwriter Amy Winehouse.

A portrait of Ian Brown, lead singer of the 1980s British band the Stone Roses, created from the unspooled reel of one cassette tape.

Rock 'n' Roll Reel

Music fan Erika Simmons from Atlanta, Georgia, has found a way to re-use all her old cassette tapes, by making them into pieces of art. Using an unspooled cassette reel per piece, Erika has created perfect portraits of music legends such as Jimi Hendrix, Bob Dylan, Jim Morrison, Amy Winehouse and the Stone Roses' Ian Brown. With the works, entitled "Ghosts in the Machine," Erika encourages the viewer to question if the music is on the cassette tape, in the head of the musician, or perhaps both.

® DEFYING GRAVITY

Bryan Berg of Spirit Lake, Iowa, created a gravity-defying sculpture of London landmarks Big Ben tower and the Houses of Parliament, without using any glue or sticky tape, from more than 600 decks of playing cards. It took him over five days to complete the structure that stood 12 x 7 ft (3.6 x 2.1 m) in Las Vegas, Nevada, in July 2009.

® HOLLYWOOD PROPS

Movie fan Luke Kay of Swindon, England, has collected Hollywood memorabilia worth more than $1.5 million. Among his iconic props are two costumes worn by Luke Skywalker actor Mark Hamill in the *Star Wars* movies and one of the original "KITT" cars from the 1980s TV series *Knight Rider* starring David Hasselhoff.

Gallery

MONA LEAVES
Sculpted in Chris Naylor's very own back garden in London, England, in July 2008, this very grassy representation took two days to make using only a small lawn mower and a selection of garden tools.

MONA-KIN
Daniel Hamlin cleverly carved the smiling lady into a pumpkin in 2005 to create a spooky Halloween masterpiece.

MONA EASEL

THE MOST FAMOUS PAINTING IN THE WORLD, "THE MONA LISA," IS AN UNMISTAKABLE PIECE OF ART, BUT WOULD YOU RECOGNIZE HER IF SHE WERE MADE OUT OF COMPUTER PARTS? INSTEAD OF USING TRADITIONAL PAINT AND WATERCOLORS, THESE RESOURCEFUL ARTISTS HAVE USED ANYTHING BUT. FROM VEGETABLES TO RUBIK'S CUBES, THESE BIZARRE PORTRAITS SHOW LEONARDO DA VINCI'S MASTERPIECE AS YOU HAVE NEVER SEEN IT BEFORE.

MONA CAR
In 2006, artist Scott Wade created this dusty impression on the back window of a dirty car. He created his canvas by driving over a mixture of limestone dust, gravel and clay, which settled onto the car windows. He molded the dust into the art piece allowing the rain to soften the edges and lighten his work.

MONA RICE
Since 1993, farmers in the rural Japanese town of Inakadate have created various amazing artworks just before the annual harvest. Using a canvas of 3.7 acres (15,000 sq m), purple and yellow rice plants are planted alongside normal grains. As the rice grows, so does the art.

MONA VISTA

Made from hundreds of tilted ASUS computer chips, "Technology Smiling" was shown at the China Beijing International High-Tech Expo in May 2006.

MOCHA LISA

Made entirely from cups of coffee, this portrait, measuring 20 x 13 ft (6 x 4 m), took three hours to complete, and used 3,604 cups of coffee and 564 pt (267 l) of milk. Displayed on the floor at the Rocks Aroma Festival in Sydney, Australia, in 2009, the portrait has a sepia effect that was cleverly created by pouring varying amounts of milk into each cup.

MONA TOFU

With noodle hair and pepper eyes, Chinese artist Ju Duoqi's veggie Lisa is made out of rice, sea kelp and tofu. The portrait, which uses everyday Chinese vegetables, was displayed at the Vegetable Museum exhibition in Beijing in 2008.

DRAGON LISA

Mona Lisa becomes a fiery dragon in this digitally enhanced portrait, known as "Le Jocondausaure." This was one of 100 parodies, impressions and re-creations at the "100 Smiles of Mona Lisa" exhibition at Tokyo's Metropolitan Museum in 2000.

MONA'S CUBE

Known as Rubikcubism, the "Invader" is a mystery street artist who re-creates famous masterpieces, historic events and celebrities out of Rubik's cubes. This "Mona Lisa" impression took two days to create in 2009—with only six colors to choose from, each of the 800 cubes had to be twisted to the correct color to complete the masterpiece.

MONA TOAST

Using 1,426 pieces of toast, Tadahiko Ogawa from Kyoto, Japan, burned slices of bread and scraped them carefully to create the shaded effect of Leonardo da Vinci's masterpiece in 1983.

MONA GREASER

In 2009, artist Phil Hansen from Minneapolis, Minnesota, re-created Leonardo da Vinci's famous painting the *Mona Lisa* from burger grease! He used his hands to smear the grease from 14 burgers on to an 11-ft (3.35-m) canvas made from butcher's paper.

MAGIC MOSAIC

Children helped to build a giant mosaic of Harry Potter author J.K. Rowling in 2009—from 48,000 LEGO® bricks. Composed of white, yellow and gray bricks, the portrait was so tall that visitors to LEGOLAND® theme park in Berkshire, England, had to use a ladder to add extra pieces.

CREMATION CREATIONS

Val Thompson from Tyne and Wear, England, paints beautiful works of art using the ashes of loved ones her clients have lost. By mixing the cremated remains with paint, she not only acquires additional texture on the canvas but is also able to create a unique, personalized and lasting tribute.

FAMILY TREE

Peggy and Peter Newman from Somerset, England, have spent 25 years and around $150,000 displaying their family tree in a series of amazing 1:12 scale model houses. Each house in the collection, which spans five centuries and 13 generations of relatives dating back to the reign of King Henry VIII, took Mr. Newman six months to carve by hand and is accurate down to the last brick.

JUNK MAIL

Free Paper, an art exhibit by Annette Lawrence of Austin, Texas, was created entirely from a year's worth of unsolicited junk mail. She cut the pieces of paper into strips 2 in (5 cm) wide and displayed them in 12 neat stacks.

SINGLE HANDED

French composer Maurice Ravel (1875–1937) wrote the "Piano Concerto For The Left Hand" in 1930 for his friend, the Austrian musician Paul Wittgenstein, who lost his right arm in World War I.

HEAVY ALBUM

In Orlando, Florida, Dodge opened a photo album that measured 9 x 12 ft (2.7 x 3.6 m). Produced to celebrate the launch of the 2008 Dodge Grand Caravan, the album featured 20 pages of photographs tracing the history of the Dodge minivan and was so heavy that it required at least two adults to turn each page.

HEAVY METAL

A busker in Cambridge, England, sings and plays his guitar while squeezed inside a small metal garbage bin. Charlie Cavey discovered his unusual musical venue after watching garbage men emptying the street bin. At 5 ft 9 in (1.75 m) tall, he decided he could fit inside it and, although he finds his job cramped, his singing style has proved a real hit with passersby.

GREAT TOME

The Great Encyclopedia of Yongle, compiled in China during the Ming Dynasty, took four years to complete (1403–07) and spanned 11,095 books.

TOOTHPICK TAIL

GREG LEWIS FROM CHESTERFIELD, VIRGINIA, CREATES STUNNING SCULPTURES FROM EVERYDAY MATERIALS THAT NOBODY WOULD THINK OF USING FOR ART. NAMED "HATTERAS," THIS MERMAID FIGURE TOOK THREE YEARS TO BUILD AND CONSISTS OF 67,000 TOOTHPICKS. GREG HAS DEVELOPED A TECHNIQUE THAT ENABLES HIM TO MOLD SHARP TOOTHPICKS INTO SMOOTH AND INCREDIBLY LIFELIKE SHAPES THAT AT FIRST GLANCE APPEAR TO BE CARVED FROM SOLID WOOD.

Massive Model

Former oil-rig worker David Reynolds from Southampton, England, drew on his experience at sea to build a scale model of a North Sea drilling platform from more than four million matchsticks. David took 15 years to complete his creation, working for up to ten hours a day, on one section at a time, in his sitting room. By the time the 21-ft-long (6.4-m) platform was finished, it weighed 2200 lb (1000 kg) and stood 12 ft (3.65 m) high.

℞ LINE DRAWING

Sethu Subramaniyan of Bangalore, India, spent six months illustrating a portrait of Qaboos Ibn Sa'id, the Sultan of Oman, drawn in one continuous, unbroken line beginning and ending at his signature with no overlap.

℞ PAINTED EGG

In 2009, the Romanian city of Suceava unveiled a huge glass-fiber decorated Easter egg that stood 23 ft 8 in (7.25 m) tall, had a diameter of 15 ft (4.6 m) and weighed 1.8 tons.

℞ OBAMA SKETCH

George Vlosich III from Lakewood, Ohio, has drawn an incredibly detailed picture of Barack Obama, complete with the presidential seal, Abraham Lincoln and the Stars and Stripes—on an Etch A Sketch®. It took him 80 hours to draw using the toy's two dials—all in one unbroken line. He has previously created Etch A Sketch® portraits of such superstars as The Beatles, Tiger Woods, Will Smith, Elvis Presley and boxing legend Muhammad Ali.

℞ BEAD FLAG

Jeyaraman Ravi, an Indian expatriate living in Abu Dhabi, United Arab Emirates, spent 14 months creating a flag by threading together 288,400 beads. The flag measured 10 x 5 ft (3 x 1.5 m) and weighed 22 lb (10 kg).

℞ BOTTLE-CAP NATIVITY

Barbara Knecht of Mountain Falls, Virginia, built a Christmas nativity scene from bottle caps, using the different-colored beer brands to create the display.

Magic Sticks

A dedicated Harry Potter fan has created his own incredibly detailed copy of the child magician's school, Hogwarts, from 602,000 matchsticks. Patrick Acton of Gladbrook, Iowa, spent two years creating the matchstick masterpiece, which is held together by 15 gal (57 l) of glue and rises over 7 ft (2.4 m) tall and 10 ft (3 m) wide. He managed to replicate every minute detail of the fictional school, from the tiny mullioned windows to the chimes on the clock tower.

Birds on a Feather

An artist in North Wales uses discarded swan feathers as a canvas for his intricate paintings. After collecting the white feathers from a swannery near his home, Ian Davie cleans them and straightens them out individually with tweezers to make the perfect natural canvas. He then uses acrylic paint to protect and coat the feathers, applying the fine detail of his composition with a tiny 000-size brush. Each work of art takes about a week to create and can sell for $900.

Trashy Lingerie

Daring designer Ingrid Goldbloom Bloch from Massachusetts fashions stylish and colorful underwear from trash, such as soda cans, and although they might look incredibly uncomfortable, they are put together in an ingenious way. Ingrid is inspired by the beauty of everyday objects and uses various scrap metals in her art. If you look closely at her bright-red bustier, you can see that it is made from tiny slivers of cola cans carefully threaded through a wire frame.

R TRICKS OF THE EYE

Californian artist John Pugh specializes in trompe l'oeil—or "trick of the eye"—art, deluding the viewer into seeing 3-D scenes that are actually painted on flat surfaces. On the side of an intact building in Los Gatos, he created the illusion of earthquake damage, depicting crumbling walls that revealed a Mayan temple. Another work, featuring a huge wave about to crash onto a sidewalk in Honolulu, Hawaii, was so lifelike that a passing fire crew stopped to try to rescue some children in danger—only to find that neither the wave nor the children were real.

R SOUND OF MOOSIC

An Austrian farmer plays the accordion to his herd of dairy cows to keep them calm and improve their milk yield. Franz Koeberl and his family stage live concerts for the animals in the hills around the farm at Birkfeld and have discovered that the livestock prefer classical music, especially Strauss. The concerts have proved so successful that Koeberl has even compiled a CD of his cows' favorite tunes.

R PRETTY SHED

Artist Sarah Hardacre from Salford, England, knits cozies for trees and has covered an entire garden shed in knitted squares.

R GORILLA HEAD

Scottish artist David Mach created an amazingly lifelike sculpture of a gorilla head—from 30,000 matchsticks. It took him three months to complete the head, which is 15 in (38 cm) high and has flared nostrils and a fierce open mouth, by painstakingly gluing each match onto a mold. He re-creates animals' features and different skin shades by using matchsticks with different colored tips. His works, which have also included grizzly bears and rhinos, sell for up to $50,000.

R PIANO MAN

Colin Huggins takes his full-size upright piano to the parks, street corners and even subway stations of New York City—to play music for fun. The crazy piano guy, as he is known, amazes commuters by transporting his 250-lb (115-kg) piano down to subway platforms in the elevator.

℞ MASSED CHOIR

More than 160,000 people assembled to form a massed choir in India in May 2009. The vast ranks of singers chanted hymns in honor of a Hindu deity in the southern city of Hyderabad.

℞ CLOSE-KNIT COMMUNITY

Twelve women have spent 23 years knitting a perfect replica of their home village of Mersham in Kent, England. They have created more than 60 woolen properties, including a church, two pubs, a shop, a school, a large manor house and dozens of cottages with gardens full of flowers.

℞ ORNATE HUBCAPS

Ken Marquis of Wilkes-Barre, Pennsylvania, collects art created from car hubcaps. As part of his Landfillart project, artists from 51 countries plus every state in the U.S.A. have sent him their individually decorated hubcaps. Some have painted animals onto their hubcaps, while others have added jewelry, wings and even an hourglass.

℞ PAINFUL MEMENTOS

After splitting up with her boyfriend, artist Olinka Vistica from Zagreb, Croatia, decided to open The Museum of Broken Relationships in Berlin, Germany, to house mementos of breakups. Exhibits include a wedding dress, engagement rings, love letters, a fax, a pair of inline skates, a toy tiger and gall stones. Also on display is an ax used by one woman to break up her ex-girlfriend's furniture, along with the smashed furniture.

℞ EXTRA-LARGE WAIST

In 2009, Tunisian fashion designer Larbi Boukamha created a pair of pants that were equal to the height of a 22-story building. He worked eight hours a day for two whole months to make the oversized pants, which measured 164 ft (50 m) in length, had a waist of 118 ft (36 m) and used a mile (1,600 m) of fabric.

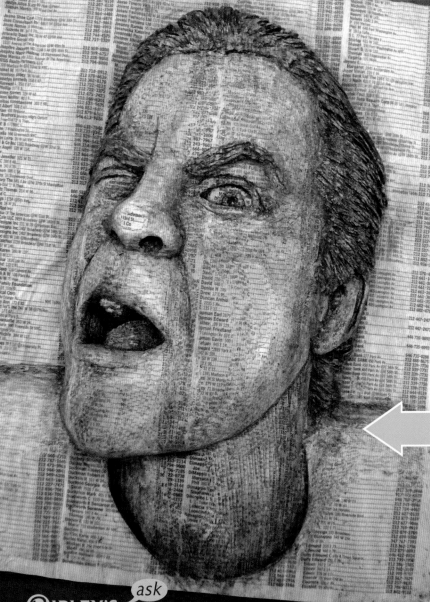

PHONEBOOK FACES

ARTIST ALEX QUERAL FROM PHILADELPHIA, PENNSYLVANIA, CREATES PORTRAITS THAT POP OUT OF THE PAGE AT YOU. WHEN HE WORKED WITH CONVENTIONAL PAINTS, HE ALWAYS TRIED TO GIVE REAL PRESENCE AND TEXTURE TO THE FACES IN HIS PORTRAITS, BUT IN DOING SO HE WAS USING A LOT OF EXPENSIVE PAINT, SO HE BEGAN TO LOOK AROUND FOR A DIFFERENT MEDIUM. WHEN THE YEAR'S NEW PHONEBOOKS STARTED TO ARRIVE IN THE NEIGHBORHOOD, ALEX REALIZED THAT THEY WERE LIKE SOFT BLOCKS OF WOOD, AND AS THERE WERE A LOT OF SPARES LYING AROUND, HE HAD AN IDEA TO USE THEM IN PLACE OF A REGULAR CANVAS. HE FOUND HIS FIRST PHONEBOOK IN A RECYCLING BIN AND RECYCLED IT INTO ART, CARVING THREE-DIMENSIONAL FACES INTO THE BOOKS RATHER THAN BUILDING THEM UP WITH PAINT.

℞IPLEY'S ask

How do you make your pictures? "I liked being able to see the lists of names and phone numbers on the faces themselves and became intrigued with the idea of the face manifesting in the book, as if it were trying to assert itself in the anonymous list of names. I carve out the face using craft knives and ordinary razor blades, using the binding of the book to hold it together, then brush on an acrylic varnish to glue it and go back into it with the cutting tools. It goes back and forth like this until it's done, then I seal it with several layers of the acrylic varnish. I use a bit of black paint to bring out the details in the eyes, mouth and hair. To me they seem like three-dimensional drawings."

R TRAIN WUNDERLAND

Since 2000, twin brothers Frederick and Gerrit Braun from Hamburg, Germany, have been building a model train set that has more than 6 mi (10 km) of track. Built from 4 tons of steel, their "Wunderland" has over 160,000 model people, 700 locomotives, 10,000 carriages and wagons, 2,800 buildings, 900 signals and three-quarters of a ton of artificial grass. It has six regions, including the U.S.A. and the Alps—featuring models of the Grand Canyon, Las Vegas, Mount Rushmore and a 20-ft-high (6-m) replica of the Matterhorn mountain.

R MODEL TOWN

A romantic English couple have spent 20 years building a 20-ft (6-m) model town based on the area of west London where they first met. Stanley and Christine Buck have constructed their replica of Greenford in the garden shed of their new home in Cambridgeshire. The model has cafés, shops and a cinema—with billboards advertising the movies the couple watched on their first dates in the 1950s.

R STILL LIFE

Australian artist Mike Parr staged an exhibition at the Artspace Gallery in Sydney that consisted of him having one arm nailed to a wall for 36 hours.

R HAIR TOWER

Chinese hairdresser Huang Xin created a detailed model of Beijing's Tiananmen Gate Tower from hair collected in his shop. It took five months and 24 lb (11 kg) of hair to make the model, which stands 2 ft 10 in (86 cm) long, 1 ft (30 cm) wide and 2 ft (60 cm) high. After washing and dying the hair—he used only women's hair because it was softer—he glued it on to paper before rolling it into different shapes.

R TOILET HORROR

A Japanese company has printed a horror story on toilet paper. *Drop*, a nine-chapter novella by Koji Suzuki, is set in a public restroom and takes up about 3 ft (1 m) of toilet roll. It can be read in just a few minutes.

R WHALE OF A TIME

Homeowner Nicki Leggett from the town of Whitstable in Kent, England, took three years of careful pruning to shape a garden hedge into the shape of a whale.

R LEGO JESUS

A church in Sweden marked Easter 2009 by unveiling a life-size LEGO® statue of Jesus Christ. Over a period of 18 months churchgoers at the Oensta Gryta Church in Vaesteras donated nearly 30,000 LEGO® bricks to build the statue, which was 5 ft 10 in (1.78 m) high and based on a Danish sculpture depicting Christ's resurrection.

R SOCK MONKEY

Cherylle Douglas from Merritt, British Columbia, Canada, has created a giant sock monkey that stands 8 ft 10 in (2.7 m) high— that's nearly 3 ft (1 m) taller than the average man. The monster stuffed toy was sewn together from 32 pairs of woolen socks and weighed 51 lb (23 kg).

R HELP YOURSELF

In November 2008, popular London artist Adam Neate left 1,000 pieces of art across the city for people to take for free. Over the years, Neate has scattered more than 6,000 of his works, which are printed on cardboard, around the English capital.

R BLOOD SAMPLE

A large-format book measuring 20 x 20 in (50 x 50 cm) published by Kraken Opus about Argentinean soccer legend Diego Maradona offered a sample of the player's blood and hair to the first 100 buyers.

R FLOOR LICK

Korean-born artist Hoon Lee staged an exhibit at the Bemis Center for Contemporary Arts in Nebraska that consisted of him licking yellow cake frosting off a floor area of 2,500 sq ft (230 sq m).

R OBAMA IN MELTDOWN

A waxwork of Barack Obama was unveiled in Paris, France, in the summer of 2009, at the height of a heatwave. The model had to be protected from the sun by umbrellas to stop the President's face melting.

R TILL RECEIPT

A $100 grocery receipt listing 36 white shopping items including boil-in-the-bag rice and toilet roll was exhibited at a prestigious gallery in London, England, in 2009 by Pakistani-born artist Ceal Floyer. The conceptual artwork, entitled "Monochrome Till Receipt (White)," was displayed at Tate Britain and was valued at $45,000.

CRACKING UP

EDGAR MUELLER'S PAINTINGS ARE OFTEN THE SIZE OF A WHOLE STREET. THE ARTIST CREATES ILLUSIONS OF DEPTH AND MOVEMENT SO CONVINCING THAT VIEWERS FEEL AS IF THEY REALLY COULD FALL INTO THE GIANT ICE CREVASSE CREATED AT EAST PIER IN DUN LAOGHAIRE, IRELAND, IN 2009. THE ARTIST WORKED WITH ASSISTANTS FROM SUNSET TO SUNRISE FOR FIVE DAYS TO FINISH "THE CREVASSE," WHICH COVERED 2,690 SQ FT (250 SQ M) OR ABOUT THE SAME SIZE AS A TENNIS COURT.

RIPLEY'S RESEARCH

THIS TYPE OF ART IS KNOWN AS ANAMORPHOSIS. THE IMAGE WORKS ONLY WHEN SEEN FROM A PARTICULAR ANGLE. IF YOU VIEWED MUELLER'S WORK FROM ANY OTHER DIRECTION, IT WOULD JUST LOOK LIKE PAINT ON A PAVEMENT—THE IMAGE WOULD APPEAR DISTORTED AND FLAT. THE ILLUSION OF DEPTH REQUIRES GREAT PRECISION, AND, AFTER USING A DIGITAL CAMERA TO CAREFULLY PLAN THE CORRECT ANGLES, EDGAR DRAWS CHALK LINES ON THE GROUND BEFORE ADDING LAYERS OF ACRYLIC PAINT TO COMPLETE THE THREE-DIMENSIONAL IMAGE.

Insect Illusion
Edgar Mueller and Manfred Stader created this vision of a giant butterfly rising out of a crack in the earth at an arts festival in Saskatchewan, Canada. From a different angle you can clearly see how the illusion is created from a painting that is is flat and stretched.

Enno uses acrylic paints on regular cardboard egg boxes, using the dimpled surface to help give his characters expression.

As well as portraits, Enno paints still life pictures, such as this bowl of fruit, onto his egg cartons.

YOLK
Art

Dutch artist Enno de Kroon has come up with a novel way of recycling old egg cartons—he uses them as canvases for his paintings, and sells them for around $1,000 each. Enno's art studio in Rotterdam, the Netherlands, is full of discarded cardboard egg boxes ready to be painted with vibrant portraits. The lumpy shape of the cartons makes the resulting paintings change shape according to the angle from which you view them. Enno, who is inspired by famous early 20th-century cubist artists, such as Picasso, has dubbed his creations "Eggcubism." The paintings often look best when viewed from a strange angle, not straight on like a regular two-dimensional painting. Enno's intention is that his egg cartons reveal different faces that seem to follow the viewer around the room.

The face appears only when the egg tray is viewed at a particular angle.

Enno's unconventional style means that the paintings are distorted when viewed head on.

RIPLEY'S *ask*

Why did you start using egg cartons for your art? The egg cartons had been lying around my studio for some time ready to be painted, but it took some courage before I could take the plunge. I've always played with distortions of perspective, which puts the viewer on the wrong foot.

What do you like about using egg cartons instead of a regular canvas? As a painter I consider egg cartons as two-and-a-half dimensional objects that offer me remarkable possibilities. The waves of the egg cartons limit the viewer's perception; they also make him aware of his positioning toward the image. The egg boxes create problems that require a new approach by the painter, which in turn leads the viewer to have to take a new approach to looking at the art.

What kind of reactions have you had to your work? The reactions are amazing; I get worldwide attention. They seem to focus on the "recycled art" aspect now, to which I seem to give an extra dimension. As for sales, I do sell a lot of my works, they provide me my income now. One German art collector has bought 36 of my "eggcubism" pieces.

The egg cartons reveal faces from several different perspectives.

HOTEL DISPLAY

In January 2009, a British couple visiting New York City were put on display to passersby in a mocked-up hotel room. In return for a complimentary stay at Manhattan's Roger Smith Hotel, Duncan Malcolm and Katherine Lewis agreed to occupy a replica of one of the hotel's rooms on the ground floor of a nearby building, where for three hours every afternoon for five days, they kept the curtains on the room's large glass windows open so that thousands of pedestrians and motorists could watch their every move.

PHOTO MOSAIC

In June 2009, a giant photo mosaic measuring 175 x 125 ft (53 x 38 m) and covering an area of 21,875 sq ft (2,030 sq m) was unveiled in the Philippines. Printed on tarpaulin, the mosaic was made up of more than 1,000 photographs taken by artist Revoli Cortez of Filipine president Gloria Macapagal-Arroyo.

JUMBO JEANS

In June 2009, workers in Zagreb, Croatia, created a pair of jeans the size of six tennis courts. Stitched together from 8,023 pairs of jeans that had been donated for charity, the giant denims boast a leg length of 150 ft (45 m) and a total width of 110 ft (34 m).

YOUNG ARTIST

Kieron Williamson of Norfolk, England, had an exhibition of watercolor landscape paintings displayed at a Cambridgeshire gallery in August 2009—even though he was just six years old. Remarkably, he had not drawn a thing until he was five.

BREAD & INSECTS

FRENCH ARTIST PETRA WERLE CREATES BEAUTIFUL WORKS OF ART FROM NOTHING BUT BREAD CRUMBS AND INSECT PARTS. HER FAIRYTALE CREATURES ARE MOLDED INTO SHAPE USING BREAD AND THEN DECORATED WITH THE BODY PARTS OF BUTTERFLIES, SCARAB BEETLES AND MOTHS, OR SOMETIMES BUG COCOONS AND WINGS.

BACON BOOKMARK

A copy of Len Deighton's World War II book *Blood, Tears and Folly* was returned to a library in Worthing, West Sussex, England, with a piece of bacon as a bookmark.

WOOLY BRAIN

Psychiatrist Dr. Karen Norberg of the National Bureau of Economic Research in Cambridge, Massachusetts, spent a year knitting an anatomically correct replica of the human brain. The two sides of the 9-in (23-cm) woolen brain—one-and-a-half times life size—are joined together by a zipper and Karen used different colors of wool to represent the various areas of the complex organ. She said that using wool rather than clay helped her achieve the desired "rippling" effect of certain parts of the brain.

SPEED VIOLINIST

Nikolai Rimsky-Korsakov's famous violin piece "Flight of the Bumblebee" normally takes 80 seconds to play, but German violinist David Garrett can play it in just 66 seconds, averaging more than 13 notes per second.

RHYMING TWEETS

Romanian website developer Andrei Gheorghe has created a poem by pairing up random rhyming Twitter posts. The finished piece is more than 350,000 verses long.

DRUM ENSEMBLE

A total of 582 drummers beat the same rhythm together for five minutes at the National Indoor Arena in Birmingham, England, in July 2009. Among them was Don Powell, drummer with the 1970s U.K. band Slade, who said: "It isn't difficult getting everyone playing at the same speed—getting them to stop at the same time is the problem!"

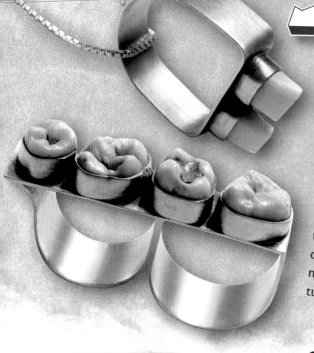

Jaw Dropping

Polly van der Glas makes items of jewelry that are embedded with human teeth! She has created a knuckle-duster ring set with four teeth, a sterling-silver single tooth signet ring and a single incisor necklace. The Australian artist, who also collects hair and fingernails, says that most of the teeth she uses are donated by friends and family. The molars are then sterilized before being turned into jaw-dropping jewelry.

FIVE LANGUAGES

South Africa's national anthem incorporates five different languages—Xhosa, Zulu, Sesotho, English and Afrikaans—all in one song.

CAN CONSTRUCTION

A structure built from more than 54,500 cans of food was unveiled in Wellington, New Zealand, in 2009. The work occupied around 3,875 sq ft (360 sq m) of the city's Civic Square and took more than 24 hours to assemble. The cans were then distributed to needy local families.

JACKSON GLOVE

A bejewelled white glove worn by Michael Jackson the first time he performed the moonwalk, in 1983, sold at auction in 2009 for $350,000.

JACKSON STATUE

In memory of the late pop icon, a statue of Michael Jackson standing 39 ft (12 m) high and weighing around 4 tons was unveiled in the small village of Regensdorf, Switzerland.

SCREAM COMPILATION

In 2009, New York City artist LeRoy Stevens compiled an album of musical screams. He spent six months visiting every record store in Manhattan asking workers to nominate their favorite musical scream. The result— "Favorite Recorded Screams"—is a three-and-a-half-minute compilation of 74 howls, screeches, grunts and yells from songs by such artists as the Who, Slayer, the Pixies and Bjork.

GIANT ACCORDION

Italian Giancarlo Francenella built an accordion more than 8 ft (2.5 m) high and weighing about 440 lb (200 kg). It has 45 treble keys and took 1,000 hours to make.

RADIO GAGA

U.S. country singer Jack Ingram gave 215 consecutive radio interviews in 24 hours between 8 a.m. on August 25, 2009 and 8 a.m. on August 26, 2009. From the base of the Brooklyn Bridge in New York, he spoke by telephone with radio stations in most of the 50 U.S. states and with others in Canada, Australia and Ireland.

TANGO EXTRAVAGANZA

After six months of practice, some 200 children (about 100 pairs) danced the tango simultaneously in Medellin, Colombia, in July 2009.

SEOUL SINGER

A South Korean housewife sang nonstop for more than 76 hours at a karaoke bar in Seoul in February 2009. Kim Sun-Ok sang a total of 1,283 tunes over a three-day period before finally giving up because her family was concerned about her health.

LEGO®CELLO

New York artist Nathan Sawaya has built a life-size working cello from thousands of LEGO® bricks. The cello, made from brown, black and yellow bricks, sounds different to normal cellos, which are usually made from spruce and maple wood.

FARM SOUNDS

For his composition "Earth Machine Music," Finnish classical musician Kimmo Pohjonen incorporated the sounds of farm animals and machinery. The noises of cows and sheep, plus the whirring of tractors and milking machines, all feature in the piece, along with more traditional instruments.

Tiny Dancers

Mexican artist Enrique Ramos will paint on just about anything. He has painted on spider webs, snake skins, vampire bats, grains of rice and, in 2009, he started on cockroaches, ants and crickets, which are called "chopolinas" in his home state. Influenced by the death of Michael Jackson, Ramos created these crickets to show the evolution of the famous singer between 1982 and 2009.

BEACH PATTERNS

Over the past six years, San Francisco artist Andres Amador has used a rake to draw more than 100 giant patterns on Californian beaches. He plans the elaborate designs on a computer and then rakes them into the sand in a race against the tide. Some of his beach images measure 500 x 300 ft (150 x 90 m).

LONG TRAIN

For her wedding to Zhao Peng in Jilin, China, Lin Rong wore a dress with a train that stretched more than 1.3 mi (2.2 km) behind her. The gown, which cost nearly $6,000 and took guests over three hours to roll out, was the groom's idea. As an added romantic gesture, it had 9,999 red silk roses pinned to it.

LEGO® HOUSE

British TV presenter James May built a full-size LEGO® house—featuring a working toilet, a hot shower and low-level lighting—from 3.3 million plastic bricks. Around 1,000 volunteers helped him construct the 20-ft-high (6-m), two-story house in Surrey, England. He even lived in the LEGO® house for a short while.

CREAT1NG

BELGIAN PHOTOGRAPHER NICHOLAS HENDRICKX HAS BEEN CREATING A BUZZ IN THE ART WORLD WITH HIS WACKY PICTURES OF FLIES. INSPIRED BY THE SIGHT OF A FLY LANDING ON A FLOWER IN HIS GARDEN, HE DECIDED TO EMPLOY LIVE INSECTS AS PHOTOGRAPHIC MODELS IN HIS SHOTS. WITH HIS BEDROOM AS A STUDIO, HENDRICKX USES TINY PROPS TO PHOTOGRAPH FLIES APPARENTLY PLAYING

GUM LADY

Artist Ally Rosenberg from Prestwich, England, has created sculptures of an old woman from chewing gum and an old man from used teabags. To obtain the raw materials for the model of the old woman, Ally challenged 50 friends to chew 1,000 pieces of gum in two weeks.

LONG PLAYER

The recording of "You've Lost That Lovin' Feelin'" by The Righteous Brothers has been played so frequently on radio stations across the world that it amounts to the equivalent of more than 45 years of continuous airplay.

SKULL SAUNA

Dutch artist Joep van Lieshout has built a 15-ft-tall (4.5-m) human skull featuring a built-in sauna. The white "Wellness Skull" is made of wood and synthetic material, and when the eight-person-capacity sauna is in use, steam emanates from its eye sockets. The skull also houses a bathtub and shower on either side of its neck.

SAME ROLE

English actor David Raven played Major Metcalfe in the Agatha Christie stage play *The Mousetrap* for 4,575 performances between July 22, 1957, and November 23, 1968.

TOWER HERMIT

In 2009, artist Ansuman Biswas from London, England, lived as a hermit for 40 days and 40 nights in the Gothic tower of Manchester Museum in Manchester, England. Each day he studied one object from the museum's collection of 4.5 million artifacts and posted his thoughts about it on an Internet blog.

HAIRY DOG

In May 2009, London's Royal College of Art unveiled a sculpture by Gareth Williams of a dog created using human hair clippings from his own head and stuck together with used chewing gum.

R FRIENDS MARATHON

TV fan Steve Misiura from London, England, watched every episode of "Friends" in a marathon 84-hour session. He watched all 238 episodes of the hit U.S. sitcom back-to-back for 3½ days, during which he experienced nausea, stomach aches and even hallucinations.

R WHITTLED CHAIN

Skilled wood-carver John Selvey of Port Orange, Florida, has created a chain made from 10,034 hand-carved wooden links that measures an impressive 407 ft (124 m) long. John spent 825 consecutive days carving his chain from 2-ft-long (60-cm) pieces of wood.

R SISTINE STITCH

Canadian Joanna Lopianowski-Roberts from San Francisco, California, has created an accurate version of Michelangelo's Sistine Chapel ceiling using simple cross-stitch. Measuring 40 x 80 in (1 x 2 m), the project took Joanna a total of 3,572 hours, working for more than one hour a day for eight years.

A BUZZ

MUSICAL INSTRUMENTS, RIDING BIKES OR RELAXING ON A BEACH. "IT TOOK QUITE SOME TIME," HE ADMITS. "SOME FLIES WERE GREAT TO WORK WITH, WHILE OTHERS WERE VERY FRUSTRATING. I GUESS IT'S NORMAL—FLIES AND HUMANS AREN'T MADE TO WORK TOGETHER. FLIES ARE MADE TO ANNOY US WITH THEIR BUZZING AND POOPING ON STUFF."

R VOLUMINOUS VASE

The Monte Palace Tropical Gardens, near Funchal, Madeira, has a vase that is 17½ ft (5.4 m) tall and weighs 1,225 lb (555 kg). The huge vase was made in South Africa.

R MASS DANCE

A total of 7,770 people assembled at the Cebu City Sports Center in the Philippines in 2009 for a dancesport class.

R BLOOD MONEY

Instead of paying cash, music fans in Poland were able to buy tickets to a 2009 concert by British-Polish duo John Porter and Anita Lipnicka by donating blood.

R TOOTHPICK CITY

For more than four years, Stan Munro of Syracuse, New York State, used over 4 million toothpicks and 45 gal (170 l) of glue to create "Toothpick City II—Temples and Towers," an exhibition featuring toothpick models of some 40 famous buildings from around the world. The landmarks—all created to a precise 1:164 scale—include London's Tower Bridge, the Vatican and a 19-ft-tall (5.8-m) model of the Burj Khalifa tower in Dubai.

R OVERDUE BOOK

A man returned a book to a library in Derby, England, 46 years after he had borrowed it. David Hall took out the book *Engineering Workshop Practice* for his father in 1963. In the intervening years it had built up a fine of nearly $4,000, but the penalty was waived.

R GOLDEN SILK

British art historian Simon Peers has produced a piece of gold cloth measuring 11 x 4 ft (3.3 x 1.2 m) from natural spider silk. Over a period of four years, more than a million female Madagascan golden orb spiders were captured and carefully placed in harnesses, where their abdomens—which produce the golden-colored silk—were lightly squeezed. The filaments of silk were then extracted and 24 filaments were twisted by hand into a single strand, and then twisted again with three other such strands to produce a thread that was wound onto a small reel ready for weaving. Each spider produced about 80 ft (24 m) of silk filament.

Pulp Art

Two artists from Rapid City, South Dakota, have developed a unique technique that enables them to mold paper into amazing sculptures. Allen Eckman and his wife Patty create incredibly detailed figures inspired by the old American West. The sculptures are all made entirely from paper, and many stand life-size. Each element of the artworks is molded separately, so the largest pieces can take several months to complete. Ripley's asked Allen how he puts together one of his artworks...

1

"First we sculpture *Little Bird*—and here you can see the mold complete with hands, ears and eyeballs being extracted. This will now be cast in pulp, dried in the mold and then posed in its final position."

4

"The *Little Bird* at Oak Creek figure finished."

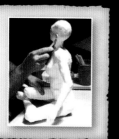

ter the figure is formed, I d the posed hands. Here I am cing the eyes and ears on the ad. Before I add the hair, I will se and sculpt for smoothness d then clothe the figure."

"Here I am adding more finely cut dry, hard paper, which serves as the hair. It is applied in layers in the same way that hair grows."

5

Finally, *Little Bird* is placed within the finished work that measures 4 x 5 ft (1.2 x 1.5 m) by 12 in (30 cm) in relief."

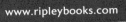

Fancy Dancer, Northern
Plains, 4 ft (1.2 m) tall.

Catch of the Day: the everyday items Tom used to make his fish

Nintendo game sleeve
Window screen
Cassette tape
1 broken clothes hanger
Woman's dress shoe
Daughter's piggy bank
Plastic toy
Tote
Decorative ribbon
Tabs from clothing tags
Pieces of plastic from
   a clothes hamper

Fabric from dress pants
1 brass button
Sequins
3 plastic utensils
8 bottle caps
Milk jug
Pieces of serving platter
Coffee container
Cut plastic cup
Häagen Dazs®
   ice-cream lid

Ball-point pen cap
Magic marker
Tape glue
Handle to paintbrush
Pen top
Ruler
Film canister
Compact disks
Square stencil sheet
   Scrap wood
      Screws
         Hot melt glue

Rubber raft
Plastic pail
Gutter mesh
Prescription pill container
Children's sneaker found
   on the beach
Buttons from clothing
   factory that went out of
   business

Trash Trout

Tom Deininger from Boston, Massachusetts, created this beautiful sculpture of a rainbow trout using only items found lying around his house (see list, above). Artist and environmentalist Tom recycled everyday items to make his fish and applied absolutely no resins or paint to the work—the trout is quite simply a product of Tom's trash!

ℝ VIDEO PROPOSAL

When movie buff Pete Simson wanted to propose to his girlfriend Hannah McDonagh, he hired out a theater in Bristol, England, to screen his own five-minute-long spoof video. Hannah was expecting to see an arty film but instead saw her boyfriend on screen in his underpants miming to Daniel Bedingfield's song "If You're Not The One." At the end of the screening, he got down on one knee and proposed to Hannah to a round of applause. She said yes!

ℝ BIG BRUSH

Artist He Wenjun used a massive 12-ft-long (3.6-m), 115-lb (52-kg) paintbrush to write calligraphy at an exhibition in Nanchong, China, in September 2009. He created the brush himself, using hair from the tails of 300 horses, and says that it can soak up enough ink to add more than 100 lb (45 kg) to its weight.

ℝ DALEK MODEL

Brian Croucher of West Sussex, England, spent more than two years building a full-size model of a Dalek from the British TV science fiction series *Doctor Who*—out of 480,000 matchsticks. The sinister 5-ft-3-in (1.6-m) alien is the latest in a line of Brian's matchstick creations. He has also built a 5-ft-long (1.5-m) boat, a full-size rocking horse and a grandfather clock.

ℝ TOILET BREAK

A website tells movie-goers with weak bladders when is the best time to go to the toilet during a particular film. Runpee.com picks the quiet moments in current movies when you can be absent for up to four minutes without missing much. It can even provide a summary of what you missed on your iPhone.

ℝ TWITTER NOVEL

Unable to find a publisher for his first novel, *The French Revolution*, Matt Stewart of San Francisco, California, put the entire book on the social networking device Twitter—140 characters at a time. It took around 3,700 "tweets" to transmit all of the 480,000 characters in the book.

ℝ MOON ROCK

A book published to mark the 40th anniversary of the first Moon landing contained pieces of genuine Moon rock that crashed to Earth as meteorites. Publishers Taschen America produced 1,969 copies of the book—to represent the year of the landing—but only the final 12 contained a piece of rock. Titled *Moonfire*, the tome was based on accounts of the Apollo 11 mission by U.S. writer Norman Mailer. It was signed by Buzz Aldrin, the second man to walk on the Moon, and went on sale for $1,000.

ℝ LIVING STATUES

As part of a new artwork designed by artist Antony Gormley, members of the public stood on an empty plinth in London's Trafalgar Square for an hour at a time, 24 hours a day for three months in 2009. Some 2,400 people took turns to occupy the 22-ft-high (6.7-m) plinth. One man dressed as a panda and carried a sign bearing his cell-phone number so that passersby could call him and another landed a job after displaying a giant copy of his resumé.

TOILET PAPER PEOPLE

FRENCH ARTIST JUNIOR FRITZ JACQUET USES A PARTICULARLY UNGLAMOROUS OBJECT FOR HIS WORK—CARDBOARD TUBES FROM THE INSIDE OF TOILET PAPER ROLLS. INSPIRED BY THE TRADITIONAL JAPANESE PAPER-FOLDING ART OF ORIGAMI, JUNIOR MOLDS AND FOLDS THE 4-IN (10-CM) TUBES INTO CHARACTERS THAT EACH DISPLAY DISTINCTIVE FACIAL EXPRESSIONS. HE THEN COLORS THE MASKS WITH DIFFERENT PAINTS BEFORE SELLING THE PIECES FOR AROUND 60 EUROS EACH.

RECYCLED CREATURES
London Zoo's Recycled Sculpture exhibition featured a polar bear made from plastic bags, a shark from discarded automobile hubcaps and a dinosaur from old tires.

DON'T JUMP!
A life-size plastic art installation in Vienna, Austria, showed a smartly dressed businessman clutching a briefcase and apparently about to jump from the top of a four-story real-estate company building. The work of artist Ronald Kodritsch was inspired by the international financial crisis of 2009.

PLASTICINE GARDEN
British TV presenter James May created a garden for the 2009 Chelsea Flower Show—out of plasticine. Flowers, vegetables, bushes, a lawn and even a pond were all made from plasticine, which was supported with wires to prevent it from wilting.

BICYCLE SYMPHONY
Argentinean composer Mauricio Kagel wrote a symphony to be played on bicycle bells. His work "Eine Brise" ("A Breeze") is a 90-second outdoor piece, described by the composer as a "fleeting action for 111 cyclists."

MASS MARIACHI
Nearly 550 mariachi musicians gathered in the Mexican city of Guadalajara in August 2009 to perform a repertoire of songs. Guadalajara is home to mariachi music, featuring bands of violinists, guitarists and trumpeters, who wear silver-studded outfits and wide-brimmed hats.

METAL ARMADILLO
Known as "Scrap Daddy" for his work with waste materials, Mark Bradford of Houston, Texas, created the sculpture "Carmadillo," a shiny 50-ft-long (15-m) armadillo built from a pickup truck and a van.

This curious creation was captured by photographer Corrie White from Ontario, Canada, and is simply a droplet of colored milk falling into water in a piece of blue glassware. Working for hours at a time, Corrie uses a pipette to create the splashes in a variety of kitchen containers. Milk is used because it reacts more slowly than pure water, but the splashes still only last an instant. As a result, the camera misses 95 percent of the colorful droplets as Corrie does not rely on any electronic gadgets for timing.

EYE TECH

FILMMAKER ROB SPENCE FROM TORONTO, CANADA, HAS DEVELOPED A CAMERA TO REPLACE THE EYE THAT HE LOST AS A CHILD. ROB BEGAN WORKING WITH ENGINEER KOSTOS GRAMMATIS TO CREATE THE "EYEBORG," AND IS NOW THE PROUD OWNER OF A WIRELESS BIONIC EYE MADE WITH ONE OF THE SMALLEST DIGITAL CAMERAS IN THE WORLD, WHICH IS CAPABLE OF RECORDING AND TRANSMITTING VIDEO DIRECTLY FROM HIS EYE SOCKET.

℞ FAKE FISH

A shoal of 5-ft-long (1.5-m) robot fish have been built that are fitted with tiny chemical sensors so that they can detect pollutants in the water. Developed by the University of Essex in England and modeled on carp, the robot fish cost around $30,000 each to make and are designed to be lifelike in appearance and swimming behavior so as not to alarm real fish. They can swim at about 3 ft (1 m) per second and run on batteries that are recharged every eight hours.

℞ ILLUMINATED DRESS

British fashion student Georgie Davis has designed a dress that lights up when the wearer's cell phone rings. The right shoulder of the dress, which is connected to the phone by wireless technology, has translucent white scales that move and light up.

℞ EMOTIONAL ROBOT

Scientists at Waseda University in Japan have developed a robot that can express seven different human emotions. The Emotional Humanoid Robot, named Kobian, uses motors to move its lips, eyelids and eyebrows into various positions and can also strike a range of poses to back up its expressions. To show delight, Kobian puts its hands over its head and opens its mouth and eyes wide; to express sadness, it hunches over, hangs its head and holds a hand up to its face.

℞ LIQUID VISION

Professor Josh Silver of England's Oxford University has invented inexpensive, fluid-filled eyeglasses that can be adjusted to anyone's vision needs. The lenses contain circular sacs filled with fluid that are connected to a small syringe attached to either arm of the eyeglasses. The wearer adjusts a dial on the syringe to increase or reduce the amount of fluid, thus altering the power of the lens.

℞ ONION POWER

To save electricity, some people have started powering up their MP3 players with onions. They bore two holes in the onion, soak it in an energy drink and then stick a USB cable into it—and by doing that they can charge their iPod for an hour. Most vegetables can power iPods because they contain ions that react with the energy drink to create a charge.

℞ INVISIBLE DOORWAYS

Using a technique called transformation optics, researchers in China have discovered a way of altering the pathway of light waves that could eventually enable them to create doorways or portals that are invisible to the human eye—like the one to platform $9^3/_4$ in the *Harry Potter* books.

Digital Digit

When Finnish computer engineer Jerry Jalava lost half a finger in a motorcycle crash in 2008, he decided to make a unique replacement. He embedded a computer memory stick in his prosthetic finger, concealed beneath the nail, and now any work he wants to carry around with him is always at hand.

℞ MECHANICAL INSECTS

Scientists at Japan's Tokyo University are creating a range of insect-machine hybrids by rebuilding their brains and programming them to carry out specific tasks. Already they have rewritten the brain circuit of a male silkmoth to react to light instead of odor.

℞ ROBOT TEACHER

Children at a school in Tokyo, Japan, had a new teacher in 2009—a robot called Saya. Beneath a humanlike face, Saya has a system of 18 motors that work like muscles to give her facial expressions including surprise, fear, anger, happiness and sadness. She has a vocabulary of 700 words, has the ability to speak in any language and is programmed to respond to words and questions.

℞ MAGNETIC IMPACT

After suffering massive head injuries in a car crash in 2005, Josh Villa of Rockford, Illinois, was eventually roused from the coma into which he had fallen by a magnetic field. An electromagnetic coil was held over the front of his head to stimulate the underlying brain tissue, and within a few weeks he was responding to simple commands.

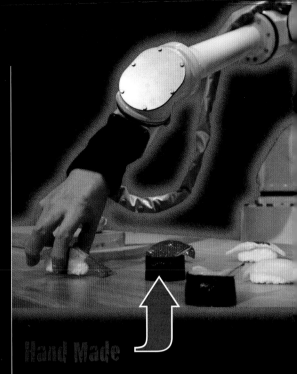

Hand Made

A robot with eerily lifelike, soft silicon hands was unveiled at an exhibition in Tokyo, Japan, in 2009. With more than 20 artificial muscles and a lack of hard metal parts, the air-powered robotic hand can pick up delicate foods such as sushi with great sensitivity, and is capable of movements ranging from a careful pinch to a full-hand squeeze.

Jerry Jalava displays his torn motorcycle glove and his hi-tech replacement finger.

The prosthetic digit can be taken off his hand to slot into a computer.

TUNNEL VISION

The Herrenknecht Gripper tunnel boring machine (TBM), called Gabi 1, drilled through 4¹/₂ mi (7.2 km) of hard mountain rock in just 18 months as part of the construction of two adjacent 35¹/₂-mi-long (57-km) train tunnels through the Gotthard mountain range in the Swiss Alps. The massive machine—measuring nearly 33 ft (10 m) in diameter—managed 130 ft (40 m) of excavation in one 24-hour period, and averaged an impressive 46 ft (14 m) a day. The drill is so accurate that the alignment axis at breakthrough deviated from perfect by just 0.16 in (4 mm) horizontally and 0.32 in (8 mm) vertically. The face of the drill contains a small door through which workers can crawl to replace the 15 or so cutters that wear out every day. The tunnel should be operational by the end of 2017.

RIPLEY'S RESEARCH

The gripper machine braces itself against the rock using two gripper plates. Then hydraulic cylinders push the cutter head into the tunnel face at high pressure, grinding the rock with hardened metal cutter rings. Using this process, TBMs produce more than 1,600 tons of rubble an hour.

Shock Tactics

An intelligent new shock-absorbing material known as D3O changes its molecular structure when subjected to a heavy blow. Under normal conditions the material's molecules flow freely, making it soft and flexible, but they lock together on shock to absorb all of the impact energy. The material is expected to be worn by sportsmen and also by soldiers under their body armor.

℞ TEQUILA DIAMONDS

Mexican scientists have turned the country's national drink, tequila, into diamonds. They discovered that, when deposited on a stainless steel base, the heated vapor from tequila blanco can form tiny diamond crystals.

℞ GIANT ORGANISMS

Researchers in The Bahamas recently discovered giant single-celled organisms the size of grapes living on the sea floor. If a person's cells were that size, the human body would stand 3½ mi (5.6 km) tall!

℞ TINY LAMP

Scientists at the University of California in Los Angeles have created a tiny incandescent lamp that utilizes a carbon filament only 100 atoms wide—one one-hundred-trillionth of the size of the carbon filament used by Thomas Edison in his original lightbulbs. To the naked eye, the UCLA filament is invisible when the lamp is turned off, but it appears as a tiny point of light when the lamp is turned on.

℞ CATWALK QUEEN

Among the models at Japan's Tokyo Fashion Week in 2009 was a robot. Standing 5 ft 2 in (1.57 m) tall and weighing 95 lb (43 kg), the $2-million HRP-4C humanoid was able to imitate the expressions, gait and poses of a supermodel as it sashayed along the catwalk thanks to battery-powered motors in its body and face.

℞ HOT METAL

The metal tungsten does not melt until it reaches a temperature of 6,192°F (3,422°C)—that's more than twice the melting point of iron.

℞ PENGUIN POOP

Scientists were able to locate the breeding colonies of Emperor penguins in Antarctica after spotting giant poop stains from space. Satellite images picked up huge, red-brown stains on the ice, which helped identify 38 breeding colonies, totaling up to 400,000 breeding pairs of penguins.

℞ LOW MAINTENANCE

The Beverly Clock, located at the University of Otago in Dunedin, New Zealand, is a working mechanical clock that has not been wound since 1864. It is powered solely by changes in pressure and temperature.

℞ THIN SHEET

A new material, called graphene, is a carbon sheet that is just one-atom thick, but is stronger than diamond and conducts electricity 100 times faster than the silicon in computer chips. Graphene is so thin that just a few grams of it could cover a football field.

℞ STEEL VELCRO

German scientists have developed a steel version of Velcro that is strong enough to support buildings. Using the same hook-and-loop fastening system as Velcro, Metaklett can bear loads of around 3.6 tons per sq ft (35 tonnes per sq m) at temperatures as high as 1,472°F (800°C).

Microscopic Snowman

Scientists in London have created a tiny snowman, measuring just 0.0004 in (0.01 mm) across—about one-fifth of the width of a human hair. The snowman is made of two tiny tin beads, welded together with platinum. A focused ion beam was used to carve the snowman's eyes and smile, and to deposit a minute blob of platinum for his nose.

ACTUAL SIZE!

Just 0.01 mm across!

R HALL OF FAME

There's a robot hall of fame at Carnegie Mellon University in Pittsburgh, Pennsylvania. Inductees in 2009 included a robot surgeon and a robot vacuum cleaner.

R MOUSE WINDOWS

Researchers at Yeshiva University in New York City surgically implanted glass windows into the skin of lab mice in order to monitor directly the development of cancer tumors.

R COMPUTER WORM

The laptop computer of Mark Taylor from Somerset, England, crashed after an earthworm crawled into its air vent and wrapped itself around a cooling fan.

R CLONED MOUSE

Japanese scientists have created clones of a mouse that had been frozen for 16 years. The same method of extracting brain cells and injecting their nuclei into female egg cells could be used to bring back extinct animals such as the wooly mammoth or the sabre-toothed tiger.

R QUICK READ

It takes only 200 milliseconds to read emotion from a person's facial expression, according to researchers at the University of Glasgow, Scotland.

R SNAIL MAIL

Vicky Isley and Paul Smith of Bournemouth University, England, created a computer relay system that used living snails to deliver email messages to the Internet. The snails were fitted with tiny capsules that held radio-frequency identification chips, and as the snails passed within range of an electronic reader located in their tank, the emails attached themselves to the chips. When the snails then passed close to a second reader, the messages were sent.

R FOLDING BATHROOM

Paul Hernon from West Yorkshire, England, has invented a fold-away bathroom that could be ideal for small apartments. The space-saving unit, called the Vertebrae, stacks a sink, water cistern and showerhead into a single 8-ft (2.4-m) steel column.

R CRAZY HORSES

The Madagascar Institute, a New York-based arts group, has created a high-speed fairground carousel where the horses are powered by jet engines!

R DISAPPEARING DIAMOND

Diamonds will actually burn at high enough temperatures, but instead of leaving ash behind, they turn into carbon dioxide gas.

Spy Tooth

The U.K.'s James Auger has devised a new concept in secret communication— an audio tooth implant. A surgeon implants a device into your tooth, the data is retrieved from a cell phone, radio or computer and the vibration resonates through your jawbone to your inner earbone, meaning that only you can hear the information.

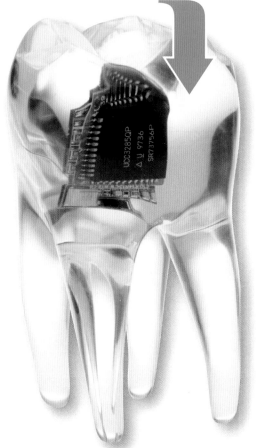

R FLIGHTLESS LADYBUG

By disrupting the insect's gene for wing development, researchers at Nagoya University, Japan, have produced a wingless ladybug. Although ladybugs have been employed as eco-friendly pest killers for years, farmers had previously been unable to stop them from flying away.

R SOLAR FLIGHT

A U.S. firm has devised an unmanned surveillance plane that can fly for five years nonstop. The solar-powered aircraft has a 500-ft (150-m) wingspan designed in a Z-shape so that it absorbs as much solar power as possible by day. Then, at night, it changes shape to a flat line for aerodynamic efficiency.

Bionic Fingers A company from Scotland has invented bionic fingers, which enable people with missing digits to pick up a glass, hold cutlery and even write. The $70,000-fingers are directly controlled by the brain and can write and grip, thanks to a special sensor that allows them to detect when they have closed around an object.

BLUE HEAVEN

In December 2008, a British artist took an abandoned apartment in London and turned it into a glittering cave of crystals. Roger Hiorns created his work, entitled *Seizure*, by pumping 18,000 gallons (70,000 L) of blue, hot copper sulphate solution into the apartment, in order to create beautiful crystalline growths on the walls, floor, ceiling and bath.

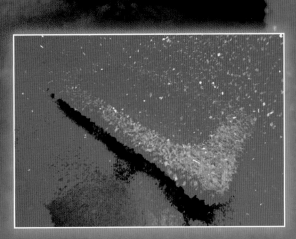

The crystals covered absolutely everything, including the bathroom sink.

FATAL STING

Microscopic nanobees, made from perfluorocarbon—a material used in artificial blood—have been used by scientists at a university in St. Louis, Missouri, to kill cancer tumors by stinging them. The nanobees, measuring just three millionths of an inch across, are armed with melittin, a toxin found in bee venom, which destroys cancerous cells by drilling holes through them.

TRICKY PROBLEM

Capable of 200 trillion calculations per second, a computer network in Jülich, Germany, spent more than a year computing the answer to a single physics question.

PHONE VIRUSES

There are over 600 kinds of cell phone viruses, which can access phone books and spread through networks by sending themselves to other phones via Bluetooth or MMS.

PIGEON SERVICE

A carrier pigeon in South Africa proved faster at delivering data than broadband Internet. The pigeon took 1 hour 8 minutes to fly the 50 mi (80 km) from Pietermaritzburg to Durban with a data card strapped to its leg—and including download, the transfer took just over two hours. In that time only four percent of the data had been transferred using the country's leading Internet service provider.

ADAPTABLE BRA

Elena N. Bodnar, Raphael C. Lee and Sandra Marijan of Chicago, Illinois, have invented a bra that, in an emergency, can be quickly converted into a pair of gas masks—one for the bra wearer and the other for a needy passerby.

PRECISION WORK

Modern surgical robots move with such precision that they now have the ability to peel the skin from a grape.

UNCHANGED UNDERPANTS

Despite being huddled together on the International Space Station with as many as 12 colleagues, Japanese astronaut Koichi Wakata wore the same underpants for a month—and nobody complained. Called J-ware, the type of odorless underwear he was wearing has been developed by Japanese scientists and is designed to kill bacteria, absorb water, insulate the body and dry quickly.

BODY BOMBS

Newly discovered species of marine worms use bioluminescent "bombs" to distract attackers. The worms, which live on the floor of the Pacific Ocean more than 1.8 mi (3 km) beneath the surface, cast off green glowing body parts when disturbed. Scientists from the University of California, San Diego, who made the find, say the worms are able to regenerate the body parts.

...MAD INVENTIONS...MAD INVENTIONS...MAD IN

Low Flyer

This peculiar contraption, photographed in 1922, is one of the earliest helicopters. Spaniard Raul Pescara's machine used four sets of blades, rather than the single blades used on modern helicopters. Unfortunately, his invention managed to get only 5 ft (1.5 m) off the ground.

Bent Barrel

In 1953, an M3 submachine gun was manufactured with a barrel that curved at right-angles. It was designed for shooting over obstacles and around corners!

Bag of Tricks

In 1963, John H.T. Rinfret came up with an unusual invention to foil opportunistic robberies. His anti-bandit bag could be instantly pulled open with a chain, spilling all the contents onto the ground.

℞ SKUNK STENCH

Israel has developed a new organic weapon called Skunk, which smells so horrible that, when sprayed from a water cannon, the stench cannot be removed for at least three days. The offensive weapon is a mix of yeast, baking powder and a few secret ingredients.

℞ CLIMBING LIQUID

In its liquid form, cool helium becomes a superfluid that can climb up and over the sides of its container.

℞ SEASICK FISH

While studying the effects of weightlessness in water as part of his research into how humans are affected in space, zoologist Dr. Reinhold Hilbig from Stuttgart, Germany, discovered that even fish can become seasick. A number of aquarium fish that went up in a plane became disoriented and lost their sense of balance when the plane went into a steep dive.

℞ WARNING SUIT

To make people aware of the threat of skin cancer, a Canadian company has designed a two-piece bathing suit that changes color to warn women when the sun's rays are too strong. The bikini is held together with pale decorative beads that turn dark purple if the UV rays reach dangerous levels.

℞ BULLET PROOF

An Icelandic inventor has designed a breast pocket handkerchief that can stop a bullet. Sruli Recht has created a handkerchief made from Kevlar, which is five times stronger than steel and can withstand temperatures of 750°F (400°C).

℞ LASER BLAST

British scientists have made a transparent form of aluminum by bombarding the metal with a laser producing brief pulses of X-ray light. Each pulse is more powerful than the output of a power plant supplying electricity to an entire city.

℞ NAVAL STUDY

To discover how lint accumulates in the human navel, Dr. Georg Steinhauser of the Vienna University of Technology in Austria spent three years studying 503 pieces of fluff from his own belly button. He concluded that there is a particular type of body hair that traps pieces of stray lint and draws them in.

℞ SPRAY WATCH

To deter attackers, Serge Cotaina of France invented a wristwatch that can release a burst of pepper spray. A small cartridge hidden inside the watch's housing emits the spray from the side of the timepiece.

℞ ROBOT ACTORS

Robots appeared on stage alongside human actors in a play that premiered in Osaka, Japan, in 2008. The machines were specially programmed to speak lines with humans and move around the stage.

MAD INVENTIONS... MAD INVENTIONS...

Ice Ride

The famous Ford Model T car was converted into an early version of the snowmobile in 1937. The vehicle had caterpillar belts around the regular rear tires, and metal skis were used in place of the front wheels. Such modified classics could reach around 18 mph (29 km/h) in thick snow.

Visionary

Science-fiction author Hugo Gernsback was way ahead of his time when he invented these television glasses, for portable TV viewing, which he unveiled in 1963.

Lisa Courtney from Hertfordshire, England, has spent the last 13 years accumulating more than 13,400 items of Pokémon cartoon memorabilia, and she is still adding to her collection. Pokémon was originally a Japanese creation, so 21-year-old Lisa has traveled to the country five times to satisfy her obsession with the cartoon creatures.

R CHARMED LIFE

Ninety-year-old grandfather Alec Alder from Gloucestershire, England, reckons he has cheated death no fewer than 14 times. He has survived several car crashes, a 15-ft (4.5-m) fall from a tree as a boy, war-time bombing, being run over by a tank, and he even walked away after a fighter jet smashed into the side of his house as he slept. Perhaps his narrowest escape came in 1939 when his wedding prevented him from being sent to Dunkirk, where his whole army squadron was killed.

R PIGEON FANCIER

Former U.S. boxing champion Mike Tyson once booked a hotel suite in Louisville, Kentucky, for his eight favorite pigeons.

R DOUBLE VISION

A set of identical twin brothers married a pair of twin sisters in a military ceremony in Pechora, Russia, in 2009. Lilia and Liana Kobozevsa were indistinguishable in their matching white dresses, while the only slight difference between Alexei and Dmitry Semyonova was the shade of their dark suits.

R SHREK WEDDING

Living up to his name, Keith Green married Christine England in Devon, England, in April 2009 dressed up as the movie character Shrek. He and his bride —who was dressed as the ogre princess Fiona also from the movie *Shrek*—spent three hours having their faces and hands painted green.

R DIVIDED HOUSE

A couple in Cambodia who separated in 2008 after nearly 40 years of marriage decided to divide their belongings equally— by taking the unusual step of sawing their house in half. The wife stayed in the remaining upright half of the house while her husband carried away his half to a field on the other side of the village where he planned to start a new life.

R PRIZED MUSTACHE

Many police departments throughout India offer bonuses and prizes for officers that grow mustaches.

Hairy Meal

An 18-year-old girl was so addicted to eating her own hair that a massive hairball measuring 15 x 7 in (38 x 18 cm) formed in her stomach. The teen had complained to doctors of abdominal pains and vomiting and that's when they discovered the 10-lb (4.5-kg) mass of dark, curly hair, which filled almost her entire stomach.

15 INCHES!

R COMPUTER CASKET

The family of a computer geek have stored his remains inside an old PC. The computer displays a plastic plaque bearing his name, Alan, and the dates of his birth and death. Friends were encouraged to pay their tributes by writing messages on post-it notes and slipping them through the floppy drive slot.

R SPACE ODDITY

Canadian circus tycoon Guy Laliberté was blasted into space as a space tourist in 2009, dressed as a clown. The founder of the Cirque du Soleil wore a bulbous red clown nose and took along more red noses for his crew mates on the International Space Station.

R FEIGNED DEATH

A 22-year-old Japanese man feigned death for three hours in a failed attempt to avoid being arrested for driving into a police motorcycle. After fleeing the scene of the accident, he collapsed and pretended to be dead even after a catheter was inserted into his urethra by paramedics.

R KEEPING ACTIVE

Xie Long from Chongqing, China, kept fit for 30 years using two old mortars as dumbbells— until a friend noticed the weapons were still live. Police defused the mortars, which could have exploded at any time.

R TRAIN ORDEAL

An American tourist survived for $2^1/2$ hours clinging to the outside of a train as it sped through the Australian outback at up to 70 mph (110 km/h). Chad Vance from Alaska jumped on to The Ghan, which travels from Adelaide to Darwin, as it was pulling out of a station in June 2009. As the express train gathered speed, he squeezed himself into a precarious stairwell until a crew member finally heard his cries for help and brought the train to a halt.

R ALCOHOLIC SOAP

A hand gel intended to combat swine flu was withdrawn from use at a British prison in 2009 after inmates realized it contained alcohol and starting eating it. Instead of rubbing the liquid soap on their hands, inmates at Verne Prison, Dorset, England, put their mouths over the dispensers and started consuming significant quantities of the gel, with the result that a number became involved in a drunken brawl.

R KNUCKLE CRACKER

Donald L. Unger of Thousand Oaks, California, cracked the knuckles of his left hand—but never his right—every day for more than 60 years to investigate whether frequent knuckle cracking could lead to arthritis of the fingers.

R BACK FROM THE DEAD

Found lying in a pool of blood from a head wound at her apartment in Cernavoda, Romania, 84-year-old Elena Albu was declared dead by a doctor. However, when a forensic photographer took her picture, she opened her eyes and complained of a headache.

GIANT HAND

LIU HUA FROM JIANGSU, CHINA, HAD AN OPERATION TO REMOVE 11 LB (5 KG) OF TISSUE FROM THE INDEX FINGER, MIDDLE FINGER AND THUMB OF HIS LEFT HAND. BEFORE THE OPERATION HIS THUMB MEASURED 10½ IN (26 CM) LONG, HIS INDEX FINGER WAS 12 IN (30 CM) AND HIS MIDDLE FINGER 6 IN (15 CM)—AND HIS THUMB AND INDEX FINGER WERE THICKER THAN HIS ARMS! THE TOTAL WEIGHT OF HIS LEFT ARM WAS A WHOPPING 22 LB (10 KG).

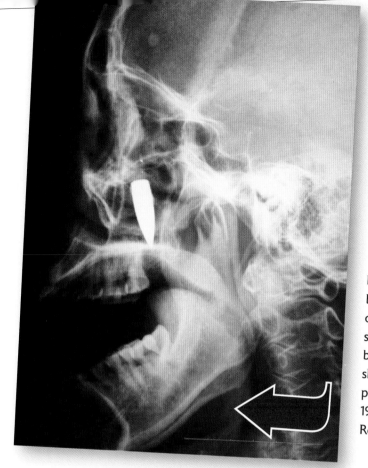

Bullet Pain

A bullet 1⅓ in (3.3 cm) long that had been lodged in a Chinese woman's face for 42 years was finally removed after she complained of blinding headaches. Hou Guoying had been mystified by the presence of the bullet until she remembered being accidentally shot with a starting pistol during the 1967 Cultural Revolution.

ⓇIPLEY'S RESEARCH

LIU SUFFERS FROM MACRODACTYLY ("LARGE FINGERS"), A CONGENITAL CONDITION IN WHICH TOES OR FINGERS ARE ABNORMALLY LARGE. IT IS BELIEVED TO BE CAUSED EITHER BY AN ABNORMAL NERVE SUPPLY TO THE AFFECTED DIGIT OR BY ABNORMAL BLOOD VESSELS.

Wily Coyote

A coyote struck by a car at 75 mph (120 km/h) near the border of Nevada and Utah was found embedded in the front fender eight hours later—still alive! The coyote not only survived the impact and the 600-mi (965-km) journey, it was even well enough to escape from its rescuers.

$500,000 DOG

A woman in China paid over $500,000 for a Tibetan mastiff dog in 2009. Mrs. Wang had spent years scouring China for the perfect specimen, a dog called Yangtze River Number Two. When the pet arrived by plane at Xi'an airport, it was met by banners, a welcoming committee of local dog-lovers and a motorcade of 30 luxury limousines sent by the new owner's wealthy friends.

BOG CHAMPION

Bride-to-be Casey Squibb of Dorset, England, went bogsnorkeling on her bachelorette party—and ended up recording the fastest time ever for a woman at the Irish Bogsnorkelling Championships in Castleblayney, Monaghan. She took 22 friends to Ireland and 15 of them entered the race along a 360-ft (110-m) trench. Casey wore a wetsuit and flippers, and a mask with a white lace veil.

EXPENSIVE HAIRCUT

The Sultan of Brunei, one of the richest men in the world, pays over $13,000 every month for a haircut. He pays the huge fee to fly his favorite barber, Ken Modestou, first-class, from London's Dorchester Hotel to Brunei and to have him stay in a hotel. Modestou normally charges $45 for a trim.

GRATE DRAIN ROBBERY

Between 2007 and 2008, thieves stole more than 2,500 manhole covers and storm drain grates from the streets of Philadelphia, Pennsylvania, to sell as scrap metal.

HOSPITAL CRECHE

The state of Nebraska has a law that allows a person to leave a child of any age at a hospital without risk of prosecution for abandonment. One of the first parents to use it dropped off nine children aged one to 17!

PERSONAL URNS

Cremation Solutions of Arlington, Vermont, offers a unique memento of the dearly departed—an urn shaped like their head. A full-sized head, created from photographs of the deceased and able to hold the ashes of any adult, costs $2,600, and the company can even add a wig to the urn if the customer wishes.

Human Kebab

A wayward throw from a classmate left athlete Jian Liao writhing in agony on the track at Guilin, China, as a 5-ft (1.5-m) javelin went through his kneecap. Rescue workers tried to cut the spear off with bolt cutters, but when Jian screamed in pain, they set fire to it instead and burned it in half before they moved him.

℞ HUMAN WEIGHTS

In January 2009, a fitness gym in London, England, set up weight-lifting machines using people as weights. The five differently sized human weights—ranging from a 66-lb (30-kg) man to one weighing 340-lb (155-kg)—not only helped gym goers visualize the weight they were lifting, but also shouted words of encouragement.

℞ SILENCE IN COURT!

Annoyed by repeated interruptions in court, a judge ordered the defendant's mouth be taped shut. Judge Stephen Belden, of Canton Municipal Court in Ohio, decided that putting duct tape over the mouth of robbery suspect Harry Brown was the only way to restore order.

℞ WEDDING TOAST

Opening their presents following their wedding at Howden Minster, East Yorkshire, England, in 2009, Claire and Stuart Linley were amazed to discover that they had been given no fewer than 24 toasters. They kept one and returned the other 23.

℞ RESTING PLACE

Jack Woodward's last wish was honored when his ashes were buried in the pub where he had spent many hours nearly every day of his life. The former landlord's remains lie beneath a flagstone in the bar at the Boat Inn in the village of Stoke Bruerne, Northamptonshire, England, with a plaque saying: "Stand here and have a drink on me."

℞ CANINE TUXEDO

Having first met while walking their dogs on the beach, Harriet and Andrew Athay of Dorset, England, chose their pet dog Ed to be best man at their wedding. Ed wore his own miniature tuxedo, while the couple's two female dogs, Humbug and Goulash, dressed in pink sparkly collars.

℞ FIVE WEDDINGS

Simone and Ryan Feeney from Buckinghamshire, England, got married five times in less than a year. They first tied the knot in March 2008 at the Little White Wedding Chapel in Las Vegas, Nevada, and followed it up over the next ten months with ceremonies in Turkey, Britain, the U.S. (again) and Australia.

℞ SCREAMING CONTEST

Russian Sergey Savelyev can scream at 116.8 decibels – that's about as loud as an ambulance siren. He demonstrated his shrieking ability when picking up $900 for winning an international screaming contest in Pattaya, Thailand, in August 2009.

℞ MILK ROUND

Eighty-one-year-old milkman Derek Arch has been delivering milk to homes in the city of Coventry, England, for nearly 70 years. Driving the same van he has had for more than 50 years, he rises at 2.30 a.m. to make his daily deliveries, seven days a week, visiting more than 400 houses and walking 8 mi (13 km) each day.

℞ UNBELIEVABLE OFFER

A four-star hotel near Venice, Italy, lost $129,000 after mistakenly offering a romantic weekend for just one cent. The Crowne Plaza received over 1,400 room reservations as soon as the offer—the result of a human error at their head office in Atlanta, Georgia—was posted on its website.

℞ LLAMA GUARD

Two of farmer Terry McCrone's llamas served as the honor guard at his funeral in Plymouth Township, Ohio.

Daredevil Falls

SINCE 1901 A SUCCESSION OF "NIAGARA DAREDEVILS" HAVE MADE LIFE-THREATENING ATTEMPTS TO CONQUER THE RAPID WATERS OF THE CANADIAN HORSESHOE FALLS, THE HIGHEST DROP AT NIAGARA FALLS, IN VARIOUS OBJECTS. MOST SEEK FAME, FORTUNE OR PUBLICITY, SOME SEEK THE THRILL, AND ALL OF THEM ARE FULLY AWARE OF THE RISK THEY TAKE WHEN THEY PLUNGE OVER THE TOP. THE CHANCES OF SURVIVAL ARE SO SLIM THAT THE JUMP IS STATISTICALLY MORE LIKE SUICIDE, WITH AT LEAST 12 TO 15 SUICIDES RECORDED AT NIAGARA EACH YEAR. INDIVIDUALS WHO MADE EARLY ATTEMPTS WERE APTLY NAMED "DAREDEVILS" WHEN THEY SURVIVED, WITH THOSE THAT DIED BEING SEEN TO HAVE COMMITTED SUICIDE. ALTHOUGH NIAGARA FALLS ARE NOT THE HIGHEST IN THE WORLD, THEY ARE ONE OF THE MOST DANGEROUS. THE FLOW OF WATER IS SO POWERFUL THAT NO MAN HAS EVER BEEN ABLE TO COMPLETELY CONTROL IT—NOT EVEN TRAINED ENGINEERS.

BOBBY LEACH and his Barrel after his perilous trip over Niagara Falls, July 25th. Copyright 1911, U.S.A. & CANADA by Bobby Leach

A HEAD FOR HEIGHTS – 1886

The first man to conquer the Niagara Falls Rapids in a barrel was Carlisle Graham from Philadelphia. In July 1886, he took on the lower Great George Rapids through Lewiston, New York, in a 5½-ft (1.7-m) barrel made of oak and iron hoops, despite being about 6 ft (1.8 m) tall. The stunt took more than 30 minutes and, surviving the ride, he decided to do it again in August of the same year. This time he did it with his head hanging out of the top—the continuous force of the rapids on the side of his head damaged both his ear drums, leaving him deaf.

FORTUNE FALL – 1901

In October 1901, Annie Edison Taylor was the first person to drop down the Falls in a barrel—and survive. Annie was looking for some money and attention when she decided to conquer the falls at 63 years old (although she claimed to be in her forties). She emerged from the airtight wooden barrel with only a scratch on her forehead. Despite this, she never really became famous and spent the rest of her life selling souvenirs on the street.

IN A SPIN – 1930

After helping Bobby Leach (see above) retrieve his barrel in 1911 and survive the fall, William Red Hill Sr. was in awe and decided to go over himself in 1930. He chose a 6 x 3 ft (2 x 1 m) steel barrel, with a 14 x 18 in (36 x 46 cm) manhole, and air holes that were secured with removable corks. More than 25,000 people watched him drop and within 90 seconds he was in the whirlpool at the bottom of the Falls where his barrel was trapped. After spinning for over three hours with his barrel half full of water, he finally emerged alive with only a few bruises.

STEEL SQUEAL – 1911

In July 1911, Bobby Leach was the second person to take on the Falls in a barrel, but this one was made of steel. Leach was a performer with the Barnum & Bailey Circus and was sure he could complete the Falls even better than Annie had. The drop resulted in him breaking both his knee caps and his jaw. However, he managed to use his experience to tour Canada, the U.S.A. and New Zealand, telling people his story and posing with his barrel. He died later in life after contracting gangrene in his leg when he slipped on an orange peel.

BARREL OF NO RETURN – 1920

Charles G. Stephens was the first daredevil to lose his life going over the Horseshoe Falls in a barrel. On July 11, 1920, Englishman Stephens thought that he could save his 11 children from poverty and find fame by taking the plunge. Thousands watched as Stephens clambered into his large wooden barrel, tying his feet to an anvil for extra security. However, this turned out to be his fatal mistake, and when the barrel was recovered all that remained was his right arm.

INFLATABLE TALE – 1928

On July 4, 1928, Jean Lussier, a 36-year-old from Massachusetts, went over the Falls in an inflatable rubber ball 6 ft (1.8 m) in diameter. Although three of the 32 inner tubes burst, he survived.

HOW MUCH WATER?

The Canadian Horseshoe Falls is the highest drop of all at Niagara, descending 180 ft (55 m) and measuring 2,500 ft (760 m) across. However, the precise drop can vary by as much as 30 ft (9 m) depending on the season or even, sometimes, on the time of day. Around 45 million gallons (170 million liters) of water flows over the edge each minute—that's equivalent to about a million bathtubs of water tipping over the Falls every minute!

BALL OF FUN – 1961

In June 1961, Nathan Boya decided to attempt the Falls in a large ball. He declared that he was not seeking fame or fortune, but that it was "just something he had to do." He used a steel sphere wrapped in rubber that allowed him oxygen for 30 hours. After nearly dropping down the American Falls (the wrong one) and having to be towed back to the Horseshoe Falls, Nathan survived unscathed, yet incurred a $100 fine and $13 in court costs for illegally going over the Falls.

DOUBLE TROUBLE – 1989

In September 1989, two men took the plunge in the same barrel for the first time. Peter DeBernardi and Jeffrey Petkovich positioned themselves head to head wearing hockey helmets in a 10-x-5-ft (3-x-1.5-m) barrel. They emerged without serious injury.

JET JUMP – 1995

Robert Overacker, a 39-year-old school graduate, used a jet ski to drop over the Falls in October 1995. However, the rocket-propelled parachute strapped to his back failed to open and Robert fell 180 ft (55 m) to his death, a fall that is said to feel like hitting cement.

WORTH THE WEIGHT – 1984

Canadian Karel Soucek went over the Falls in July 1984 in a lightweight wooden and plastic barrel, using a weight to ensure he went down feet first. His fall took about 3.2 seconds, going over at 75 mph (120 km/h). He suffered cuts and bruises, and an arm injury, as well as a $500 fine for stunting without a license!

DOUBLE DIVE – 1985 & 1993

Not content with going over the Falls once, Canadian Dave Munday did it twice! In 1985, Munday tumbled 173 ft (52.7 m) down Horseshoe Falls in five seconds in a 7-ft-long (2.1-m) steel barrel. In 1993, he did it again, in a diving bell. He had no helmet and there was just a 2-in (5-cm) layer of padding inside the bell to soften the impact.

GOING IT ALONE – 2003

In October 2003, Kirk Jones became the first daredevil to take on the Falls without any protection whatsoever but the clothes on his back. Climbing under the barrier, Kirk floated down the 175-ft (53-m) drop on his back and when he reached the bottom swam to some rocks. Refusing a helping hand from a *Maid of the Mist* tour boat, he climbed out to land on his own. He had only a couple of bruises, yet received a fine of $2,300 and was banned from Canada for life.

R TYPO SQUAD

As part of their campaign to eradicate bad spelling and punctuation, Jeff Deck of Somerville, Massachusetts, and Benjamin Herson of Virginia Beach, Virginia, toured the U.S.A. for two months in 2008, removing typographical errors from public signs.

R WASP DIET

An eight-year-old Indian boy, Ravi Singh, is addicted to eating wasps. He says they have a sweet taste and he enjoys the sensation of the wasp's sting on his tongue. He can eat up to seven at a time and, although five wasp stings can kill a grown man, Ravi's body has developed a resistance to their poison.

R LIFELIKE COSTUME

A man dressed as a gorilla for a charity run through England was stopped by police, who had received calls from passing motorists thinking he was a real ape that had escaped from a zoo! Rory Coleman was running to support the Gorilla Organization.

R LIGHT RIDDLE

For five years, farmer Mo Zhaoguang from Nandan, Hubei Province, China, was mystified as to who kept turning on the light in his barn—until he finally realized it was his buffalo. Mo says the buffalo turns on the light when it is hungry or thirsty and then turns it off again afterward to go to sleep.

R MOBILE ZOO

Police officers who stopped a motorist in Bari, Italy, found no fewer than 1,700 animals squeezed into the trunk of his car. Inside were more than 1,000 terrapins, 300 white mice, 216 budgies, 150 hamsters, 30 Japanese squirrels and six chameleons.

R GARBAGE COLLECTOR

Officials made Merv Jones move out of his home in Lincolnshire, England, while they cleared out 100 tons of rubbish that had been collected over decades and stacked floor-to-ceiling throughout the house. The stench from the waste, which included old ammunition, samurai swords and propane gas canisters, was so bad that it could be smelled more than a mile away.

R CANINE BRIDE

Two-year-old Sagula Munda was married to a dog at a ceremony in Jajpur, India, in 2009 to protect the boy from ghosts and further bad luck following the discovery of a rotten tooth in his gum.

R USEFUL BONES

In 2009, seven years after his death, Gordon Krantz, a professor of osteology from Port Angeles, Washington State, received his dying wish that the bones of he and his dog become a museum display when he was exhibited in the Smithsonian Museum of Natural History.

R CATTLE OFFER

During U.S. Secretary of State Hillary Clinton's 2009 visit to Kenya, 39-year-old Godwin Chepkurgor, a former Nairobi councilor, offered her 20 cows and 40 goats in exchange for the hand of her daughter Chelsea in marriage.

RIPLEY'S ask

Why did you start taxidermy art?
I started making taxidermy after I met a beautiful girl in college who was doing it. I wanted her to like me, so I used this thing she liked to get her attention. As I remember it, she was using a stapler to connect parts of different animals, and then submerging them in jars of rubbing alcohol. So I sewed together an opossum tail by hand and gave it to her. She liked it—but not enough to date me!

Where do you get your animals?
I get animals from everywhere possible, so it is a lot of places. They can be found in Chinatown fish markets and their garbage, Florida roadkill, live poultry houses in New York City, taxidermy supply websites, supermarket meats, sympathetic veterinary clinics, and probably more places.

What are the problems caused by using dead animals?
There are many problems. Exposure to disease and parasites is always a concern, but I have not had a problem yet. I store my animals in rubbing alcohol, and the fumes are not healthy to breathe. But the worst is the smell from the animals that are in the rubbing alcohol, which release a smell of rotting flesh into my life.

Dead Art

New York artist Nate Hill scours backstreet trashcans for animal carcasses, which he then sews together in unique, grotesque creations. Nate presented his grandest creation, the A.D.A.M. project, at his apartment in January 2008. A life-sized man with fish for shoulders and a deer-fur torso, A.D.A.M. is also part chicken, conch, cow, crab, duck, eel, frog, lobster, rabbit and shark.

Cheesy Crawlies

CASU MARZU CHEESE IS A GOURMET TRADITION ON THE ISLAND OF SARDINIA, ITALY. WHILE MANY CHEESES ENCOURAGE THE GROWTH OF BACTERIA, CASU MARZU IS NOT READY TO EAT UNTIL IT IS FULLY INFESTED WITH THE MAGGOT LARVAE OF THE CHEESE FLY. AS THE MAGGOTS PROCESS THE CHEESE, THEY GIVE IT THE REQUIRED MOIST TEXTURE, AND THEN IT IS EATEN, MAGGOTS AND ALL. IT IS ONLY WHEN THE MAGGOTS DIE THAT THE CHEESE BECOMES UNFIT FOR HUMAN CONSUMPTION.

R ZOO QUEST

Marla Taviano and her family from Columbus, Ohio, visited 55 U.S. animal parks in 52 weeks. They began their 22,000-mi (35,405-km) safari at Louisville Zoo, Kentucky, in August 2008 and, after visits to zoos in Dallas, New York and San Diego among others, ended it a year later at their hometown Columbus Zoo and Aquarium.

R STOLEN SAND

Environmental enforcement officers supported by the Mexican Navy put crime tape around a Cancun hotel beach in 2009 on suspicion that the hotel had stolen the sand for its beach by pumping it illegally from the sea floor.

R CROC JAILED

Police in Gunbalanya, Northern Territory, Australia, threw a 6½-ft-long (2-m) saltwater crocodile in jail for three days in October 2009 after it was found loitering in the town.

R BIG BUBBLE

In August 2009, professional bubble maker Sam Heath (aka Samsam Bubbleman) of London, England, made a free-floating, multicolored soap bubble measuring 20 x 5 x 5 ft (6 x 1.5 x 1.5 m). He used a secret mixture—that he has spent 20 years perfecting—and a piece of rope tied between two sticks.

R DOG BAN

A judge banned a small Pomeranian dog from the resort of Aspen, Colorado, in 2009 for repeatedly biting. Municipal Judge Brooke Peterson told the dog's owner that if the animal was seen again in Aspen, it would have to be put down. The dog, named Gizmo, had previously been sent to an animal shelter for ten days in a bid to curb its aggressive behavior.

R RAPID BOUNCE

Ashrita Furman of New York City bounced a basketball 339 times in just 60 seconds in February 2009.

Carry on Canine

Irish customs officers were extremely surprised to see a Chihuahua dog clearly visible on the luggage X-ray screen at Dublin airport in October 2009. The dog had been smuggled out of Spain inside a passenger's hand luggage. Despite its unconventional method of travel, the dog was reported to be in good health.

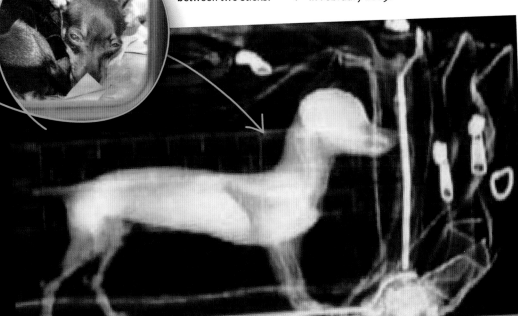

Drinking Hole

A 46-year-old man woke up stuck from the waist down in a gully in Bochum, Germany, after a night of drinking in July 2009. With no knowledge of how he ended up jammed down the drain, the man was finally pulled out by baffled firefighters. Police are still confused as to how the drain cover was removed when he claims he did not touch it!

℞ SNAKES BLAMED

A motorist who lost control of his sports utility vehicle in Hartford, Connecticut, in 2009 blamed the accident on two pet baby snakes that he said escaped from his pants pockets as he was driving. He claimed the snakes slithered near the gas and brake pedals and, while he and a passenger tried to catch them, the vehicle veered into some parked cars and overturned.

℞ NEW NAME

After a night out, 19-year-old Tom Hayward, a computer-games design student from Leicestershire, England, changed his name by deed poll to N'Tom The Hayemaker Haywardyouliketocomebacktomine. He forgot all about it until he received a formal letter confirming his new name.

℞ YOUNG LECTURER

Aman Rehman of Dehradun in Uttarakhand state, India, started teaching adult students computer-generated animated film at Dehradun's College of Interactive Arts in 2009—when he was just eight years old! The son of an illiterate mechanic, Aman mastered his first animation program at age three and a half and has since made more than 1,000 animated films.

℞ UNDERPANTS SMUGGLER

In 2009, a man was caught wearing 15 pairs of contraband underpants, four tracksuits and three pairs of pants as he tried to smuggle them into Belarus from Ukraine. He was sweating so heavily and waddling so badly that he could hardly walk, thus attracting the attention of customs officials.

℞ THRIFTY BRIDE

Heather Saint, a 20-year-old bride from Teesside, England, beat the recession in 2008 by buying her wedding dress on the Internet auction site eBay for just five pence (8 cents).

℞ PENGUIN MAN

For over 35 years, Alfred David of Brussels, Belgium, has lived life as a penguin. Monsieur le Penguin, as he is known, walks the streets in a penguin costume, likes to eat raw sardines and preens himself to keep clean. He believes he has a telepathic connection with penguins, has a collection of more than 3,000 ornamental penguins and has even hosted penguin exhibitions in Belgium and abroad. He wants to be buried in a penguin-shaped coffin and is convinced that he will eventually be reincarnated as a penguin.

℞ JAWS BURGLAR

Police investigating a series of baffling burglaries through caged windows around Chongqing, China, discovered that the culprit had gained entry by biting through steel bars. When arrested, the man revealed that he could chew any steel bar up to $3/8$ in (1 cm) thick by tearing open the welding spots with his powerful teeth.

℞ BOMB ANCHOR

A fisherman in Johor, Malaysia, had been using an unexploded bomb from World War II as a boat anchor for months before he realized what it was.

Smelly Nelly

In August 2009, a baby elephant was walking to work with his trainer in Rayong Province in Thailand when he slipped and fell into a manhole. His owner had taken his eyes off him for just a moment when he turned to find the calf firmly stuck in the 3-ft-wide (90-cm) drain. It took three hours for rescuers to get him out, eventually having to use a bulldozer to widen the hole. The elephant miraculously survived without any injuries.

® PETTY CASH

When two women were laid off from their jobs at a ceilings-installation company in Vladivostok, Russia, their former boss paid them the $1,150 he owed them—in 33 heavy bags full of low-denomination coins.

® VEGAS CRAZY

Anette and Kenneth Lund from Vejle, Denmark, got married four times in one day in 2008 in Las Vegas, Nevada. They wed in a hotel, in a limousine with the service conducted by an Elvis impersonator, in a helicopter and while skydiving. They said they plan to get married once a year for the rest of their lives to keep their relationship exciting.

® CLOWN STOLEN

An inflatable clown stolen from a Russian circus in Alice Springs, Northern Territory, Australia, in 2009 was found a few days later on a nearby golf course—along with a handwritten note in which he demanded better working conditions.

® SLEEPING ON THE JOB

In 2009, Roisin Madigan, a student from Birmingham, England, was paid $1,500 to sleep in designer beds every day for a month. She spent eight hours a day in bed to help with a sleep survey being carried out by a luxury bed manufacturer.

® PRISONER RETURNS

Jail guards in Camden County, Georgia, caught a prisoner in March 2009 as he was sneaking back into jail after he had escaped to steal cigarettes from across the street.

® ELECTION DRAW

When a 2009 council election in Cave Creek, Arizona, ended in a tie, the result was decided by invoking a 1925 local statute and drawing from a deck of cards. Adam Trenk was elected after his king of hearts beat rival candidate Thomas McGuire's six of hearts.

® KITCHEN DIG

To reach an underground river full of fish, Li Huiyan of Chongqing, China, hired 30 villagers to dig a 50-ft (16-m) hole in his kitchen. After digging down to the river, he placed a fishing net across it and hauled out enough fish every day to support his family.

IN JULY 2009, FREE DIVER YANG YUN WAS SUFFERING DANGEROUS PARALYZING CRAMPS WHEN A BELUGA WHALE, MILA, HEROICALLY GUIDED HER TO THE SURFACE. DIVING 20 FT (6 M) WITHOUT ANY BREATHING EQUIPMENT, YUN WAS FACING CERTAIN DEATH WHEN HER LEGS FROZE FROM THE ARCTIC TEMPERATURES OF THE AQUARIUM POOL IN HARBIN, NORTHEAST CHINA. MILA CLEVERLY SENSED THE PROBLEM, WELL BEFORE THE ORGANIZERS DID, AND USED HER DOLPHIN-LIKE NOSE TO PUSH YUN TO SAFETY.

Whale Watch

SPIDER SKIN

It might look like this man's skin has been scraped away to reveal a superhero suit, but it is actually a most extraordinary life-like tattoo by Dan Hazelton from Milwaukee, Wisconsin. The talented skin artist inked the startling design, known as a "tear out," on a tattoo-mad client's chest in 1996. The design took ten hours of work over three sessions.

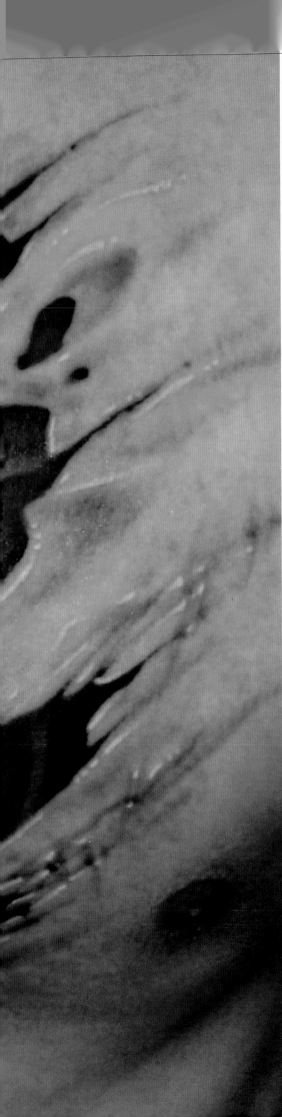

℞ SAME TIE

Attorney Bob Flournoy of Lufkin, Texas, wore the same U.S. flag tie every day for more than six years. With daily wear, the tie started to disintegrate, forcing Bob to cut portions out and hold it together with Velcro, but by 2007 it was only half its original size and was too fragile even to tie.

℞ GNOME RESCUE

When an elderly Australian lady died in 2009, the 1,500 ornamental gnomes she had collected over the years faced eviction from their home in Cootamundra, New South Wales, and the prospect of being thrown in a dumpster. However, local people came to the rescue and in a four-hour operation they rounded up the gnomes with a view to finding foster homes for them.

℞ BAMBOO BALANCE

Three couples got married on the Xiangjiang River in Zunyi City, China, in January 2009 while balancing on bamboo poles that measured 8 in (20 cm) in diameter. The couples, who wore traditional wedding attire, are all members of the local single bamboo rafting club and chose to get married on the water to demonstrate their skill at the sport.

℞ FAST-FOOD CEREMONY

Paul and Caragh Brooks got married in Normal, Illinois, in 2009 in their favorite restaurant—a branch of the Mexican fast-food chain Taco Bell.

℞ FRIDGE PARTY

Paul and Val Howkins from Coventry, England, invited friends and family to a 50th birthday party—for their fridge. They had banners, party poppers and even a cake to celebrate the milestone birthday of the still-working fridge, which they bought for around $100 in 1959.

℞ CHAMELEON CHAOS

A fire brigade in Hampshire, England, sent 18 officers, three trucks and a unit wearing special chemical protective clothing to a house in Basingstoke—to clean up a broken jar containing a pickled chameleon that had been preserved in formaldehyde.

℞ QUIT SMOKING

After smoking for 95 years, 102-year-old Winnie Langley from London, England, finally decided to quit in 2009. Since her first puff in 1914, she smoked on average five cigarettes a day, making a total of more than 170,000.

℞ CAT CALLS

Police broke into a home in Sussex, England, after a cat dialed the emergency number 999 four times in the space of a few minutes. The owner, who was perfectly safe and well the whole time, said her cat Watson, who enjoys playing with the phone, must have accidentally called the number.

℞ ROBOT DANCERS

A total of 269 people dressed as robots on the Bournemouth and Poole College campus, in Dorset, England, in July 2009 and gave a five-minute performance of robot dancing.

℞ THREE POLES

British explorer Adrian Hayes reached the three extreme points of the Earth—the North and South Poles and the summit of Mount Everest —in the space of just 19 months. He climbed to the top of Everest in May 2006, arrived at the North Pole in April 2007 and reached the South Pole in December 2007—a daunting triple challenge that takes most explorers several years to attempt.

℞ BARE HANDS

On November 21, 2008, expert knife thrower the Rev. Dr. David Adamovich—aka The Great Throwdini—from Freeport, New York, caught a thrown knife, a flying arrow and a fired .22 caliber bullet—all with his bare hands.

℞ CLOVER BUNCH

Ten-year-old Mabel South picked more than 120 four-leafed clovers in the garden of her home in Hertfordshire, England, in less than half an hour. The bunch included three five-leafed clovers and one six-leafed clover.

℞ BLINDFOLD SKATER

Nine-year-old limbo skater Rohan Ajit Kokane squeezed his body under a car with a clearance height of just $6^3/_4$ in (17.1 cm) at Belgaum, India, in 2009—while blindfolded.

℞ SOLO SAILOR

Southern Californian sailor Zac Sunderland completed a 13-month, 28,000-mile (45,000-km) solo voyage around the world in July 2009—at age 17. Zac, who was just 16 when he set off from Marina del Rey in June 2008, endured many dramas on his 36-ft (11-m) boat *Intrepid*, not least during the leg from Australia to the Coco Islands when he was followed by pirates and forced to call the Australian authorities to scare them off.

SCRAP YARD

INNOVATIVE IRISH COMPANY ROBOSTEEL WELD SCRAP STEEL RECYCLED FROM OLD CARS, MOTORBIKES AND AIRPLANES INTO GIANT SCULPTURES OF FILM ICONS AND FANTASY CHARACTERS, SUCH AS *TRANSFORMERS*, *PREDATOR* AND *ALIEN*. THE TEAM USES THOUSANDS OF PIECES OF STEEL PER SCULPTURE, WHICH CAN TAKE OVER TWO MONTHS TO COMPLETE. EACH FIGURE IS ENTIRELY UNIQUE AND SOME STAND OVER 8 FT (2.4 M) TALL.

"TRANSFORMER"

℞ CAVEMAN RECAPTURED

An escaped prisoner was recaptured in northern Portugal in 2009 after 16 years on the run. The bearded, long-haired fugitive had been hiding out in caves and living mainly on fruit.

℞ MONKEY MUGGER

A visitor to the Chengdu Wildlife Park in China plunged 20 ft (6 m) after being pushed off a cliff by a monkey. Zhou Juchang broke three ribs and fractured her hip after being mugged by the monkey for bags of food.

℞ MR. BIG

A Chinese man wanted on suspicion of stealing dozens of electric bicycles in Anyang, Henan Province, nearly evaded arrest because police officers didn't recognize him as he had put on 28 lb (13 kg) in weight in a month. He had changed his appearance by remaining in his motel room, getting meals delivered and not exercising.

℞ BULL GUEST

A runaway bull spent an entire night in a hotel room in Jinan, Shandong Province, China. The bull casually strolled into a room at the hotel without being noticed and was not discovered until the following morning.

℞ RETURN VISIT

A burglar who stole a man's valuables returned to the house in Pensacola, Florida, a few hours later and took what he hadn't been able to carry on his first visit—a 100-lb (45-kg) plasma-screen TV. A police investigator was at the house by then, but the TV was unattended in the backyard (where the burglar had put it the first time around) so that it could be dusted for fingerprints. Police offered to pay for the TV.

℞ EMU CUFFED

Police officers used a stun gun and handcuffs to capture an emu that was running loose on a highway in central Mississippi. Deputies surrounded the bird as it dodged traffic on Interstate 20, but had to resort to a Taser and cuffs to get it off the road.

MONSTERS

℞ DEAD-END JOB
In 2009, a London, England, tourist attraction offered an annual salary of $45,000 to the successful applicant for the post of resident zombie. Job seekers were asked to turn up for the auditions with the London Bridge Experience in blood-soaked costumes and scary makeup.

℞ FAMILY REUNION
Gary Nisbet discovered his long-lost brother when he turned up as his new workmate 35 years after the two boys had been adopted by different families. Lookalike Randy Joubert's arrival at the bedding retailer in Waldoboro, Maine, prompted remarks that the two could be brothers, which they laughed off—until they discovered they were.

℞ FREAK DRAW
The same winning numbers were drawn in Bulgaria's national lottery two weeks in a row—at odds of more than four million to one. The freak occurrence saw the numbers 4, 15, 23, 24, 35 and 42 selected, in a different order, by machine, live on TV on September 6, 2009, and again four days later.

℞ DILLINGER'S DERRINGER
A small pistol belonging to notorious 1930s U.S. bank robber John Dillinger was sold at auction for $95,600 in 2009. The Remington .41 caliber Double Derringer was said to have been hidden in one of Dillinger's socks when he was arrested in 1934 in Tucson, Arizona.

℞ THE WRONG NEIL
Neil A. Armstrong, a 38-year-old financial services worker from Symmes Township, Ohio, receives dozens of letters and phone calls every year intended for famous astronaut Neil A. Armstrong who lives just 11 mi (18 km) away. When he moved from West Virginia over 15 years ago, Mr. Armstrong said he had no idea that the first man to walk on the Moon lived in the area, but now he has to field inquiries from autograph seekers, journalists, even NASA's Johnson Space Center.

℞ BULLET COLLISION
David Olson of Riverton, Wyoming, found a pair of 9mm bullets that had collided in midair.

℞ SUN INSURANCE
French travel agencies offer insurance to reimburse sun-lovers whose vacations are marred by bad weather. Travelers can claim back up to $550 if they suffer at least four days of rain in any one week.

℞ SUPERHERO GATHERING
To raise money for charity, more than 100 students and staff at Bournemouth University, England, crowded into one room dressed as superheroes, including a number of Batmen and Supermen.

SPACE "SOLDIER"

INDEX

Page numbers in *italic* refer to illustrations

ACKNOWLEDGMENTS Cover © DivaNir4a–istockphoto.com; **Page 5** (t/r) AFP/Getty Images, (b/l) Reuters/Luke MacGregor; **10** Quirky China/Barcroft Media Ltd; **12–13** Patrick Koster/Barcroft Media Ltd; **14** (t) © UPPA/Photoshot, (b) heartlessmachine.com; **15** Blank Archives/Getty Images; **16** Kevin Beresford; **17** Wenn.com; **18** (t, c) Mark Moffett/Minden Pictures/FLPA, (b/l) Norbert Wu/Minden Pictures/FLPA, (b/r) Photolibrary.com; **19** (t/l) Pascal Goetgheluck/Science Photo Library, (t/r) Dr Robert A. Patzner, (b/l) © NHPA/Photoshot, (b/r) Professor Nico Smit; **20** (b) Imagine China; **21** (t) Caters News, (b) Reuters/Pawan Kumar; **22** Werner Forman Archive/Formerly Hooper Collection/Sold at Christies; **24** (t) Reuters/Sukree Sukplang, (b) © EuroPics[CEN]; **25** Narinder Nanu/AFP/Getty Images; **26** © EuroPics[CEN]; **27** (c) © EuroPics[CEN], (b) Wenn.com, (t) Monica Rueda/AP/Press Association Images; **28** (t/l, t/r) Ian & Louise Fairburn, (b) © Extreme Cello; **29** (r) Caters News; **30** Photolibrary.com; **32** (b) Feliciano Guimarães, (t) Reuters/Bruno Domingos; **33** Tim Graham/Getty Images; **34** (t, c) Furious Earth, (b) Courtesy Alexander Turnbull Library, Wellington, New Zealand; **35** NASA/JSC; **36–37** Over Schiehallion, Perthshire, Scotland. © Ken Prior; **38–39** Rhett Dashwood/© Google Maps; **38** (b/r) GeoEye Satellite Image, (b/l) Keystone/Getty Images; **39** (c, b) GeoEye Satellite Image; **40** John R. Chu; **42** Wenn.com; **43** Jerry Ting; **44** International Fiber Collaborative; **45** www.style-your-garage.com; **46** (t/l) © Roberto–Fotolia.com, (b/r) © Julien Scaperrotta–Fotolia.com, (b/l) © Stefanie Leuker–Fotolia.com; **46–47** Photos by Keith Ducatel www.keithducatel.com; **48** (t) © Jeremy Horner/Corbis; **49** (sp) Photo by Deb Hall, (c/r) Sharon O'Dea/Bizarre Magazine, (b/r) Elizabeth Mackenzie-Barrett; **50** © EuroPics[CEN]; **52** (t) Jung von Matt/Neckar, (b) Melissa Smith; **53** Brendan Beckett/Barcroft Media Ltd; **54** (t) Barcroft Media Ltd, (b) Bournemouth News/Rex Features; **55** Zak-n-Wheezie hatched on 6/14/07 to Frank and Barbara Witte of www.fresnodragons.com; **56** (b) Wenn.com, (l) Todd Mecklem, (r) Christopher Hall; **57** Picture by Ian McLelland on behalf of PDSA; **58** Wenn.com; **59** (t) Caters News Agency Ltd/Rex Features, (b) Gary Florin/Rex Features; **60** Cardoso Flea Circus, by Maria Fernanda Cardoso Produced by the Fabric Workshop and Museum, Philadelphia. Collection of the Tate Gallery London. Photo credits: Ross Rudesch Harley; **61** (t) © Nicole Duplaix/Corbis, (c) © Hulton–Deutsch Collection/Corbis, (b/l) Hannah Grace Deller/Starstock/Photoshot, (b/r) © Bettmann/Corbis; **60–61** © Bettmann/Corbis; **62** (l) Ringland Life Images, (b) Drew Fitzgibbon/Newspix/Rex Features; **63** © NHPA/Photoshot; **64** (b) Eric Cheng/Barcroft Media Ltd; **65** (t) ChinaFotoPress/Photocome/Press Association Images, (b) Heng Sinith/AP/Press Association Images; **66** (t/l, b) Dana Fineman Courtesy of The Venice Beach Freakshow, (t/r) Priscilla Cermeno-Shakur; **67** (t/l, c/r, b/l, b/r) Dana Fineman Courtesy of The Venice Beach Freakshow, (t/r, c/l) Asia Ray Courtesy of The Venice Beach Freakshow; **68** (t) Apichart Weerawong/AP/Press Association Images, (b) Barry Bland/Barcroft Media Ltd; **69** www.redfernnaturalhistory.com; **70** (t) © EuroPics[CEN], (b) Caters News; **71** (sp) Wenn.com; **72** (l, r) © UPPA/Photoshot; **73** (t) Reuters/Cathal McNaughton, (b) Martin Birchall/Rex Features; **74** (t) Rex Features, (b) Chris Ison/PA Archive/Press Association Images; **75** Caters News Agency Ltd/Rex Features; **76** Cindy Lane/Newspix/Rex Features; **77** Newspix/Rex Features; **78** Vaclav Silha/Barcroft USA Ltd; **79** Kelly Tarlton's Antarctic Encounter and Underwater World; **80** Getty Images; **82** (sp) Topher Donahue/Getty Images, (t/l) Photolibrary.com; **83** (t, b) Norman Kent/Barcroft Media Ltd; **84** (t) Shaun Curry/AFP/Getty Images, (b) Reuters/Chaiwat Subprasom; **85** Dave Thompson/PA Wire/Press Association Images; **86** (t) www.lloydimages.com, (b) Marcus Brandt/DPA/Press Association Images; **87** (t) www.jw-sportfoto.de, (b) Marcus Brandt/DPA/Press Association Images; **88–89** Michael Martin/Barcroft Media Ltd; **90** (b/l) National Museum of the United States Air Force, (t/l, b/r) wetsuits bydiddo.com ©; **91** Mery Nunez/Barcroft Media Ltd; **92** Getty Images; **94** © NHPA/Photoshot; **95** Rex Features; **96** (b/r) © EuroPics[CEN], (t/l) Beretta/Sims/Rex Features; **97** Kevin Smith/Solent News/Rex Features; **98–101** Simon de Trey-White/Barcroft Media Ltd; **102** Reuters/Yiorgos Karahalis; **103** Eileen Darby/Time Life Pictures/Getty Images; **104** (b/r) © Andy Rain/epa/Corbis, (b/l) Archive Holdings Inc./Hulton Archive/Getty Images, (t/r) Geoffrey Swaine/Rex Features, (t/l) Wierzbicki/BEI/Rex Features; **105** (t/l) Wenn.com, (b/r) Rex Features, (b/l) FPG/Staff/Hulton Archive/Getty Images, (t/r) ©Sky1/Andi Southam; **106** James Elsby/Newspix/Rex Features; **107** Picture courtesy de Pury & Luxembourg, Switzerland & Studio Wim Delvoye, Belgium; **108** Photographer: Sridar Sri; **109** (t/l, t/r) Jaime Puebla/AP/Press Association Images, (b, b/r) Lane Jensen/BizarreArchive.com; **110** (r, l) Miami New Times/Colby Katz; **111** (l) © EuroPics[CEN]; **114** (t/l, t/r) Richard Drew/AP/Press Association Images; **115** (t/r) Dazed & Confused/Rex Features, (b) © EuroPics[CEN]; **117** D. B. Denholtz Collection; **118** (b/l) D. B. Denholtz Collection, (t/l) Time & Life Pictures/Getty Images, (b/c) Getty Images; **119** D. B. Denholtz Collection; **118–119** (t, b) Time & Life Pictures/Getty Images; **120** © EuroPics[CEN]; **121** Reuters/Supri Supri; **122** Photographer Jan Letocha; **124** (t) Wenn.com, (c) Reuters/Nozim Kalandarov, (b) Reuters/Nir Elias; **125** (t) Wenn.com, (l) Top Photo Group/Rex Features, (r) Reuters/Adrees Latif; **126** (t) Rex Features, (b) Marc Cameron/Mark Brown/Rex Features; **127** (b) John MacDougall/AFP/Getty Images, (t) Chris Jackson/Getty Images; **128–129** Concept, design, sculpture by John Towers of Blue Flame Alley Studios, Florida/Photos courtesy of Horst Rösler, Germany/Special thanks for Kate Towers for her endless support; **130** Mark Malkoff; **131** (sp) National Geographic/Getty Images, (t,c) Canadian Press/Rex Features; **132** Johnny McCormack; **133** Scubacraft 2010; **134** Jeff Barnett-Winsby; **135** (t) Courtesy of NASA-JSC, (b) Khalid Tanveer/AP/Press Association Images; **136** Hulton Archive/Getty Images; **138** Andrew J.K. Tan; **139** (sp) Walt Seng/Getty Images; **140** (r) D.J. Struntz/Barcroft Media Ltd, (l) Simon de Trey-White/Barcroft India/Barcroft Media Ltd, (r) Photolibrary.com; **142–143** PPL Media; **144** (t) Wenn.com, (b) Barry Bland/Barcroft Media Ltd; **145** (t) Lisa Rastl/Barcroft Media Ltd; **146** (b) Niall Carson/PA Archive/Press Association Images; **146–147** The Space Cowboy; **150** AFP/Getty Images; **151** Wenn.com; **152–153** Niklas Halle'n/Barcroft Media Ltd; **154** (t, b) Guinness Rishi (sp) © rawlex–Fotolia.com; **156–157** Chad Netherland; **158** (sp) Barcroft Media, (b) © EuroPics[CEN]; **159** M & Y Agency Ltd/Rex Features; **160** (l) Time & Life Pictures/Getty Images, (r) Getty Images; **161** (t/l) Chatham News, (t/c) Simon de Trey-White/Barcroft Media Ltd, (t/r) Bill Tremblay/The Independent, (c/l) AFP/Getty Images, (b/l) ChinaFotoPress/Photocome/Press Association Images; **162–163** Amy Sancetta/AP/Press Association Images; **164** SSPL via Getty Images; **166** Michelle Enemark of CuriousExpeditions.org; **167** (t) © epa/Corbis, (b) Bournemouth News/Rex Features; **168** (t) Jan Petter Jorgensen/Rex Features, (b) Reuters/Gopal Chitrakar; **169** Snap/Rex Features; **170** (l) © PixAchi–Fotolia.com, (b/r) Everett Collection/Rex Features, (t/r) Snap/Rex Features; **175** Fortean Picture Library; **176** (t) Paul Huber, (c) Reuters, (b/l) Pamela Bohnenstiehl, (b/c, b/r) Bishop Sean Manchester; **177** (t) AFP/Getty Images; **178** Olycom SPA/Rex Features; **180** Wenn.com; **181** Wenn.com; **182** Getty Images; **183** (t) Photolibrary.com; **184** Caters News; **185** (t) Zubova Zhanna, (b) Professor Andrew Davidhazy; **186** (t/l) AP/Press Association Images, (b) www.tropix.co.uk/V. and M. Birley; **187** East News/Rex Features; **188** YaYa Chou; **189** (l) Archant, (t/r) Wenn.com, (b) Vat19.com; **190** (t) Reuters/Thomas Mukoya, (b) Tony McNicol/Rex Features; **191** Wenn.com; **192** NTI Media Ltd/Rex Features; **194** (t) Heidi Hooper, (b) SWNS.com; **195** Leandro Granato; **196** Robert Bradford; **197** (b/l) Thomas Becker, Arnstadt, Germany, (b/r) Copyright Parks Victoria, (t) Solent News/Rex Features; **198–199** Caters News; **200** Benjamine Shine; **202** (t/l) David Parry/PA Archive/Press Association Images; Fotolia.com; © michanolimit–Fotolia.com, (t/ r) Jeff Moore/allactiondigital.com/Jeff Moore/Empics Entertainment ; © Studio-54–Fotolia.com; © MB–Fotolia.com, (b/l) Masatoshi Okauchi/Rex Features; © Kirill Zdorov–Fotolia.com; © angelo.gi–Fotolia.com, (b/r) Scott Wade; **203** (t/l) Ripley Entertainment; © Lou Oates–Fotolia.com; © Claudio Baldini–Fotolia.com, (t/c) ChinaFotoPress/Photocome/Press Association Images; © Lou Oates–Fotolia.com; © Le Do–Fotolia.com, (t/r) Reuters/Claro Cortes; Fotolia.com; © Raia–Fotolia.com, (c/r) Getty Images, © Kirill Zdorov–Fotolia.com; © François Roche–Fotolia.com; (b/r) © Invader/Solent News/Rex Features; © Kirill Zdorov–Fotolia.com; © Sergej Razvodovskij–Fotolia.com; **205** (r, l) Solent News/Rex Features; (b) Rex Features; **206** (t/l, b/l) Dean Powell, (r) Ian Davie; **207** Alex Queral; **208** Edgar Mueller/Rex Features; **209** Edgar Mueller/Manfred Stader/Rex Features; **210–211** Enno de Kroon; **212** Unimedia Images/Rex Features; **213** (t, c) Terence Bogue; **214–215** Nicholas Hendrickx; **216–217** eckmanfineart.com; **219** Matthieu Gauchet; **220** Solent News/Rex Features; **222** Kosta Grammatis, lead engineer for team eyeborg; **223** (b/r, b/l) Reuters/Attila Cser, (t) Reuters/Michael Caronna; **224** (t, b) Reuters/Arnd Wiegmann; **225** (t) Reuters/Luke MacGregor, (b) Dr David Cox, National Physical Laboratory, UK; **226** (l) David Cheskin/PA Wire/Press Association Images, (r) SSPL via Getty Images; **227** (sp, b) Aisling Magill/Barcroft Media Ltd; **228** (l, c) Getty Images, (r) © Photoshot; **229** (l) AP/Press Association Images, (r) Time & Life Pictures/Getty Images; **230** Paul Michael Hughes/Guinness World Records/Rex Features; **232** Wenn.com; **233** (b) © UPPA/Photoshot, (t) Wenn.com; **234** (b) Rex Features, (t) David Lovere/Rex Features; **235** (t, b) © EuroPics[CEN]; **236–237** (bgd) © filtv–Fotolia.com; **236** (l, b/c, t/r) Niagara Falls (Ontario) Public Library, (c/r) © Bettmann/Corbis; **237** (t/l, b/l, b/c) Niagara Falls (Ontario) Public Library; **238** Kevin Walsh; **239** (b, c) Irish Revenue Commissioners, (t) David McLain/Getty Images; **240** (t) © EuroPics[CEN], (b) AP/Press Association Images; **241** © EuroPics[CEN]; **242** Tattoo by Dan Hazelton; **244–245** Sculptures from recycled steel by RoboSteel www.Robosteel.com

Key: t = top, b = bottom, c = center, l = left, r = right, sp = single page, dp = double page.
All other photos are from Ripley Entertainment Inc. Every attempt has been made to acknowledge correctly and contact copyright holders and we apologize in advance for any unintentional errors or omissions, which will be corrected in future editions.

Ripley's MUSEUMS

There are 31 Ripley's Believe It or Not! museums spread across the globe for you to visit, each packed full with weird and wonderful exhibits from the Ripley collection.

Atlantic City **NEW JERSEY**

Bangalore **INDIA**

Blackpool **ENGLAND**

Branson **MISSOURI**

Cavendish **CANADA**

Copenhagen **DENMARK**

Gatlinburg **TENNESSEE**

Genting Highlands **MALAYSIA**

Grand Prairie **TEXAS**

Guadalajara **MEXICO**

Hollywood **CALIFORNIA**

Jackson Hole **WYOMING**

Key West **FLORIDA**

Kuwait City **KUWAIT**

London **ENGLAND**

Mexico City **MEXICO**

Veracruz **MEXICO**

Myrtle Beach **SOUTH CAROLINA**

New York **NEW YORK**

Newport **OREGON**

Niagara Falls **CANADA**

Ocean City **MARYLAND**

Orlando **FLORIDA**

Panama City Beach **FLORIDA**

Pattaya **THAILAND**

San Antonio **TEXAS**

San Francisco **CALIFORNIA**

St. Augustine **FLORIDA**

Surfers Paradise **AUSTRALIA**

Williamsburg **VIRGINIA**

Wisconsin Dells **WISCONSIN**

ANNUALS